ALMOST
DEPRESSED

ALMOST DEPRESSED

Is My (or My Loved One's) Unhappiness a Problem?

❖

Jefferson Prince, MD, Harvard Medical School

Shelley Carson, PhD, Harvard University

HAZELDEN®

Hazelden
Center City, Minnesota 55012
hazelden.org

Library of Congress Cataloging-in-Publication Data

    Prince, Jefferson B.
    Almost depressed : is my (or my loved one's) unhappiness a problem? /
Jefferson B. Prince, MD, Harvard Medical School ; Shelley Carson, PhD,
Harvard University.
       pages   cm.—(Almost effect)
    Includes bibliographical references.
    ISBN 978-1-61649-192-5 (pbk)—ISBN 978-1-61649-499-5 (e-book)
    1. Depression, Mental—Diagnosis. 2. Affective disorders—Physiological
aspects. 3. Psychobiology. I. Carson, Shelley, 1949– II. Title.
    RC537.P699 2013
    616.85'27—dc23

                                        2013016874

Editor's notes:
Many of the individuals described in this book are composite examples based upon behaviors encountered in the authors' own professional experience. All identifying details
and circumstances have been changed to protect the privacy of the people involved.

This publication is not intended as a substitute for the advice of health care professionals.

17 16 15 14 13   1 2 3 4 5 6

Cover design by Theresa Jaeger Gedig
Interior design by Kinne Design
Typesetting by BookMobile Design & Digital Publisher Services

Harvard Health Publications
HARVARD MEDICAL SCHOOL
Trusted advice for a healthier life

The Almost Effect™ series presents books written
by Harvard Medical School faculty and other
experts who offer guidance on common behavioral
and physical problems falling in the spectrum between
normal health and a full-blown medical condition.
These are the first publications to help general readers
recognize and address these problems.

❖

To David—
my anchor and my protective factor
S.C.

To all my teachers, with gratitude,
especially my rose, Jane
J.P.

And now here is my secret, a very simple secret:
It is only with the heart that one can see rightly;
what is essential is invisible to the eye.

—Antoine de Saint-Exupéry,
The Little Prince

contents

list of tables and figures

The Almost Effect

I once overheard a mother counseling her grown daughter to avoid dating a man she thought had a drinking problem. The daughter said, "Mom, he's not an alcoholic!" The mother quickly responded, "Well, maybe not, but he *almost* is."

Perhaps you've heard someone, referring to a boss or public figure, say, "I don't like that guy. He's *almost* a psychopath!"

Over the years, I've heard many variations on this theme. The medical literature currently recognizes many problems or syndromes that don't quite meet the standard definition of a medical condition. Although the medical literature has many examples of these syndromes, they are often not well known (except by doctors specializing in that particular area of medicine) or well described (except in highly technical medical research articles). They are what medical professionals often refer to as subclinical and, using the common parlance from the examples above, what we're calling *the almost effect.*

For example:

- Glucose intolerance may or may not always lead to the medical condition of diabetes, but it nonetheless increases your risk of getting diabetes—which then increases your risk of heart attacks, strokes, and many other illnesses.

- Sunburns, especially severe ones, may not always lead to skin cancer, but they always increase your risk of skin cancer, cause immediate pain, and may cause permanent cosmetic issues.

- Pre-hypertension may not always lead to hypertension (high blood pressure), but it increases your risk of getting hypertension, which then increases your risk of heart attacks, strokes, and other illnesses.

- Osteopenia signifies a minor loss of bone that may not always lead to the more significant bone loss called osteoporosis, but it still increases your risk of getting osteoporosis, which then increases your risk of having a pathologic fracture.

Diseases can develop slowly, producing milder symptoms for years before they become full-blown. If you recognize them early, before they become fully developed, and take relatively simple actions, you have a good chance of preventing them from turning into the full-blown disorder. In many instances there are steps you can try at home on your own; this is especially true with the mental and behavioral health disorders.

So, what exactly is the almost effect and why this book? *Almost Depressed* is one of a series of books by faculty members from Harvard Medical School and other experts. These books are the first to describe in everyday language how to recognize and what to do about some of the most common behavioral and emotional problems that fall within the continuum between normal and full-blown pathology. Since this concept is new and still evolving, we're proposing a new term, *the almost effect*, to describe problems characterized by the following criteria.

The problem

1. falls outside of normal behavior but falls short of meeting the criteria for a particular diagnosis (such as alcoholism, major depression, psychopathy, anorexia nervosa, or substance dependence);

2. is currently causing identifiable issues for individuals and/or others in their lives;

3. may progress to the full-blown condition, meeting accepted diagnostic criteria, but even if it doesn't, still can cause significant suffering;

4. should respond to appropriate interventions when accurately identified.

The Almost Effect

Normal Feelings and Behaviors	The Almost Effect	Condition Meets Diagnostic Criteria for Full-Blown Pathology

All of the books in The Almost Effect™ series make a simple point: Each of these conditions occurs along a spectrum, with normal health and behavior at one end and the full-blown disorder at the other. Between these two extremes is where the almost effect lies. It is the point at which a person is experiencing real pain and suffering from a condition for which there are solutions—*if* the problem is recognized.

Recognizing the almost effect not only helps a person address real issues now; it also opens the door for change well in advance of the point at which the problem becomes severe. In short, recognizing the almost effect has two primary goals: (1) to alleviate pain and suffering now and (2) to prevent more serious problems later.

I am convinced these problems are causing tremendous suffering, and it is my hope that the science-based information in these books can help alleviate this suffering. Readers can find help in the practical self-assessments and advice offered here, and the current research and clinical expertise presented in the series can open opportunities for health care professionals to intervene more effectively.

I hope you find this book helpful. For information about other books in this series, visit www.TheAlmostEffect.com.

Julie Silver, MD
Associate Professor, Harvard Medical School
Chief Editor of Books, Harvard Health Publications

acknowledgments

First and foremost, we would like to thank our editor at Harvard Health Publications, Dr. Julie Silver. Her amazing writing and editing talents were instrumental in conceptualizing and shaping this book. Sid Farrar, our editor at Hazelden, provided valuable feedback, support, and belief in the value of this project. Thank you so much, Sid! We would also like to thank Natalie Ramm, Mindy Keskinen, and the great staffs at both Harvard Health Publications and Hazelden who were always there to assist in matters great and small. Thanks to our great literary agent, Linda Konner, who helped make this book and the entire Almost Effect™ series a reality.

We would like to thank our colleagues at Harvard Medical School, the Harvard Department of Psychology, Massachusetts General Hospital, and North Shore Medical Center who gave us feedback and advice and who were kind enough to share their expertise with us. We also thank our friends and family members Jane Prince, Nacie Carson, and Dave Carson for their valuable feedback and perspective.

We could not have written this book without the emotional support of our families. Dave, Nacie, Davey, Jane, Jake, and Sophie, as well as my (JP) parents Joyce and Bruce—we send our gratitude and love for your patience, understanding, and support as we spent the long hours on research, hand-wringing, collaborating, and writing this book. You truly are our protective factors!

We would like to send special thanks to artist Sally Loughridge and others (whose identities have been changed in the text) for allowing us to share their stories. Your stories will resonate with readers, give them hope, and help them realize they are not alone.

Finally, we would like to express our deep gratitude to our patients, students, and clients, who have taught us so much about depression in its early stages and in its attenuated states. We wish you each a long, resilient, and rewarding journey as each day takes you further from the shadows of almost depression and into the land of future possibilities!

■ ◆ ■

introduction

In between a state of positive well-being and a full-blown major depression lies a large gray area of persistent negative mood that has not been fully charted by modern medicine. Although many attempts to define parts of it have been put forth—using diagnostic titles like "dysthymia," "minor depression," "depression NOS" (not otherwise specified), "depressive CNEC" (depressive conditions not elsewhere classified), and "depressive personality disorder"—we feel this gray area, which we are calling *almost depressed*, needs to be recognized and identified both by individuals who may suffer from it and by physical and behavioral health professionals.

Our purpose is not to propose or promote yet another diagnostic entity, but simply to bring awareness to this gray area of mood disturbance and to outline some proven strategies to decrease its symptoms and improve lives. There are two very important reasons to do this.

First, being almost depressed, in and of itself, is a source of distress and suffering. To look at how much stress and suffering it causes, we invited 200 individuals from the Harvard community to participate in a study of depression symptoms and quality of life. In this study, we found that almost depressed

1

people, not surprisingly, reported lower life satisfaction and less satisfying interpersonal relationships. They also had more symptoms of anxiety and distress and less of a sense of control over their lives than those who were free of symptoms. Clearly, even what mental health professionals would call "subclinical" (and we would translate into "not very noticeable") levels of depressive symptoms exact an unacceptable toll on individuals and families.

The second reason to bring awareness to what it means to be almost depressed is that we know from previous research that in about three out of every four cases, low-grade subclinical depression eventually evolves into major depressive disorder. This means that if you suffer with some symptoms of depression— even if it's not that bad right now—you are more likely than not to develop more severe symptoms in the future. Major depression is a mental health diagnosis that involves significant suffering and unhappiness; however, there are other reasons to avoid this serious disorder, including the accompanying high suicide rate, elevated risk of heart disease, and the chemical changes in the brain that increase the likelihood of future episodes. As we also note in chapter 4, people who are feeling depressed often try to cope with those feelings by self-medicating with alcohol or other addictive substances. Yet alcohol and substance abuse can lead to additional sources of misery.

As behavioral health professionals, we encounter people with almost depression daily in our work and have seen first-hand the distress associated with it. Jeff is an instructor in psychiatry at Harvard Medical School; a researcher, teacher, and staff member of the department of psychiatry at Massachusetts General Hospital; and the director of child psychiatry at Mass

General for Children at North Shore Medical Center in Salem, Massachusetts. The treatment of depression is a primary focus in his clinical practice, as well as his research in psychopharmacology. During his own struggles with almost depression, Jeff was introduced to mindfulness-based techniques. Now, along with his colleagues at North Shore Medical Center, he offers yoga, pranayama, meditation, and Mindfulness Based Stress Reduction (MBSR) programs for children, adolescents, and adults.

Shelley is a Harvard research psychologist and lecturer whose teaching and research focus on the interface between psychopathology, creativity, and resilience. Her work on these topics has been published in both national and international scientific journals. She is the author of the book *Your Creative Brain* and counsels highly creative professionals on how to become more productive in their work. Through this, Shelley has found that subclinical depressive symptoms are often at the heart of writer's block and creative blockade. She is also a consultant for the Department of Defense, developing Web-based interventions for people in the military and their families. Many of the interventions that Shelley has developed focus on how to detect and improve symptoms of depression, post-traumatic stress, and relationship problems for service members who are returning from Iraq and Afghanistan. Throughout her work, Shelley has seen the subtle but significant way that almost depression negatively affects people's lives—whether those people are students, creative writers, movie directors, or military members and their families.

In this book, we will share our own personal stories, as well as stories from our work with people who are almost depressed. Some of the stories are composites of several people from our professional experiences. In all cases, names and details have been changed to protect the privacy of the people involved. We will also share the often simple, but very effective and helpful, strategies that people have used to lift the hovering cloud of subtle depressive symptoms—improving their mood, renewing their energy, and restoring their vigor.

We have divided the book into two parts. In the first part, we describe almost depression, as well as other aspects of the depressive continuum, and provide examples based on our professional experiences. We discuss many of the risk factors for depressive symptoms, the role that stress plays in depression, and a number of physical conditions that mimic depression. In the second part of the book, we describe common barriers to dealing with depressive symptoms and how to overcome these barriers.

If you think that you, or someone you love, may be suffering unnecessarily, we'll explain step by step how you can start making positive changes that will aggressively combat almost depression. The strategies we encourage you to use have been studied and proven to help people improve their mood, feel happier, and become more productive. We incorporate the latest findings from clinical research and neuroscience studies to bolster our recommendations. Just as there are many pathways that lead to a downward spiral into depression, there are numerous pathways *away from* depression, and we describe a variety of these paths that can guide you out of almost depression and toward brighter days. While the pathway you choose may vary depending upon your individual traits and symptoms, all the strategies we describe in this book have been shown to be effective. There is a great deal that people who are almost depressed can do to feel happier.

Some of the strategies we recommend may seem to contradict each other at first glance. For example, in chapter 5 we talk about becoming *more* active and engaged, while in chapter 8 we recommend *slowing down* a little to reduce your stress level. Likewise, in chapter 9 we talk about *changing* your thoughts through positive reframing, while in chapter 10 we discuss *accepting* your thoughts and feelings through mindfulness practice. How is it possible that all of these strategies, even when they contradict each other, can work? The answer lies in understanding that depression and almost depression are indications that the healthy systems of our brains and bodies have become imbalanced. Just as you can rebalance a scale by either adding weight to one side or taking away weight from the other side, there is more than one way to rebalance your brain and body systems to regain a healthier emotional state.

In fact, although this book is intended to help people who are struggling with mild depressive symptoms, the research-based strategies we recommend are good for all of us—regardless of our usual mood fluctuations. So, no matter what your mood is now or in the future, we believe the strategies outlined in this book will help you and your loved ones live fuller and more zestful lives.

◆

Part 1

The Grays:
More Than Just "the Blues"

| 1 |

What Is Almost Depression?

Life is full of misery, loneliness, and
suffering—and it's all over much too soon.
—Woody Allen

Life inevitably has its ups and downs. We all have had bad days, an occasional bad week, and times when we feel a little "off," unmotivated, or blue. This is normal. And because you know it's normal, you might not notice when these bad days, bad weeks, or off times begin to string together. You might go on for months—sometimes even years—in a state of just getting by, without experiencing the pleasure and contentment that you used to take for granted. This *isn't* normal, even though you may have come to accept it as so; it's *almost depression*. And, unlike Woody Allen's analysis in the quote above, it isn't over much too soon; it may continue to cause you to feel a bit dreary and gloomy until you finally recognize it in yourself (or a loved one) and decide to take specific steps to restore the well-being and positive emotions that you used to experience.

Like a lot of people, you may think that a person is either depressed or they're not. In the old days, many doctors and scientists shared this perspective and viewed mental health problems in a "categorical" manner—meaning that someone was either normal or depressed. If we were to draw a picture of this view, it would look like this:

Figure 1.
Categorical View of Depression

Normal Mood	Depressed

Today, however, most experts believe that it is more accurate to look at psychological health as occurring along a "spectrum." On the far left of the spectrum would be normal mood symptoms, including the usual ups and downs that occur day to day or when something quite good or particularly bad happens to someone. On the far right of the spectrum would be severe depression—the diagnosis of "clinical depression" or "major depression." When someone moves from the left into the middle zone, this is where things get a bit dreary. We call this part of the spectrum *almost depression*.

Figure 2.
Spectrum View of Depression

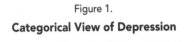

Normal Mood	Almost Depressed	Major Depression

As behavioral health professionals, we see people who are almost depressed on a regular basis. And we know the subtle—and sometimes not so subtle—distress that this condition bestows upon its victims and their families. We have dubbed the condition *almost depression* because it shares many of the symptoms, signs, and negative feelings of clinical depression, but lacks the intensity of a full-blown depressive episode. Almost depression is not just feeling blue or sad for a few days; it's not a state you can simply "snap out of." It is the gray part of the depression continuum that, if left untreated and unrecognized, may eventually degrade into the full-blown dark state of clinical depression. As mental health professionals, we are particularly concerned about this because when people become more depressed, the likelihood that they will take their own lives also increases. In fact, between 6 and 9 percent of people who are diagnosed with clinical depression will eventually commit suicide.[1] We pause here to say that depression is a life-threatening condition, and we encourage you to talk to your doctor about symptoms that you may be having. However, even when feeling depressed does not turn into full-scale clinical depression, it causes far too much suffering, and you may be experiencing more distress and unhappiness than normal. Furthermore, your mood affects the people around you, and vice versa. So if you are experiencing any symptoms of depression, this is probably affecting your loved ones. Alternately, you may be reading this book because someone you love is struggling with depressive symptoms, and you realize that it's affecting not only your loved one but you as well.

Our intention is not to present almost depression as a new diagnosis; there are already a number of identified disorders on the depression spectrum, which we'll look at in the next chapter. Rather, our intention is to (1) bring attention to the distress and impairment that even subclinical symptoms of depression (symptoms that don't qualify for a diagnosis of clinical depression) can cause and (2) help individuals and clinicians recognize these symptoms so they can take action to reduce suffering.

The symptoms we're talking about may come on gradually or they may appear rather quickly as a response to a negative event or situation. You may not even realize that you have slipped into this gray mood state. However, like a six-cylinder car that is working on only four cylinders, almost depression ultimately extracts a price both in performance efficiency (in all areas of life) and in terms of physical health. Without knowing it, you may be devoting more and more internal resources to just getting through the day, leaving little energy for delighting in the richness of life.

Almost depression can take many forms. To get an idea of how it affects performance and enjoyment of life, take a look at how it affected two very different people: Remy and Saul.

Remy's Story

Remy is a thirty-six-year-old mother of three who has a small photography business. She photographs weddings and special events on the weekends, and she used to be passionate about her work. "I wanted each picture to capture the spark of new love and the promise of the future that I saw in young couples' eyes. I wanted to seize the joy of the event for them to keep forever" was how Remy described her work.

Remy also used to be passionate about her home and creating a warm and beautiful place for her family to come together, relax, and feel secure. She has always loved to entertain and worked to make holidays and birthdays special events with lots of decorations and special food.

The struggling economy seems to have changed all that. When she and her family were forced to downsize and move to a smaller home, Remy started to tackle the job of decorating their new house with her usual artistic flare. However, somewhere along the way she lost the passion that has always been a sustaining quality for herself and her family. She complains that her creativity is blocked and that her inspiration has left and seems unlikely to return. Although she is still keeping her house clean, she has lost interest in adding the little touches that have always set her decorating and entertaining apart. Her family feels like the light inside the house is gradually dimming. Recently, her daughter told Remy that now she seems like a normal mother rather than the Super Mom she used to be. And her son describes the change in his mom as going from four-dimensional to two-dimensional. She is still photographing weddings but says it feels like she is clicking the shutter with her eyes closed. The love and joy aren't jumping out at her like they used to. With these symptoms, Remy wouldn't qualify for a diagnosis of major depression, but it is clear that she is *almost depressed*.

Notice that Remy continued to do her work, but she lacked energy and enthusiasm; she was functional, but seemed to be winding down. The zest was missing. Now let's look at Saul, who reacted to almost depression in a different way; he actually picked up the pace of his work—almost to a frenzied level.

Saul's Story

Saul, a young lawyer, was on his way to a promising future. Ten years after graduating from law school, he'd married a fellow lawyer, bought a house in an upscale neighborhood, and found an engrossing job at a human rights organization. What could go wrong?

Plenty. The urgent demands of his job, plus the workaholic tendencies that had won him honors in college, took over his life. He spent more and more time at the office or overseas on business. When he did spend time with his wife, he was distracted and often irritable. They'd once talked of having children. Now, in her mid-thirties, she badly wanted to start a family. But he felt too involved in work for such a time-consuming change and wanted to wait. She pleaded. They argued. Finally she filed for divorce.

Saul was shocked. He blamed her. He blamed himself. But instead of learning from his mistakes and trying to restore balance to his life, he drove himself even harder at work and distracted himself from his loneliness and feelings of failure by getting wrapped up in the lives of his refugee clients.

Saul's life is functioning. He's a valued employee with many grateful clients. He has friends who try to set him up on blind dates. But he is unhappy. He has difficulty falling asleep at night and goes around in a funk. The more he tries to avoid facing his negative feelings with overwork, the more imbalanced his life becomes and the more solid and fixed his unhappiness gets. Saul's unhappiness isn't serious enough to be considered a medical condition. But he's clearly suffering and is unable to have a loving and nurturing relationship with a woman or to create the family that he so desires. Saul is *almost depressed.*

· · ·

Remy and Saul are not savoring life to its fullest. They are going through the motions of living and working but aren't currently able to experience the full spectrum of color and richness that their lives could afford them. They are stuck in a gray mental state—between the black of full depression and the bright light of positive well-being. In this book, we'll share other stories that illustrate the gray landscape of almost depression. We'll also show you that there are many roads leading out of this landscape. And the good news is that by taking one or more of those roads, you will not only improve your mood and your life in the present, but you will protect yourself against future forays into almost depressed territory.

Could You Be Almost Depressed?

Here's a quick quiz to help you consider whether you may be almost depressed[2] (the next chapter offers a more scientific assessment). Read through the following statements and place a check mark by any that have applied to you in the past month. (You can also download this assessment at www .AlmostDepressed.com.)

Table 1.
Almost Depressed: A Quick Assessment

☐ Recently I find that I am getting frustrated over little things that don't usually bother me.

☐ I used to enjoy going out with friends, but I find that I am avoiding my friends now.

☐ I have not been sleeping well lately.

☐ Nothing tastes very good these days.

☐ I'd like to just "stop the world" and get off for a while.

☐ When someone tells a joke, I laugh to be polite, but nothing seems very funny to me these days.

☐ Nothing seems very interesting or exciting to me lately.

☐ My fuse seems shorter than it used to be, and I get easily irritated.

☐ I'm not as interested in having sex with my partner as I used to be.

☐ I'd really like just to be left alone.

☐ I have trouble concentrating on a book or TV show.

☐ I just feel tired all the time for no reason.

If you checked two or more of these statements, you may fall somewhere in the gray-to-black range of the depression spectrum. The good news is that there are many steps you can take to get your life back. That's why we've written this book. We want you to be able to recognize the signs of depression in both yourself and the people you care about. And then we want you to know how to take action on your own to restore and maintain your emotional health and vibrancy. Finally, we want you to know which signs suggest the situation is serious enough to warrant a talk with your doctor. It's important to share both physical and emotional symptoms with your doctor, who can help you figure out if you need a referral to a mental health professional.

Almost Depression versus Clinical Depression

The concept of what is now called clinical depression has been described since at least the time of the ancient Greeks. The physician Hippocrates provided the first known description of the condition, which he called *melancholia* (from the Greek words *melas* or dark, and *kholé* or bile) because he believed it resulted from too much black bile in the body. Aristotle also wrote about melancholia (and was the first to associate it with creativity, suggesting that poets, playwrights, and philosophers were prone to it).[3]

Today, clinical depression is based on a diagnosis of major depressive disorder as it is described in the *Diagnostic and Statistical Manual for Mental Disorders* (called the *DSM* for short). The *DSM* is compiled by the American Psychiatric Association and is updated regularly to reflect recent scientific findings. The current *DSM* (the fifth edition, *or DSM-5*) lists the following criteria for the diagnosis of a major depressive episode.[4]

A person must have experienced at least five of the following symptoms for a two-week period or longer. (Of course, most people who are depressed will have suffered for considerably longer, but the two-week demarcation allows mental health professionals to distinguish between true depression and a few days of simply being sad or blue.)

- depressed or irritable mood most of the day, nearly every day (that is, feeling sad, empty, or tearful)

- diminished interest or pleasure in all, or almost all, activities most of the day, nearly every day (the clinical name for this symptom is "anhedonia")

- significant and unintended weight loss or weight gain (this is usually accompanied by a change in appetite)

- extreme fatigue or loss of energy

- significant changes in sleep patterns (either insomnia or hypersomnia—sleeping much more than is usual for the person)

- psychomotor retardation (a slowing down of behavior and speech that is noticeable by others) or psychomotor agitation (extreme restlessness and agitation)

- feelings of worthlessness or guilt that are excessive and unwarranted
- difficulty concentrating and making decisions
- suicidal ideation (recurrent thoughts of death or suicide) and/or making a plan for suicide

For an official diagnosis of major depressive episode, one of the five symptoms has to be either depressed mood or loss of pleasure. The symptoms also have to represent a change from the person's normal functioning. Finally, the symptoms must cause significant distress or problems in functioning, such as difficulty in making or keeping relationships or difficulty fulfilling work obligations.

DSM-IV-TR and *DSM-5* describe another lesser form of depression called "dysthymia," a well-studied clinical disorder characterized by either chronic depressed mood or anhedonia for more days than not, lasting for at least two years. In *DSM-5*, dysthymia and chronic depressed mood are called "persistent depressive disorder." Dysthymia is often referred to as "depression light" because sufferers experience many of the symptoms of major depression. However, the symptoms of dysthymia are not as severe as those of major depression and do not include thoughts of death or suicide: thoughts that may occur in major depression.

We introduce the concept of almost depression to describe the gray area of mood disturbances that is bounded at its most severe edge by dysthymia and at the milder edge by a persistent state of low-grade dysphoria (negative, irritable, or unpleasant mood) and/or anhedonia (loss of pleasure in most activities). This range of disturbed mood is currently considered "subclinical," yet clearly interferes with a person's ability to savor life or carry out responsibilities at his or her optimum capacity.

Figure 3.

Almost Depression

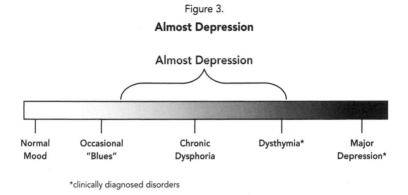

*clinically diagnosed disorders

Almost depression is distinct from the ordinary mood swings of daily living in that the negative mood is chronic (perhaps lasting months or even years) and the person cannot simply "snap out of it." Although the person at the mild end of almost depression experiences some symptoms of clinical depression, these symptoms are not intense, frequent, or persistent enough to qualify as major depression. Nevertheless, these symptoms adversely affect the person's quality of life and, often, that of his or her family members, friends, coworkers, and others who interact with the person. The condition has a significant, though often subtle, effect on all aspects of a person's life, including mood, perception, thought processes, emotions, physical condition, motivation, work performance, and social life.

Almost depression is also distinct from the sadness that may immediately follow a personal loss. It is normal for a person who has suffered a loss to feel sad, to withdraw, or to have trouble sleeping or concentrating. These feelings are an adaptive part of the grieving process and, unlike almost depression, will improve with time.

How Common Is Almost Depression?

So how prevalent is almost depression? It has not been as well studied as clinical depression, but we can make an estimate based on the results of a recent study conducted by the U.S. Centers for Disease Control. This study surveyed a representative cross-section of more than 235,000 adults in the United States and found that just over 9 percent of those surveyed are suffering from two or more symptoms of depression.[5] Further evaluation revealed that approximately 4 percent of individuals surveyed qualified as clinically depressed. This means that 5 percent of respondents had some symptoms of depression but didn't meet the full criteria for a diagnosis. Those 5 percent (which, if we extrapolate the survey results, amounts to more than 12 million people in the United States) are the people we would call almost depressed; they have some symptoms but won't be diagnosed with full-blown depression.

Although the 5 percent statistic is derived from a U.S. study, we acknowledge that people who live in other countries face different challenges and may be either more or less at risk for almost depression. For example, a study of over 3,000 Australians found that 12.9 percent of those surveyed currently qualified as having subclinical depression.[6]

When you consider that each person who is almost depressed is probably interacting with several family members, coworkers, and close friends, the total number of individuals who are affected by this negative condition rises to tens of millions just in the United States. The effect of social networks is powerful, and we believe that if you and others recognize almost depression and take steps to counter its negative effects, you can be part of a tremendous positive shift *away* from much of the distress and misery in society.

Distress, Dysfunction, and Almost Depression

We've already mentioned that being almost depressed causes distress and prevents people from functioning at their peak level. We also saw earlier in this chapter how this mood condition caused distress for Remy and Saul. In general, studies have found that people with dysthymia (the more severe boundary of almost depression) experience a lower quality of life in a number of areas, poorer physical health, lower levels of psychological well-being, and poorer relationships with family and friends. They also show higher levels of marital discord, poorer work performance records, and more on-the-job problems than control subjects without dysthymia.[7]

People on the less severe boundary of almost depression also show distress. In the Australian study mentioned above, people with two or more symptoms of depression (but who did not qualify for major depressive disorder) scored lower on all aspects of quality of life than those who had fewer than two symptoms, missing more days of work due to health-related issues, having poorer interpersonal relationships, and having poorer psychological well-being. Finally, in our study of members of the Harvard community, we found that those who fell within the almost depressed range expressed less satisfaction with their relationships, lower marital satisfaction, less intimacy, more physical and emotional pain, and lower self-esteem than those who had no mood disturbance.

Clearly, almost depression is associated with significant distress and problems in functioning, although it is not as severe as the distress and dysfunction found in major depression. It is an identifiable, common, and distressing condition. However, it's also very treatable. If you or a loved one is struggling, you have every reason to believe that things can get better, and we'll show you a number of routes you can take to psychological well-being. In the next chapter, we'll look at some of the risk factors for depression, and you'll have the chance to take a validated assessment (a tool that is used in research studies) to see where you fall on the depression continuum.

❖

| 2 |

Understanding the
Depression Continuum

Even a happy life cannot be without a measure of darkness.
—Carl Jung

To get a feel for the range of distress and dysfunction that exists on the depression continuum, let's look at Inez and Joey. These two bright young people suffered from depression symptoms, but there is a clear difference in the intensity of their symptoms and their level of suffering.

Inez's Story

Inez is a young college math professor. All through college and graduate school, she was a serious, diligent student who always did more than expected. She was also shy and spent most of her time at home alone, studying. When she landed the job she really wanted, as an assistant professor at a liberal arts college, she quickly became overwhelmed. Her skills as a student were now liabilities. Instead of spending hours alone studying in her room or at the library, she was now expected to step up and be a leader, to mentor students and contribute as an equal at department meetings. Meeting these expectations would mean going against her natural shyness and inclination to follow the directions of others. Now she was expected to initiate direction herself. Her reaction was to retreat and put on an arrogant, indifferent front to hide her fear and sense of inadequacy.

Each day, she fled from the college as quickly as she could, feeling self-conscious and awkward at campus activities or faculty social events. In her student days, she could always lose herself in the elegance of mathematical calculations and equations; now Inez was concerned that she was starting to lose interest in math, a pursuit that had formerly filled her with wonder. She spent her evenings worrying that she would lose her position, and she began to have trouble sleeping. She realized that the arrogant demeanor she was projecting was not a reflection of her true self, and that made her feel false and guilty. However, she believed that if she let her colleagues know how awkward and self-conscious she felt in her new leadership position, she would lose stature in their eyes. Inez was almost depressed. She knew she needed to make some changes, but she didn't know how to begin.

Note that Inez was feeling depressed and miserable, but she was not feeling hopeless. Now compare the seriousness of her situation to Joey's.

Joey's Story

Joey, a bright twenty-year-old and strong student, had been prone to low moods and self-criticism throughout high school.

During his first year of college, he had some trouble adjusting to life at a big state university. And in his sophomore year, things got worse instead of better. Before college, he had never had to manage his own time, but now he was having trouble concentrating on his courses. There was no one to yell at him if he didn't do homework, and he just seemed to lose focus on academics.

Joey grew anxious and withdrawn. He found it difficult to sleep and often stayed up and fooled around with his guitar until early in the morning. Then he would wake up late, exhausted and dreading the day, and miss his morning classes. Soon he was missing his afternoon classes, too. He began smoking more and more marijuana to relax and escape. Weed seemed to relieve his exhaustion and the heaviness and aching in his body. In the meantime, the student down the hall who was supplying Joey with marijuana wanted to be paid. Somehow Joey had built up a $3,000 debt.

Joey didn't really care at this point. He quit taking showers, doing laundry, and cleaning his room. He ignored messages from his professors. He didn't return calls from his parents. His roommate, unable to stand the mess, moved out. Joey knew he'd gotten himself into a scary corner, but he couldn't think of a way out. How could he tell his parents he was failing his courses and owed money to a drug dealer? When he thought about the looks on their faces if he told them his true situation, his feelings of failure and worthlessness became almost overwhelming. He sometimes thought about going to sleep and not waking up. These thoughts scared him. In the meantime, he put off doing anything and continued smoking marijuana to fuzz out his fears. Fortunately, the resident assistant on Joey's hall finally realized that Joey was in a bad place and got the ball rolling to get Joey the help he needed.

. . .

Clearly, Joey was much further along on the depression continuum than Inez was. Joey was well into the realm of clinical depression (and had issues with substance abuse or dependence as well).

When trying to decide whether you or a loved one is almost depressed, it is important to understand what "depressed" really means in clinical terms, as well as where you or your loved one may fall on the depression continuum. This will help you determine whether you should focus on making the changes recommended in this book (as we'll see later, these worked well for Inez) or whether you should seek help from a medical professional (as in the case with Joey). In addition, recent studies indicate that depressed individuals who have a good understanding of the symptoms and causes of depression do better in treatment than those without this knowledge. In short, the more you know about depression, the better your outcome will be. In this chapter, we'll take a closer look at depression, including factors that contribute to depressive symptoms.

In chapter 1, we mentioned that the "official" diagnoses associated with depression are listed in the *Diagnostic and Statistical Manual of Mental Disorders (DSM)*, published by the American Psychiatric Association. The *DSM* is updated on a regular basis. This manual reflects the best information currently available, rather than facts set in stone. The latest edition, the *DSM-5*, lists a number of disorders under the category of Depressive

Disorders; however, a few other disorders also produce depressive symptoms. We have described these disorders in appendix A: *DSM* Disorders on the Depression Continuum.

All of the depression-associated disorders listed in the *DSM-5* cause significant distress and dysfunction. They also lead to considerable economic cost; the National Institute of Mental Health (NIMH) reported that depression is currently the leading cause of disability in the United States and costs approximately $53 billion a year in therapy and lost production.[1] However, a person's quality of life and functioning are also impacted by subthreshold levels of depressive symptoms, as we saw in the previous chapter. The distress, suffering, and functioning problems that come with low-level depression can often be resolved just by recognizing them and taking the simple steps we outline in the second part of this book. You can help yourself or your loved ones by recognizing when your negative mood is more than the everyday "blues" and has progressed into that region we call "the grays" (almost depression). That is the time to take action. The following assessment is an adaptation of the Quick Inventory for Depression Symptoms developed by Dr. A. John Rush and his colleagues, a reliable assessment currently used in many scientific studies. This assessment will help you determine where you currently stand on the depression continuum.

Table 2.

Where Are You on the Depression Continuum?

(an adaptation of the Quick Inventory for Depression Symptoms)

Please circle the statement under each item that best describes how you have been for the past two months. Circle only one statement under each item.

1. Sleeping

  0   I do not have any real problems with falling asleep or staying asleep.

  1   I occasionally have trouble falling asleep or staying asleep.

  1   I have been sleeping somewhat more than usual.

  2   I have trouble falling asleep or staying asleep about three times a week.

  2   I sleep around 12 hours in a 24-hour period, including naps.

  3   I have trouble falling asleep or staying asleep more than three times a week.

  3   I sleep more than 12 hours in a 24-hour period, including naps.

2. Feeling sad or irritable

  0   I generally do not feel sad or irritable.

  1   I feel sad or irritated less than half the time.

  2   I feel sad or irritated more than half the time.

  3   I feel sad, irritated, or angry nearly all of the time.

3. Weight and appetite

  0   I have not noticed any changes in my weight or appetite.

  1   I eat somewhat less often or lesser amounts of food than usual and have lost some weight lately without intending to do so.

  1   I feel a need to eat more frequently than usual and have gained a little weight without intending to do so.

  2   I eat much less than usual and only with personal effort, or I have lost 4 pounds or more over the past month without intending to do so.

2   I regularly eat more often and/or greater amounts of food than usual, or I have gained 4 pounds or more over the past month without intending to do so.

3   I rarely eat, and only with extreme personal effort or when others persuade me to eat, or I have lost 8 pounds or more over the past month without intending to do so.

3   I feel driven to overeat both at mealtime and between meals, or I have gained 8 pounds or more over the past month without intending to do so.

4. Concentration/decision making

0   There is no change in my usual capacity to concentrate or make decisions.

1   I occasionally feel indecisive or find that my attention wanders.

2   Most of the time, I struggle to focus my attention or to make decisions.

3   I cannot concentrate well enough to read or cannot make even minor decisions.

5. View of myself

0   I see myself as equally worthwhile and deserving as other people.

1   I am more self-blaming than usual.

2   I largely believe that I cause problems for others.

3   I think almost constantly about major and minor defects in myself.

6. Thoughts of death or suicide

0   I do not think of suicide or death.

1   I feel that life is empty or wonder if it's worth living.

2   I think of suicide or death several times a week for several minutes.

3   I think of suicide or death several times a day in some detail, or I have made specific plans for suicide or have actually tried to take my life.

(If you circled 2 or 3 to this question, please contact a mental health care provider, call the National Suicide Prevention Hotline at 1-800-273-8255, visit your local emergency department, or share your concerns with a trusted family member or friend who can assist you in accessing help.)

7. General interest
   0   There is no change from usual in how interested I am in other people or activities.
   1   I notice that I am less interested in people or activities.
   2   I find I have interest in only one or two of my formerly pursued activities.
   3   I have virtually no interest in formerly pursued activities.

8. Energy level
   0   There is no change in my usual level of energy.
   1   I get tired more easily than usual.
   2   I have to make a big effort to start or finish my usual daily activities (for example, shopping, homework, cooking, or going to work).
   3   I really cannot carry out most of my usual daily activities because I just don't have the energy.

9. Feeling slowed down
   0   I think, speak, and move at my usual rate of speed.
   1   I find that my thinking is slowed down or my voice sounds dull or flat.
   2   It takes me several seconds to respond to most questions, and I'm sure my thinking is slowed.
   3   I am often unable to respond to questions without extreme effort.

10. Feeling restless

    0   I do not feel restless.

    1   I'm often fidgety, wringing my hands or needing to shift how I am sitting.

    2   I have impulses to move about and am quite restless.

    3   At times, I am unable to stay seated and need to pace around.

Now add up the numbers beside the statements you have circled. Your total should be somewhere between 0 and 30.

0 to 5 points = no depression likely

6 to 12 points = almost depression

13 to 17 points = moderate depression

If you scored between 13 and 17, please bring your answers to the attention of a loved one and contact a health care provider.

More than 17 points = severe depression

If you scored more than 17 points, we urge you to bring your answers to the attention of a loved one or a health care provider.

| Normal Mood | Almost Depressed | Moderate to Severe Depression |

If you scored more than five points on the assessment, you fall in the gray-to-black area of the depression spectrum, meaning you may be almost depressed or even clinically depressed. If you scored between five and twelve points, please keep reading! A variety of strategies in this book can help you. If you scored thirteen or more points, we urge you to check in with a health care professional. This assessment can't confirm whether you have clinical depression—only a qualified health care professional can do that. However, the test can help you decide if your symptoms are severe enough to warrant a professional evaluation. If you scored thirteen or more points, you can still benefit from the information in this book, but you should also seek additional help. There are effective treatments, and you do not need to suffer.

The question we are asked most often about depression and almost depression is "What causes depression symptoms in the first place?" This is a fairly complex question with a complex answer; moreover, science hasn't totally answered the question yet. The current theory is that multiple factors combine to affect mood and the brain systems associated with depression. Some of these factors increase your vulnerability to depression (risk factors), and some protect *against* depression. Both risk factors and protective factors can be biological, psychological, or social/environmental in nature. You will sometimes hear this described as a biopsychosocial model of depression.

Current thinking also views risk factors as a kind of underlying predisposition to depression. For instance, if you have a family history of depression, you may have a genetic predisposition to depressive problems. However, this *does not* mean you are destined to have depression or any other disorder. Typically, the predisposition has to be paired with current life stressors (we'll talk about these stressors in depth in chapter 3) in order to trigger depressive symptoms. This is called the vulnerability/ stress model of depression.[2]

Figure 4.
Vulnerability/Stress Model

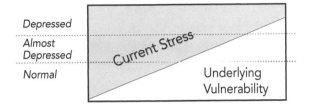

Note that in this model of depression the levels of underlying predisposition and current stress are inversely related. That means if you have a large predisposition to depression, it will take little or no stress to push you into the depressed realm. However, if you have a low level of underlying predisposition, you will need a large amount of stress to push you into the range where symptoms appear. We will discuss current life stress in chapter 3. See the sidebar "Underlying Predispositions for Depression" for a description of other risk factors.

Underlying Predispositions for Depression

As we mentioned, the underlying factors for depression can be biological, psychological, or social/environmental in nature. Although this list does not include all of the many predispositions for depression, the factors we describe here have been well documented. We'll look at some examples of biological predispositions first.

CONTINUED ON NEXT PAGE

CONTINUED FROM PREVIOUS PAGE

Biological Predispositions

Genetic. The most studied area of biological risk is genetic predisposition. If you have close relatives who have suffered from depression, you are two to three times more likely to become depressed than people who do not have depression in their immediate family. In fact, averaging across many research studies indicates that somewhere between 31 and 42 percent of the risk for depression may be due to genetic influence.[3] One particular gene has been connected to depression (although there are likely many contributing genes). This is the serotonin transporter gene. A certain version, or allele, of this gene has been shown to increase the risk of depression in people who have experienced a high number of life stressors.[4]

Neurotransmitter dysregulation. Imbalances in brain chemicals called "neurotransmitters" have been noted as a predisposition to depression. A special class of neurotransmitters called "monoamines" is the most widely studied. Monoamines include serotonin (associated with mood regulation), norepinephrine (associated with arousal and focused attention), and dopamine (associated with the brain's reward system and with motivation). These brain chemicals are often (but not always) out of balance in depression.[5]

Dysregulation of the stress system. Many people with depression appear to have abnormal levels of cortisol (the stress hormone), which is regulated by a biological stress system.[6] We will discuss this stress system in more detail in chapter 3.

Hormone fluctuations. Fluctuating or low levels of the hormone estrogen have been linked with the onset and maintenance of depression in women at various life stages, including puberty, premenstrual, postpartum, perimenopausal, and postmenopausal states.[7] A number of studies have also found an association between low circulating testosterone and depression in men, especially the elderly.[8]

Brain damage in the left hemisphere. People who have had a stroke or a head injury in the left hemisphere of the brain are more susceptible to depression than people without a head injury or with a head injury to the right hemisphere. Although there are exceptions to this, a number of research studies on brain injuries have supported this finding.[9]

Serious physical illness. As we will discuss in the next chapter, living with a serious illness can be exhausting and lead to a form of "secondary depression" (depression that occurs as a reaction to a debilitating life circumstance).

Chronic pain. Living with chronic uncontrolled pain is a serious risk factor for depression. Fortunately, pain management has become a primary focus of medical science recently. There are many new treatment options for controlling pain. Many hospitals and clinics now have dedicated pain specialists to help patients manage chronic pain.[10]

Psychological Predispositions

Pessimistic attitude toward yourself, the world, and the future. This negative attitude is called the "cognitive triad" of depression. It has been shown to reliably predict depressive symptoms.[11]

Neuroticism. Neuroticism is a personality trait associated with a tendency to have mood and anxiety disorders. People who are high in this trait are more likely to experience a broad range of negative emotions, including sadness, anxiety, guilt, and hostility.[12]

CONTINUED ON NEXT PAGE

CONTINUED FROM PREVIOUS PAGE

Low self-esteem. Low levels of self-esteem have been shown to predict depression in large studies and to be implicated in both the cause and the maintenance of depression.[13]

Social/Environmental Predispositions

Childhood neglect or physical or sexual abuse. Although childhood neglect or abuse may act as a risk factor for depression, the experience of childhood trauma by itself does not mean you are destined to suffer from depression. It is simply one of many factors that increase the risk of developing depression. However, childhood sexual abuse has been shown to interact with and increase the negative aspects of life stressors, especially in women.[14]

Orphanhood. Losing a parent at an early age is another factor in depression.[15]

Depressed parent. Growing up with a depressed parent is a risk factor on two counts: first it may indicate a genetic predisposition, and second, the depressed parent may not be emotionally available for the child during crucial stages of development.[16]

Poverty. Living in poverty is a risk factor for depression, especially, according to one recent survey, if you live in an urban area.[17]

Let's turn our attention to Robert, a patient who was suffering from a major depressive episode, to see how an underlying predisposition can interact with current life stressors to create a perfect storm for depression.

Robert's Story

Robert, the only child of a blue-blood Boston mother and Wall Street mogul father, sought therapy after he had purchased a gun with the intention of killing himself. He had recently learned that his wife of six years was planning to divorce him. Although they had been having difficulties almost from the beginning of their marriage, he thought they could work out their latest bout of problems and give their relationship another go. His wife, apparently, did not agree.

Robert's father had committed suicide when Robert was ten years old, after having lost the family fortune in a questionable investment scheme. Robert's mother had insisted that Robert keep his chin up; he wasn't allowed to grieve the loss of his father. Meanwhile, his mother began to drink heavily and was emotionally unavailable to Robert as he matured. She became a hermit, according to Robert, locking herself in her suite of rooms with a bottle and refusing to admit that the family was no longer on the "A list" of Boston society.

Robert had done well for himself, getting a degree from a top-tier school and following his father's footsteps into a prominent Wall Street firm. But he had always felt like an imposter and reported that if he let his guard down, he was sure people would eventually discover how frail he was.

• • •

Robert was clinically depressed by the time he sought help and was long past the almost depressed days of his youth at college. However, his case demonstrates how underlying predispositions (he has many, including losing a parent at an early age, growing up with alcoholism, and having low self-esteem) can combine with current stressors (his marital problems) to lead to a serious depression.

However, there is reason for hope: even in the presence of

a strong predisposition and current life stressors, having strong protective factors can help you weather the storm. A more recent model of depression incorporates protective factors into the vulnerability/stress model. This newer work is called the vulnerability/stress/coping model.

Figure 5.
Vulnerability/Stress/Coping Model

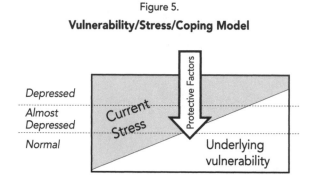

Notice that in the vulnerability/stress/coping model of depression, underlying predisposition and current life stressors still combine to increase the risk of depression; however, in this model that risk is pushed down again by the presence of protective factors. Although the research on protective factors is relatively new, we already know that many protective factors are behaviors and skills that can be *learned*. So even if you have a large predisposition to depression, you can counter this risk by increasing your protective factors. Many protective factors—and ways you can implement them in your life—are described in part 2 of this book.

Protective factors, like risk factors, can be biological, psychological, or social in nature. Briefly, here are some of the protective factors for depression that have been identified:

- physical well-being (we'll discuss this in chapters 5 and 14)
- an optimistic but realistic attitude (in chapter 9)
- a proactive problem-focused coping style (in chapter 8)
- self-efficacy (in chapter 6)
- a strong social support system (in chapter 12)
- a belief in something greater than yourself (in chapters 6 and 16)

Brittany's Story

Brittany, a twenty-year-old waitress, had always dreamed of going to college and escaping the poverty and alcoholism that defined her family. When she was twelve years old, her father, who often came home drunk after work, began sexually abusing her. When her mother, who was also an alcoholic, found out about the abuse, she took Brittany and moved out of the family apartment to a rented trailer in a poorly maintained trailer park. Brittany claims that the rankness of their home in the trailer park was actually a blessing. She hated to be home so much that she spent as many hours as she could in the local library, where she honed her writing and study skills.

Brittany saw college as the way out of her impoverished circumstances. Unfortunately, she initially received rejection letters from all the colleges to which she had applied. This was at first a devastating blow to her. But she soon recovered and decided to support herself by working in the coffee shop and taking courses at her local community college. She planned to send out another batch of college applications the next year, by which time she also expected to have saved more money toward her future education. Happily, Brittany was accepted to a four-year college the next year and also received financial aid. She feels confident that she can make a good life for herself and hopes to be able to someday make life easier for her mother as well.

. . .

Brittany's story illustrates how vulnerability factors (childhood sexual abuse, family alcoholism, and poverty) can interact with life stressors (college rejection) to create an opening for depression. However, it also illustrates how protective factors (Brittany's optimistic attitude, social support from a mother who would not allow abuse to continue, and Brittany's sense of self-efficacy) can temper the one-two punch of vulnerability and stress to keep a person's head above the waters of depression.

There are many risk factors for depression in its many forms, and sometimes the combination of risk factors and life stressors is simply too overwhelming to be managed. However, learning strategies that will strengthen your protective factors will give you the best shot at keeping depression at bay. If you are almost depressed, and are not yet in the deep waters of full-blown depression, now is the time to take action and use some of the strategies in this book. At any time, however, if you feel you are losing the battle with depression, please seek help from a mental health professional. There are a number of effective treatments, and you don't have to fight the battle against depression alone.

■ ◆ ■

3

Almost Depression and the Role of Stress

There cannot be a stressful crisis next week.
My schedule is already full.
—Henry Kissinger

We've all felt "stressed out" from time to time in our lives, and most of us know that too much stress that lasts too long isn't healthy. But what exactly is stress? How does it contribute to almost depression? And how can we tell whether our stress level is unhealthy?

We'll address all of those questions in this chapter, but first meet Pia, a doctor who is under a great deal of stress both at work and at home.

Pia's Story

Pia is an emergency department (ED) physician with two young children and a poorly trained cocker spaniel named Woo. Her husband, who is in the import/export business, travels for months at a time. Pia's mother-in-law has recently moved in to help with the kids while Pia works. Pia had originally joined a group of ED doctors with the expectation of a salaried position and a set number of shifts per week, which would allow her a good bit of family time. She liked the idea that she would not have to bring her work home with her or be awakened by the late-night calls that her colleagues in private practice experienced. However, when one of the partners in her group had a heart attack, Pia began to take on more shifts and work longer hours to keep the ED covered. She feels guilty if she is called to do extra work and refuses. She also feels guilty about her role as a mother, expressing remorse that she is missing out on her children's milestones, but finding she has little patience for their daily problems when she does have so-called quality time with them. And she has no patience at all with her mother-in-law, whom she views as "taking over" her household. She feels mildly resentful of her husband for traveling and is somewhat short with him when he's at home. This shortness on her part leads to more guilt. In fact, everything from her job to taking care of her family is beginning to feel like one big hassle and guilt trip, and Pia sees no hope that things will improve. She is constantly fatigued and on edge. One night, Woo had an accident on the expensive Chinese carpet, and it seemed like the last straw. Pia responded by doing something that as a physician she knew was irrational: she bought a package of cigarettes and lit up for the first time in seventeen years. Pia's stress level is leading her down a dangerous path. She is not enjoying either her work or her family: she is almost depressed.

・ ・ ・

Pia is visibly overwhelmed by the stress in her life. She has reached the point at which even minor events, such as Woo's accident on the carpet, are causing an overreactive stress response. But it's important to understand that not all stress is unhealthy. Humans actually need a certain amount of stress to function effectively. Good stress (called *eu*stress) provides energy and motivation to surmount obstacles. Most of us face a multitude of stressful situations each day and navigate them successfully. However, when stress becomes too intense or is unrelenting, it becomes *dis*tress. This type of stress is damaging and can lead to health problems, such as heart disease or ulcers, as well as the depressive symptoms—fatigue, inability to concentrate, guilt, and feelings of hopelessness—that Pia is experiencing. In fact, recent studies suggest that chronic stress precedes most (as many as 80 percent) of the episodes of both almost depression and clinical depression.[1]

Let's take a closer look at the stress response.

Perceived Stress

The stress response is a physical reaction in your brain and body to a perceived threat or challenge. These threats and challenges (called stressors) can originate in the environment (anything from a traffic jam or a deadline at work to a natural disaster) or they can originate internally within your body or mind (for instance, a stomachache or an unpleasant memory). When you're exposed to a perceived stressor, your brain sends out signals to the body to prepare for action. The body responds by secreting the stress hormones adrenaline and cortisol, increasing your heart rate and blood pressure and preparing you, in varying degrees, to respond to the threat. This response is also called "the fight-or-flight response." When the threat subsides, your body returns to its normal resting state. (To learn more about what's going on in the body during the stress response, see appendix B: The Biology of Stress.)

Notice that we use the phrases "perceived threat" and "perceived stressor." That's because one person's stressor may be another person's source of pleasure. How you perceive an event, situation, or experience will determine whether, and to what degree, the physical stress response is initiated. For example, one person may consider the morning commute in traffic to be a major source of stress, while another person may look forward to the commuting time as a pleasant chance to mentally organize the day ahead. Likewise, one person may consider giving a speech in front of strangers to be a terrifying and highly stressful event, while another person might consider the same speech as just another part of the day's work.

Researchers have found that several factors determine perceived stress:

- the objective demands imposed by an event or situation
- the individual's attitudes about the event or situation
- the individual's appraisal of his or her ability to cope with the situation

Let's look at each of these factors separately.

Objective Demands

Although there is indeed a subjective component to perceived stress, certain events or situations are universally considered to be stressful. Thus, we can say there is also an *objective* component to many stressors. In the 1960s, psychiatrists Thomas Holmes and Richard Rahe rated the amount of stress generated by a set of common life events according to how each of the events correlated to stress-related health problems, such as heart disease.[2] They found, for instance, that the most stressful life event was the "death of a spouse," while the least stressful of the forty-three events they rated was a "minor violation of the law." This table shows a few examples of the stressful life events that Holmes and Rahe identified, as well as the stress points (on a scale from 1 to 100) associated with each.

Table 3.
Common Life Events Stress Ratings

Life Event	Points
Death of a spouse	100
Marital separation	65
Personal injury or illness	53
Marriage	50
Retirement	45
Foreclosure of a mortgage	30
Trouble with boss	23
Minor violation of the law	11

Holmes and Rahe further found that an *accumulation* of stressors predicted health problems (generally, a score of 300 stress points indicated dangerously high stress). So, while no single event by itself was related to poor health, as the number of stressful life events increased, so did the health risk. One of the interesting findings of this research was that events we often think of as positive, such as vacations, weddings, or promotions, can also add to our overall stress load. The updated Holmes-Rahe Stress Inventory is still widely used and is available at no charge at several Internet sites.

In addition to life events, certain living conditions can increase stress, such as ongoing marital or family problems, health problems, chronic pain, poverty, mental or physical disabilities, or social isolation. Environmental conditions, such as noise, heat, wind, flashing lights, and noxious odors, can also increase stress. And finally, daily hassles, such as traffic, computer problems, rude salesclerks, and missed appointments, all can add to the objective stress load you are carrying.

Attitude toward Stressors

The second factor that determines whether an event or situation will activate the body's stress response is your personal attitude and thought processes concerning the potential stressor.[3] If, for example, you believe that visiting your in-laws is a hassle, then your preconceived attitude will increase the stress you feel in anticipation of this event and will actually initiate the physical stress response. Often much of the stress we experience is due to our predetermined *conviction* that the event will be stressful. In fact, a 2011 study conducted by researchers in Singapore found a strong connection between negative thoughts and perceived stress, with negative thoughts accounting for about 44 percent of stress.[4]

Perceived Ability to Cope

Finally, your perception of how well you can *cope* with a potentially stressful event determines in part whether the event will activate a physical stress response. Again, let's consider the situation in which you must give a presentation to a group of people you do not know. Public speaking evokes pretty severe anxiety in about 33 percent of the population and is used regularly in psychology experiments to induce a stress response. Yet many people, for example politicians and college professors, give public speeches on a daily basis with no apparent experience of fear and with only slight perturbations in the stress response. These professional public speakers are confident in their ability to handle public speaking, and therefore, they experience no serious increase in their stress level when doing so. Researchers Richard Lazarus and Susan Folkman have dubbed this the "transactional" model of stress.[5] Their model suggests that the stress response is a transaction between a potential stressor in the environment and the individual's *perceived ability to handle* that stressor. When you feel that you have the resources to deal with a stressor, you tend to see the stressor as a *challenge*; on the other hand, when you are unsure you have the necessary internal or external resources to cope with it, you perceive the stressor as a *threat*. This challenge-versus-threat appraisal makes a big difference in how your body responds to the situation. (See the sidebar "Stress Response: The Good, the Bad, and the Ugly.") Even a small event can initiate a stress response in those who believe they will have trouble coping. Further, even if a person perceives that he or she can cope with an individual stressor just fine, when the stressors start piling up, as they did in Pia's case, the person may feel lacking in resources to deal with all the challenges simultaneously.

Many other factors influence whether you *perceive* a situation or event to be stressful. These include, but are not limited to, your temperament and personality, early childhood experiences, your genetic predisposition, your mood, your health, the total burden of stress you are currently under, and your *self-efficacy* (your general belief in your ability to handle the slings and arrows of life). The good news is that many of these factors are controllable. As you'll learn throughout this book, it is possible to break away from your habitual perceptions and reactions to stressors, and to perceive and respond in innovative, healthful ways.

Figure 6.

Threat Appraisal

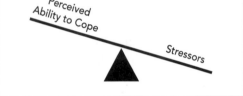
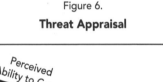

Threat appraisal leads to distress response.

Figure 7.

Challenge Appraisal

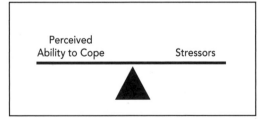

Challenge appraisal leads to eustress response.

Stress Response: The Good, the Bad, and the Ugly

Scientists have known for decades that the way you appraise a stressful situation can affect the stress response. Appraisal (that is, whether you interpret a specific event or situation as stressful and also how you interpret your ability to handle the situation or event) helps determine whether your stress system releases the cascade of chemicals that place the brain and body into "high alert" mode. Now, however, researchers here in our labs at Harvard have demonstrated that the way you appraise the stress response itself affects the physiological aspects of stress. It turns out that there is a good (adaptive) stress response and a bad (maladaptive) stress response that can affect both your current ability to respond well to a stressor and your long-term physical and mental health.[6]

When you're faced with a stressor, your body initiates the stress response and you begin to feel your heart racing. If you believe you can cope with the stressor, you experience what researchers call a *challenge* response (adaptive): your heart rate continues to increase and your blood flow becomes more efficient, enabling you to meet the challenge with increased physical strength and energy. If, however, you believe you cannot cope with the stressor, you experience a *threat* response (maladaptive): again, your heart rate increases, but your blood vessels become constricted, increasing blood pressure and preparing the body for avoidance of the stressor and defeat.[7] The *threat* response is associated with poorer decision making and, if prolonged over time, can lead to ugly results, including mental decline, heart disease, and anxiety and mood disorders.

It appears that you can actually change your physiological response from maladaptive to adaptive, however, by reframing

CONTINUED ON NEXT PAGE

CONTINUED FROM PREVIOUS PAGE

your appraisal of the stress response. In a unique study, researchers put participants through a stressful protocol in which they were required to give a public speech.[8] Some of the participants were told that feeling their heart beat faster was a positive sign and was related to better performance on the task; in other words, they were primed for a *challenge* response. Other participants were told nothing about the effects of elevated heart rate. All subjects were monitored for heart rate and blood pressure throughout the task. As expected, the group primed for the *challenge* response showed a more adaptive physiological response to the stressful task and reported feeling less anxiety. The group who had not been primed for challenge felt more anxious and had a more maladaptive physiological response to the task. While this research did not specifically look at symptoms of depression, the results nonetheless suggest that just changing the way you think about your body's response to stress may reduce your stress load and improve your mood.

Chronic Stress and Depression

The human stress response developed over evolutionary time to allow us to respond rapidly to a discrete danger (such as a predator or a natural disaster) by fighting or taking flight. However, when a person is under chronic stress—such as Pia is experiencing—the stress response never fully shuts off and the body remains "hyped up" with an overabundance of circulating cortisol. You have probably heard cortisol called "the stress hormone." That's because the amount of cortisol in the bloodstream increases when we're under stress and is often used as a marker indicating how much stress an individual is experiencing. High sustained levels of cortisol can damage brain structures such as the hippocampus, which is important for learning and memory. High sustained levels of cortisol have also been detected in people suffering from low-level and moderate depression. Which brings us to a second question we would like to address here: How does stress contribute to almost depression?

The first thing to note is that stressful events and situations have long been associated with a risk for major depression. Both major life events, such as those ranked by Holmes and Rahe back in the 1960s, and ongoing stressors, such as marital problems, financial difficulties, or health problems, have been linked to the development of depression. Chronic and unremitting stress has been shown to increase the symptoms of both clinical and subclinical depression, including fatigue, loss of enjoyment, difficulty sleeping, and trouble concentrating.

A second factor linking stress and almost depression was highlighted in a 2010 review by researchers at Temple University:[9] Not only does stress lead to depressive symptoms, but depressive symptoms *increase* your exposure to stress. This reciprocal relationship between stress and depressive symptoms suggests that becoming *almost depressed* actively contributes to generating additional stress that, in turn, increases your risk for future depression. This interaction creates a cycle of ever-increasing negative emotions, thoughts, and behaviors.

Figure 8.
Stress-Depression Cycle

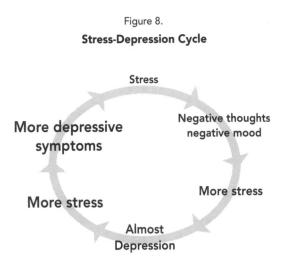

Another recent finding determined that the more *types* of stressors you experience, the greater your risk for depressive symptoms. In this study, researchers examined information on stress and depressive symptoms gathered in a national survey of over 17,000 Canadian residents.[10] They divided stressors into four categories: negative life events (such as a divorce or death in the family), chronic stressors (such as ongoing health, financial, or relationship issues), perceived job strain (such as lack of support from your boss or worries about job security), and early childhood traumas (such as sexual abuse or loss of a parent—note that early traumas have been shown to exert stress across the life span). People who reported stressors in all four categories had a risk for depressive symptoms that was *seven times greater* than those who had stressors in only one of these categories. This research may be important to individuals like Pia, who are experiencing multiple types of stressors. Reducing stressors at work may allow her to adequately manage stress at home or vice versa, while trying to manage stressors on multiple fronts may lead to almost depression and that ugly stress-depression cycle.

Positive Stress

Now let's return to the idea mentioned at the beginning of this chapter that humans need a certain amount of stress to function normally. Just as too much stress can be overwhelming, too little stress can lead to feelings of boredom and ennui. When you are overburdened with stress, like Pia, you may feel the only way to cope is simply to eliminate all stress-producing circumstances in your life—this is the "stop the world; I want to get off" approach to stress management. But if you somehow manage to stop the world and get off (we're not talking about seven days on a Caribbean island, which could very well be what the doctor ordered; we're talking about sustained low stress over an extended period of time), this lack of stress can also lead to almost depression. We need stress—*eu*stress or the type of stress we consider to be a *challenge* rather than a *threat*—to maintain our interest and sense of purpose in life. Consider the case of Kenneth.

Kenneth's Story

Kenneth, the owner of a successful commercial real estate firm, had looked forward to retirement for seven years. He had eagerly awaited the end of late-night phone calls from clients; dealing with lawyers, tax liens, incompetent employees, developers who didn't follow through on promises; working fourteen-hour days; and eating most of his meals on the run. He also looked forward to selling the large family home he and his wife had lived in for thirty-one years, describing it as "the original money pit," a constant maintenance nightmare, and a huge source of stress. When seen for counseling, Kenneth had sold his real estate firm and big house and he had been retired in Florida for two years. He now had plenty of time to pursue his dreams of golf, fishing, and leisurely meals in the area's great restaurants. However, after a few months of "the dream life," Kenneth began to feel irritable and restless. Golf and fishing were beginning to lose their appeal. And leisurely meals were less enjoyable than he had anticipated because, as he put it, "nothing tastes that good anymore." His wife complained that all he did was mope around their large condo in his bathrobe. "No matter what I suggest we do, his answer is 'Not interested,'" she related. "He used to be this cyclone of activity. . . . Now he's just like a gray cloud casting an unhappy shadow over everything I try to do." Kenneth was almost depressed—not due to too much stress but to lack of stress.

• • •

How can a lack of stress contribute to almost depression? When nothing in your environment initiates the stress response, you are either (a) not challenged by events or situations in your environment or (b) not motivated to respond to challenges in your environment. This is a state we call "boredom," or as a recent research article in the *Journal of Social and Clinical Psychology* described it, a "state of core motivational deficits accompanied by a phenomenological experience of a lack of interest or [emotional] engagement."[11] Note that, according to this rather long-winded definition, the emotional state of boredom is almost identical to one of the core symptoms of almost depression: a lack of interest in activities that you used to find interesting.

While boredom is not depression, extended periods of boredom may pose a risk for developing depression-spectrum conditions. The same brain chemicals that are present when you feel interested, engaged, and motivated are lacking in both boredom and depression. Failing to find meaningful interests and challenges in life (in other words, feeling bored and lacking stress) decreases brain arousal and is associated with reduced production of the brain chemicals dopamine and norepinephrine—both crucial to positive mental health.

Kenneth's story raises an important point about retirement. Many people look forward to retirement as a period of well-deserved stress-free time. We have talked to many clients and patients who believe that when they retire, they will finally be happy since they will be living a life of leisure. However, as Kenneth found, leisure does not equal happiness. As more and more of the Baby Boomer generation reaches retirement age, we may need to rethink what retirement should look like. We believe that people need to plan ahead for retirement, not only in a financial sense but also in a purpose-driven sense, so that retirement doesn't consist of endless days of unstructured time combined with loss of purpose. We humans feel happiest and are at our best when we are working toward goals and overcoming challenges along the way. In fact, one of the important components of treatment for depression is to help clients set goals and engage in activities that are meaningful and attainable. We'll discuss this in more detail in chapter 6.

Figure 9.

No Threat/Challenge Appraisal

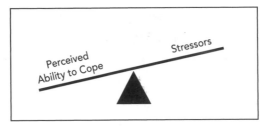

No threat/challenge appraisal leads to boredom response.

Figure 10.

Challenge Appraisal

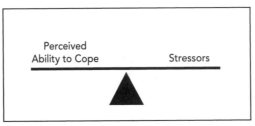

Challenge appraisal leads to eustress response.

So there is an optimal amount of stress that not only helps you to be productive but also improves your mood and reduces negative emotional states. This is the "dose-dependent" or Goldilocks effect of stress: a large, sustained dose of stress is unhealthy; likewise, too little stress is unhealthy; but a moderate amount of stress is just right.

In retirement, Kenneth has overcompensated for his former high-stress life and now needs to "up" the challenges he experiences to feel productive and engaged. The signs of chronic underarousal are boredom, low mood, irritability, and those almost depressed symptoms of fatigue, restlessness, anhedonia, and irritability. Kenneth can likely relieve those symptoms and work his way out of almost depression by setting and working toward meaningful and challenging goals in his personal, physical, social, professional, and spiritual life. For example, he may decide to work part-time again or to start a completely new business in his retirement.

Recognizing the Warning Signs of Stress

In Kenneth's story, we learned about a stress level that is too low. Now, how can you tell if your stress level is dangerously high? Research has shown again and again that we are rather bad at recognizing when we're dangerously stressed. Certainly, if we experience a serious life event or face a potential life-changing crisis, we know that we're under stress. However, less critical stressors have a way of building up gradually without our recognition until our stress load reaches the danger level and we are suddenly ready to crack. One of the best ways to keep this from happening is to learn to recognize your personal warning signs of stress. These signs can involve physical changes, emotional changes, or changes in your thinking or behavior.

Read through the following list of typical signs of stress, and using table 4 or a sheet of paper, check those you've noticed in yourself in the past. (You can also download this exercise at www.AlmostDepressed.com.) You might want to ask someone close to you to help you identify small changes in your behavior that occur when you're under stress. You may, for example, have particular little "I'm stressed!" giveaways that your loved ones recognize, but that you may not have noticed.

Table 4.

Typical Signs of Stress

Physical Changes	Behavior Changes
☐ Loss of energy or fatigue	☐ Drinking too much alcohol
☐ Stomach problems	☐ Increased tobacco use
☐ Tense muscles	☐ Eating compulsively
☐ Problems sleeping	☐ Grinding your teeth
☐ Frequent headaches	☐ Acting "bossy"
☐ Loss of sex drive	☐ Yelling or shouting at others
☐ Excessive sweating	☐ Driving too fast
☐ Loss of appetite	☐ Using drugs
☐ Shortness of breath	☐ Overdoing activities
☐ Difficulty with sexual arousal/ orgasm	☐ Sleeping too much
☐ Restlessness	☐ Nail-biting, hair-twisting
☐ Skin breakout	☐ Pacing or fidgeting
☐ Other _____	☐ Laughing or crying inappropriately
Emotional Changes	☐ Picking fights
☐ Loss of interest in activities or work	☐ Road rage
☐ Anxiety	☐ Other _____
☐ Irritability with others	
☐ Sadness or depressed mood	**Cognitive Changes**
☐ Anger or resentment toward others	☐ Trouble concentrating
☐ Sudden shifts in mood	☐ Trouble remembering things
☐ Increased mood sensitivity	☐ Confusion
☐ Overreacting to minor situations	☐ Difficulty making decisions
☐ Frustration	☐ Repeating thoughts
☐ Impatience	☐ Criticizing yourself
☐ Frequent uneasiness, restlessness	☐ Poor judgment
☐ Feeling pressured or trapped	☐ Racing thoughts
☐ Feeling emotionally numb	☐ Self-doubt or low self-confidence
☐ Feeling overwhelmed	☐ Pessimistic and negative thoughts
☐ Other _____	☐ Other _____

In a notebook or journal, write down the items you noted to create your personalized list of signs that your stress load is too high. Check yourself periodically for your stress signs, and as soon as you notice them, begin to take action to manage your stress so it doesn't lead to almost depression and beyond.

• • •

In chapter 8, we will discuss a number of steps you can take to reduce your stress level and keep it down, so that it won't contribute to future depression. In the meantime, if you find that you are under a great deal of stress due to negative life events or ongoing stressful conditions in your life, consider these recommendations:

1. *Try not to make major life decisions* when your stress level is very high.

2. *Avoid additional stress* while your stress level is high by saying no to new responsibilities. While it's hard to say no when someone asks for help or a favor, your first responsibility has to be to care for yourself; remember that you will not be able to help anyone if you are caught in an almost depressed funk. One helpful trick is to prepare and rehearse a "no" response in advance. That way, when someone asks you for a favor or tries to saddle you with a new responsibility, you will not have to think about it—you can just present your prepared response. Here are some examples of graceful ways to say no: "That sounds like a wonderful opportunity, but I'm not able to help out this time" or "My schedule just won't allow me to _____ (fill in the blank) at this time. But thank you for thinking of me."

3. *Be patient with yourself.* The more stress you're under, the more irritable or short with others you are likely to be. You may also be prone to forget small obligations or to perform everyday tasks less efficiently because of the effects stress has on concentration and memory. *This is normal.* It doesn't mean you're a bad person. Don't beat yourself up for these minor slips, apologize when necessary, and give yourself some leeway until you are able to bring your stress level down.

4. *Reduce underlying stressors where possible.* If going out with friends seems like just one more stressful thing, then gracefully beg out. If spending Sunday with your in-laws will raise your adrenaline level, then offer to stay home and fix the sink faucet instead. If the sight of your son's messy room makes you feel anxious, then shut the door and don't go in there. We are recommending that you avoid increasing your stress level until you can bring down the temperature on your stress thermometer. However, this doesn't mean that you can use "I'm too stressed" as a catchall excuse to avoid your major obligations.

5. *Build in time in each day to relax and have fun.* Each day should have moments that you look forward to, whether it's a walk in the woods, watching a favorite TV show, or taking a hot bath.

6. *Make time during the day for reflection or meditation.* Unplug from your smartphone, tablet, or computer, even if just for a few moments, and allow yourself a few precious moments to reflect on your day and give your

brain a momentary rest from the constant stream of incoming information.

7. *Enhance connection with others* by placing a brief call or sending a text, email, or card. Especially during times of high stress, reaching out by offering small thoughtful gifts, such as a smile or a friendly nod, connects us with others. It may also be helpful to consider the numerous other people in your town, city, county, or state who may be experiencing similar difficulties. These practices may help you to recognize that although you may be stressed, you are not alone.

8. *Notice changes in nature.* When stress is "too much," try investigating some aspect of nature, such as a cloud, the wind, or the light. Notice how the natural world is constantly in flux and yet remains stable and whole. Observing aspects of nature may give you a sense that, even if things are pretty stressful in your life right now, there is an underlying stability and rhythm to the world.

You have taken a big step forward if you can recognize your personal signs of stress. In part 2, we'll discuss ways you can adjust your stress level, improve your mood, and protect yourself from the negative consequences of almost depression.

■ ◆ ■

| 4 |

Almost Depression . . .
or Something Else?

Illness is the night side of life . . .
—Susan Sontag

If you're feeling almost depressed but don't have a family history of depression and haven't experienced a recent stressful life event, your symptoms may be caused by some other condition, such as a medical condition or the side effect of a medication. Fatigue, loss of motivation, weight loss, sleep difficulties, and dysphoric mood (feeling unwell or unhappy) can be caused by certain medical conditions and medications. In this chapter, we'll describe conditions that mimic depression. You can then check with your doctor to rule out any physical illnesses that might be masquerading as almost depression.

Jonas's Story

Jonas is a fifty-two-year-old African American who owns a small chain of successful convenience stores. Although he is usually a sociable and jolly family man, Jonas's personality seemed to change over a period of a few weeks. He became sullen and distant, preferring to spend evenings alone in his den rather than playing with his grandchildren who lived next door. His wife was concerned about him, but he brushed off her concern and said he just needed time alone to think. He was having trouble sleeping, and Jonas's wife could hear him pacing downstairs in the middle of the night.

One morning, Jonas announced that he was not going to work. He had lost interest in the business, he claimed, and his twenty-eight-year-old son (who helped manage the stores) could take care of things. Jonas eventually stopped getting dressed in the morning and just sat in his study all day in his bathrobe. When his wife tried to bring him meals or talk to him, he would shoo her away. She became increasingly alarmed over her husband's depression, and finally took action when their son told her that Jonas had called him and asked him to bring home a revolver that Jonas kept at the store for security.

Together, his son and wife convinced Jonas to go to the emergency room. He agreed and finally admitted that he was having symptoms he hadn't told them about, including periodic weakness in his right arm and leg. A neurological examination revealed that Jonas had sustained a series of minor strokes that had caused the weakness in his limbs and likely his symptoms of depression.

Elizabeth's Story

Elizabeth, the principal of a large private high school, visited her doctor complaining of fatigue, weight gain, difficulty sleeping, lack of motivation, and attention problems. She reported feeling irritable much of the time and felt that she was over-reacting to even small frustrations. This was a real change from her usually easygoing manner. Blood tests revealed an endocrine problem, which her doctor described to Elizabeth as "low thyroid."

Elizabeth was treated with thyroid medications, and after two months of ups and downs during which the dosage was adjusted to the right level, she was feeling like her old self.

. . .

Jonas's strokes and Elizabeth's low thyroid caused symptoms that mimicked depression. A variety of other medical conditions also mimic mild, moderate, and even severe depression. These imitators are identifiable through a medical examination, and most are treatable conditions.

The first clue in determining whether a medical condition may be causing your depressive symptoms is to review the order in which symptoms appeared. If the symptoms of almost depression or clinical depression started or worsened around the same time that medical symptoms became apparent, then it's possible that your depression symptoms may be due to an underlying medical condition.

A second consideration is the way the symptoms of depression change when the medical condition is treated. If the mood symptoms improve when the medical condition is treated, it is more likely that the medical condition caused the mood disorder. If the mood symptoms don't improve, then the depression symptoms are probably not related to the medical condition.

Here is a partial list of medical conditions that may cause depression symptoms:

- certain cancers
- thyroid problems
- disorders of the adrenal glands
- disorders of the parathyroid glands
- diabetes
- anemia (including iron deficiency)
- B12 and other B vitamin deficiencies
- low blood sugar
- mononucleosis
- HIV or hepatitis
- Lyme disease
- influenza
- heart disease
- chronic fatigue syndrome
- fibromyalgia
- neurological conditions, such as stroke
- multiple sclerosis
- Parkinson's disease
- progressive dementias
- sleep disorders, such as sleep apnea
- restless leg syndrome

Any of these conditions may produce symptoms of insomnia, fatigue, irritability, and depressed mood. If you are feeling depressed, review this list with your doctor to rule out a medical cause for your depressive symptoms. If you have one of these conditions, it is likely that appropriate medical treatment will relieve the depression.

Medical Conditions and Demoralization

Besides physically causing depressive symptoms, medical conditions may also psychologically lead to these symptoms. The burden of having a disease or condition can contribute to the stress, frustration, sadness, or hopelessness that a person experiences. Having a serious medical condition can also lead to anxiety, causing insomnia, weight loss, and confusion. It is easy to see how someone with these symptoms could easily qualify for a diagnosis of major depression.

Experts refer to the depression symptoms that go with a serious illness as "demoralization."[1] They argue that demoralization is distinct from depression because it is a normal response to being ill, similar to grief. Its main features are distress and a feeling of incompetence because the person has no control over the illness. If you are feeling demoralized because of a serious medical condition, there are things you can do to reduce your distress. First, make sure you are getting good medical care. Second, work on *accepting* the condition. Acceptance doesn't mean that you accept that your illness will not improve; rather, it means you accept your current state of health and work from there. You can find out more about acceptance in chapter 10. Then consider what is the best possible outcome given your current condition, and set goals to work toward that outcome. You can learn more about setting goals in chapter 6.

Effects of Medications That Mimic Depressive Symptoms

A variety of medications may trigger changes in mood, energy, thinking, or sleep. A person who is taking these medications can seem depressed. Common medications that can cause depressive symptoms are antibiotics, antivirals and antifungals, some blood pressure medications, and medications used to treat acne vulgaris, such as isotretinoin (Accutane).

Other medications, such as oral contraceptives and hormone replacement therapies, can also cause mood fluctuations, as can statin drugs and allergy medications. See the sidebar for a list of medications that have been noted as causing symptoms of depression.[2] It's important to note, however, that most people use these medications without experiencing depression as a side effect.

Medications That Can Cause Depression Symptoms

1. *Antimicrobials, antibiotics, antifungals, and antivirals:* acyclovir (Zovirax); alpha interferons; cycloserine (Seromycin); ethambutol (Myambutol); levofloxacin (Levaquin); metronidazole (Flagyl); streptomycin; sulfonamides (AVC, Sultrin, Trysul); tetracycline; interferon (for treatment of hepatitis C infections); mefloquine (Lariam), used to treat malaria

2. *Heart and blood pressure medications:* digoxin (Digitek, Lanoxicaps, Lanoxin); disopyramide (Norpace); methyldopa (Aldomet); clonidine (Catapres, Kapvay, Nexiclon); reserpine (many brand names include combinations of reserpine and other pharmaceuticals)

3. *Acne medications:* isotretinoin (Accutane) for treatment of acne vulgaris

4. *Hormones:* estrogens when used as oral contraceptives or for hormone replacement therapy; anabolic steroids; danazol (Danocrine); glucocorticoids such as prednisone and adrenocorticotropic hormone; estrogens (such as Premarin, Prempro)

5. *Statins* for high cholesterol: In February 2008, the Food and Drug Administration (FDA) approved a product label change for the cholesterol-lowering drugs ezetimibe (Zetia) and ezetimibe/simvastatin (Vytorin), adding depression as a possible side effect.

6. *Asthma medication:* On March 27, 2008, the FDA issued a safety alert regarding the asthma medication montelukast (Singulair). The alert was issued to inform health care professionals and patients about the agency's investigation into the possible link between Singulair use and depression and suicidal thinking.

7. *Smoking cessation medication:* Several studies have reported an increased incidence of depressive symptoms, erratic behavior, and suicidal thoughts associated with the use of varenicline (Chantix).[3]

8. *Anticonvulsants* used to treat seizure disorders; patients taking barbiturates (phenobarbital), vigabatrin, and topiramate seem to have more depressive symptoms than those on other antiseizure drugs.

9. *Opiates* used to treat pain conditions

10. *Digitalis preparations,* along with a variety of other cardiac medications

CONTINUED ON NEXT PAGE

CONTINUED FROM PREVIOUS PAGE

11. *Gastrointestinal* medications, such as cimetidine (Tagamet) for gastroesophageal reflux disease and metoclopramide (Octamide, Reglan) used for nausea

12. *Indomethacin* and other nonsteroidal anti-inflammatory medications

13. *Disulfiram* (Antabuse), used to help with not drinking alcohol; usually described by patients as more a sense of fatigue than true depression

14. *Antipsychotic medications* can cause an akathesia or inhibition of spontaneity that can both feel and look like a true depression. This is much less common with the newer "atypical" antipsychotic medications.

15. *Anxiolytics:* All sedative hypnotics, from the barbiturates (such as phenobarbital [Solfoton] and secobarbital [Seconal]) to the benzodiazepines (such as diazepam [Valium] and clonazepam [Klonopin]), have been implicated both in causing depression and making it worse in susceptible individuals. However, the benzodiazepines are often used successfully to reduce anxiety in people with anxiety and depression.

16. *Parkinson's disease medications:* levodopa or L-dopa (Larodopa)

Again, most people who take these drugs will *not* have depressive side effects. However, it's important to discuss your prescription medications with your health care professional if you are having any symptoms of depression. If you are experiencing depressive symptoms while on one of these medications, *do not* stop taking your medication until you consult your health care professional. It can be dangerous to do so.

It's also important to look at your family history to see if others in your family have had drug reactions. Many medications may be likely to cause symptoms like fatigue and malaise (meaning a general feeling of being ill or uncomfortable) or a change in appetite. These symptoms may be mistaken for depression. Check to see whether any of the following factors describe you:

- You are over the age of fifty and are experiencing symptoms of depression for the first time.
- You experience symptoms of depression after starting a new medication.
- You're taking multiple medications and beginning to feel depressed.
- You begin to feel depressed after a recent change in dosage of one or more of your medications.

You can help yourself by being aware of your medical history and your family history. If you're taking prescription drugs, check in with your body periodically to see how you're feeling. Take an active role in your treatment by letting your health care professional know about any changes in your mood, sleep, or ability to concentrate.

Psychiatric Conditions and Secondary Depression

As with medical conditions, psychiatric conditions unrelated to depression can cause distress and misery that ultimately lead to depressive symptoms. This type of depression is referred to as "secondary depression," because the depression is the result of the difficulty of coping with other disorders.

Loren's Story

Loren, a medical equipment salesperson, made a good living selling his company's products in a seven-state region in the Northeast. Loren had suffered from a mild tic disorder as a child but had outgrown it by the age of twelve. However, about a year ago, he developed a habit of clearing his throat every few minutes that his doctor thought might be tic-related. About that time, he became obsessed with checking his garage door. Each time he left home, he would convince himself that he had left his garage door open, potentially allowing strangers to enter his property and small animals to sneak in and build nests in his lawnmower engine.

His obsession caused him to return to his home—even if he had driven several miles—to make sure the garage door was closed. Over time, he developed the need to return over and over again to check on the door. He found it impossible to drive more than twenty miles from his home without being overcome with anxiety about the security of his house. His work suffered, and eventually he had to give up his sales territory, because he could no longer service his customers in other states.

Loren became distraught because of his inability to work. He felt his life was ruled by his obsession. He had trouble sleeping, he lost weight, and he felt exhausted and disheartened almost all the time. When his company finally let him go, he momentarily considered suicide. Instead, Loren decided to get medical help. When he arrived for therapy, he complained of being depressed. However, Loren's primary problem was his obsessive-compulsive disorder (OCD). He worked with a therapist specializing in the treatment of OCD and, as Loren gained control over his obsessions and compulsions, his symptoms of depression gradually receded.

. . .

Depression can, in fact, be secondary to a number of psychiatric disorders. These include anxiety disorders, such as panic disorder and social anxiety disorder, post-traumatic stress disorder (PTSD), OCD, eating disorders, and attention deficit/hyperactivity disorder (ADHD). You can often determine whether depressive symptoms are secondary to another disorder by looking at the order in which symptoms appeared. If the symptoms of the other disorder occurred before the depression, as in Loren's case, then it is likely the depression is secondary and will begin to diminish if the other psychiatric disorder is successfully treated.

Abusing substances, including marijuana, alcohol, cocaine, and amphetamines, can also lead to depression. The negative effects of substance abuse on personal relationships, health, finances, and behavior can cause secondary depression, which tends to improve as the substance abuse is controlled or, in the case of dependence, treated. However, substance abuse can also lead to primary depression because of the effect of substances on neurotransmitters in the brain. (We note that some people may use substances such as marijuana or alcohol in an attempt to self-medicate the symptoms of depression. They mistakenly believe that such substances will make them feel better. While these attempts at self-medication may provide some very short-term relief, in the long run, they can actually exacerbate depressive symptoms because of the negative effects of substance abuse on people's lives.)

If you're experiencing clinical or subclinical depression symptoms, there are many steps you can take to start feeling better. However, before you address them, it's important to rule out other causes of depression, such as the medical, drug, and psychiatric causes we've discussed in this chapter. Along with your doctor, review your medical history and prescription medications, and check for symptoms of potential mental disorders to make sure there are no other issues that should be treated before you tackle almost depression or depression.

Stopping the Downward Spiral

The vast research on depression indicates that it is a condition that affects both psychological and physical health. As we reviewed in chapter 2, there is no single cause for depression but rather a complex set of biological, psychological, social, environmental, and stress risk factors that interact with each other. As one area of your life takes a downward turn, it may affect functioning in many other areas.

Your goal is to stop the downward spiral while you are still *almost* depressed. Doing so will not only improve your quality of life, your daily functioning, and your relationships, but will also avert the even more serious effects of a full major depressive episode.

Figure 11.
The Downward Spiral of Depression

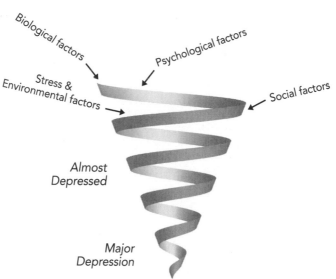

Just as there are many factors that can initiate the downward spiral of depression, there are many pathways out of depression, which you'll discover in part 2. In fact, learning skills and strategies to improve your functioning can also transform the very risk factors that started the downward spiral into protective factors that will not only lead you out of subclinical depression but will be a buffer to becoming depressed in the future. These skills and strategies are adapted from therapies that have broad scientific backing for effectiveness, including cognitive-behavioral therapy (CBT), interpersonal therapy (IPT), problem-solving therapy (PST), and mindfulness-based cognitive therapy (MBCT). What is interesting is that these skills and strategies have been shown to change the actual structure of the brain in areas associated with reasoning, decision making, emotion, and memories.[4] We also include strategies backed by clinical trials that involve the use of supplements. Each pathway offers a different approach to treating depressive symptoms; however, evidence suggests you can start with any of the pathways and experience improvement across all factors.

◆

Part 2

Moving from the Grays
to Bright

TAKING THE
Behavioral Pathway

| 5 |

Enhancing Your Mood
through Movement

My get up and go has got up and went.
—Pete Seeger (quoting "Anonymous")

One of the common signs of almost depression is fatigue and lack of motivation. It seems that you just don't have the energy or desire to do the things you used to do. And as a consequence, you find yourself becoming less and less physically active—and more withdrawn and socially isolated. We call this "behavioral *de*activation." Even if you have considered yourself a high-energy person in the past, once this downward trend in activity begins, you may find that you soon become an honorary member of the Couch Potato Club, as your ability to savor life is gradually replaced by ennui, inactivity, and apathy. Let's look at two women who experienced behavioral deactivation leading to almost depression.

Betty Ann's Story

Betty Ann is a seventy-four-year-old widow in good physical health who lives in a senior citizen housing complex outside of Boston. Her children live in distant cities and she rarely sees them. Her life has turned into a daily routine of watching daytime television shows, making occasional meals, and watching sitcoms in the evening. Once a week, a van from the senior center takes her to the mall to do her grocery shopping. Other than that, Betty Ann seldom leaves her apartment. She used to walk to the nearby library twice a week. She also used to participate in the activities, including a yoga class, provided at her local senior center. She has stopped doing this because "it's too much effort." Likewise, she rarely cooks anymore, finding it easier to make a sandwich when she gets hungry (which she seldom does). Betty Ann remembers when she used to enjoy cooking for neighbors, going to the theater, and participating in a book club with friends. But she sprained an ankle last winter and had to temporarily curtail her outings. Even though her ankle is fine now, she never got back into the swing of things. She has found that the more she stays at home, the harder it is to motivate herself to go out. She has started taking over-the-counter sleeping aids to deal with her sleeping problem. She confided that she also hopes that a good long sleep will help "fill the hours" of her boring days. Betty Ann is almost depressed.

• • •

Now let's also look at Taylor's case. Although Taylor and Betty Ann are miles apart in age and life circumstances, they share behavioral deactivation and the beginning signs of depression.

Taylor's Story

Taylor, age nineteen, is a sophomore at a private college in the Northeast. She grew up in Georgia, where she liked to play tennis and go hunting with her father and brother. During her freshman year, both the harsh winter climate and the workload of her courses kept her indoors. As a result, instead of the "freshman fifteen," she gained twenty-two pounds during her first year at school. During the summer break back in Georgia, Taylor was embarrassed to let her old high school friends see how much weight she had gained, so she "hermitted out" as she called it, and basically avoided going places where she would have to interact with friends. Although she was determined to lose weight when she returned to school in the fall, she soon slipped back into the sedentary habits of her freshman year. Most of the information she needs for her courses is online, so she rarely needs to visit the library. When she isn't studying, she plays video games or watches movies on her computer. She doesn't leave her room except to attend classes and eat at the campus cafeteria. She admits, however, that she prefers to get a pizza delivered right to the dorm. She has stopped getting dressed in the morning and, like many of her classmates, goes to class in the same sweats she sleeps in. "What's the point of getting dressed? I'm just coming back to the room right after class—it's not like I have anything else to do," she explains. Also, the sweats hide the extra pounds that seem to be piling on. Taylor admits that she hasn't even actually attended her classes for a few weeks. She can watch videos of the lectures online, so only needs to show up at the lecture hall to take exams. She realizes she is slipping into some bad habits, but she says, "It's just easier to live this way." Taylor is almost depressed.

• • •

For both Betty Ann and Taylor, their spiral toward depression began with physical inactivity. The inactivity then led to social isolation and reduced their motivation to do almost anything. Low motivation led to further decline in physical activity, and before they understood what was happening, both Betty Ann and Taylor were caught in a very common downward spiral into almost depression.

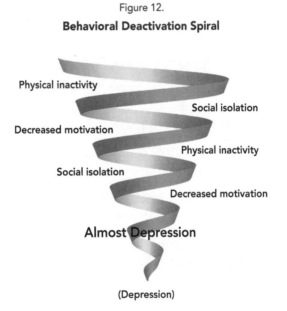

Figure 12.
Behavioral Deactivation Spiral

The good news is that, just as physical inactivity can be an entry point into this downward spiral, increasing physical activity (in other words, behavioral *activation*) and engagement in pleasurable activities can lead to an upward spiral that improves your mood, restores your motivation, and begins to lift the fog of almost depression. You can increase behavioral activation through a physical exercise regimen or simply by spending more time each day engaged in pleasurable activities that require you to get out in the world. Even when you're feeling good, it can be really difficult to motivate yourself to exercise, so we understand that this is even more challenging if you're almost depressed. But if you can make yourself do it, you will find that getting active will provide many benefits. Let's look at the benefits of physical exercise first.

The Effects of Physical Exercise on Mood

Researchers and therapists have long known that exercise improves depressive symptoms. Community studies have shown that people who are more physically active have a lower risk for depression than those who do not exercise. In fact, physically active people have 30 percent lower odds of depression than physically inactive individuals.[1] Exercise helps people of all age groups, from children to the elderly, in combating depression. There is also some evidence that exercise reduces suicidal thinking: a large 2012 study of college students indicated that the more days per week a student exercised, the lower the number of depressive symptoms, feelings of sadness or hopelessness, and thoughts of suicide.[2] Exercise has also been shown to counter the depressive effects of negative life events, such as divorce or legal problems, and medical conditions, such as asthma, arthritis, and diabetes. And if you've been depressed in the past, exercise can also help protect you from slipping back into depression in the face of stress.[3]

As an antidote to depressed mood, exercise has been found to be as effective as antidepressant medications in treating mild to moderate depression. A few years ago, researchers conducted a randomized controlled trial (the gold standard for testing the efficacy of treatments) called the SMILE (Standard Medical Intervention and Long-Term Exercise) study, in which they compared the effects of a sixteen-week treatment of either sertraline (Zoloft), exercise training, or a combination of both on depressive symptoms. By the end of the study, participants in all three treatment groups had improved significantly over those in the control group. However, in a follow-up survey conducted ten months after the SMILE study began, members of the exercise group reported significantly lower relapse rates than the medication group, especially if they had continued to exercise on their own. So exercise not only reduced depressive symptoms as well as one of the leading antidepressants did; it provided protection from a return of symptoms.[4] Another report, a review of twenty-five controlled trials of exercise in depression, found significant and sustained clinical benefits. In some of these trials, benefits from exercise were equal to those from cognitive-behavioral therapy or antidepressant medications, and in one study, exercise was more helpful than light therapy (see chapter 15) in reducing depressive symptoms.[5]

The benefits of exercise seem to extend across the depression spectrum. A recent study conducted by Portuguese researchers showed that exercise improved symptoms for people who were even moderately to severely depressed and who had not responded to drugs and other forms of therapy. When these "treatment-resistant" individuals began exercising for thirty to forty-five minutes five days a week in addition to taking medication, 26 percent of them were no longer depressed after twelve weeks.[6] If exercise can work even for severely depressed people who have not been helped by other forms of therapy, you can see how important it may be for you if you are almost depressed.

Exercise and Brain Chemistry

We hope that we've convinced you that exercise is effective in combating depression. But *why* is it so effective? Physical activity appears to help regulate the brain chemicals that moderate mood—chemicals such as serotonin, norepinephrine, and dopamine. And interesting new research proposes that exercise also affects the immune system in the brain, strengthening the brain's natural ability to fight off inflammation and oxidative stress—and thereby reducing depression.[7] Physical activity, in particular aerobic exercise, not only improves your health; it also elevates your mood and reduces depression through the regulation of neurochemicals. It also does not seem to matter if the exercise you do is mindfulness-based (such as yoga, tai chi, and qigong) or a traditional form of exercise.[8] The bottom line is that the sooner you make physical activity a part of your everyday life, the healthier your body, mind, and spirit will be. We know it's hard—but once you start exercising, the benefits you get will go a long way toward keeping your exercise routine going.

Frequency of Exercise

So how much should you exercise and how often should you do it? Participants in the SMILE study exercised three times a week. Each exercise session began with a ten-minute warm-up, followed by thirty minutes of continuous aerobic exercise, and a five-minute cool-down. While you will reap even more physical health benefits by exercising more often, the Depression

Outcomes Study of Exercise (DOSE), conducted by researchers in Colorado and Texas, found that exercising three times a week was just as effective at reducing depression symptoms as exercising five times a week. The trick is to exercise at a moderately rigorous intensity (70 to 85 percent of maximum heart rate).[9] There are many types of activity with this aerobic intensity, including walking, running, cycling, swimming, tai chi, and certain forms of yoga. While you should check with your doctor before beginning an exercise program, most people can safely engage in aerobic exercise.

Obesity, Depressive Symptoms, and Exercise

Cultural depictions of the happy obese person—including the Buddha, Santa Claus, and Shakespeare's comic character Falstaff—as well as several studies on obesity and mental health, have led to what has been called the "jolly fat" hypothesis; that is, the theory that obesity somehow provides protection against anxiety and depression. However, more recent research has found that this hypothesis is flawed. Obesity, especially in women, may actually be a *risk factor* for depressive symptoms. Indeed, a large survey of over 9,000 adults in the United States found that having a body mass index (BMI) of over 30 percent significantly increased the rate of depression in both women and men.[10]

Obesity is also associated with the lower-level depressive symptoms we are calling *almost depression*. European researchers, who studied almost 8,000 Finnish subjects, found that individuals who suffered from dysthymia and subclinical depression had higher levels of abdominal obesity (fat that collects around the waist) and greater fat mass than individuals who did not report low-level depressive symptoms. These researchers suggested that abdominal fat and low-level depressive symptoms may both operate through the same physiological pathways involving adverse reactions to extended stress and insulin resistance.[11]

Other pathways between obesity and depression have also been noted:

- Obesity affects self-esteem and body image.
- Depressed mood can lead to "emotional eating" that increases obesity.
- The stigma of obesity can lead to social isolation, especially in women.
- Obesity is associated with other physical conditions, such as diabetes, that can contribute to depression.
- Obesity also can reduce a person's perceived ability to exercise due to joint pain.
- It can lead to general behavioral deactivation, reducing a person's involvement in rewarding or pleasurable activities.

The good news is that exercise can reduce depressive symptoms, obesity, *and* many of the physical ailments that limit an obese person's ability to enjoy life. A recent Canadian study found that when people who are obese increased their moderate to intense physical activity while reducing the time they spent in sedentary activities, they significantly lowered their odds of depression.[12] Other studies have found that increasing aerobic exercise reduces depression in obese individuals, as well as reducing diabetes and increasing cardiovascular fitness.

If you struggle with weight, do *not* let obesity be a barrier to exercising! It is important to get yourself out there and moving. The Centers for Disease Control recommends that obese individuals try to exercise for thirty minutes a day at a level that increases your heart rate. Walking will do the trick. However, if you experience joint pain while walking, try an exercise that reduces pressure on joints: work out on a stationary bike, walk or do another aerobic activity in a swimming pool, use an elliptical machine, or hold on to a kitchen counter and walk in place. Be sure, of course, to discuss your proposed exercise program with your doctor.

Having struggled with weight issues most of my life, I (Shelley) would like to offer some additional tips: If you find that you can't sustain a workout for thirty minutes at a time, try breaking up the exercise into three ten-minute sessions each day. Find a friend or loved one to work out with you to increase your motivation. If possible, exercise outside rather than indoors. A recent study by Canadian researchers found that people who walked outdoors in nature had a greater sense of well-being afterward than those who walked indoors.[13] These researchers also found that people underestimate the amount of pleasure that walking out of doors will provide, and thus may deprive themselves of this beneficial mood lift. And finally, reward yourself (but not with food!) with small pleasures (for example, take a long, hot bath, meditate for a few minutes, or listen to your favorite music) each time you complete your exercise sessions. Your brain will soon make a connection between exercise and reward, and you will look forward to your workouts!

Making the Effort

A forty-five-minute aerobic workout three times a week seems like a small investment to reap the enormous benefits that result from regular exercise. However, if you're suffering from almost depression, like Betty Ann or Taylor whom we met earlier in this chapter, it may be difficult to garner the motivation to get your exercise program off the ground. You may have trouble enough getting motivated to complete daily routines— like brushing your teeth or going to the post office—let alone contemplating aerobic exercise. This is normal when you're sliding into depression. The downward spiral saps you of motivation, and even tasks that require minimal energy seem almost overwhelming. Getting yourself out of stagnation mode to do something—*anything!*—may seem like just too much trouble. You may believe that if you hold off until your energy returns and you feel better, you will be able to do the things that need doing. However, research shows that just the opposite is true: if you can force yourself to get out there and do even small activities, you will begin to feel your motivation return and your mood will brighten.

One of the key components to many therapies for depression is, in fact, behavioral activation. As we've seen in this chapter, the research on this topic is powerful; depression begins to lift as people become more physically active and engaged in their surroundings. The premise of behavioral activation therapy is this: the pathway to feeling less depressed is to develop healthy patterns of *active* engagement in enjoyable activities that lead to fulfillment and purpose.

To find out whether behavioral deactivation may be a problem for you, take the following assessment using table 5 or a sheet of paper. (You can also download this assessment at www .AlmostDepressed.com.)

Table 5.

Your Behavioral Activation Score

The following questions are taken from behavioral activation and physical activity scales. To test your behavioral activation, read each statement; then circle the number that represents your experience over the past month.

1. I force myself to do things that are good for me even when I don't want to do them.

1	2	3	4	5
Almost never	Not often	Sometimes	Often	Almost always

2. I avoid doing things that require a lot of physical effort.

5	4	3	2	1
Almost never	Not often	Sometimes	Often	Almost always

3. Most people would consider me an active person.

1	2	3	4	5
Almost never	Not often	Sometimes	Often	Almost always

4. I'm really not motivated to do much of anything.

5	4	3	2	1
Almost never	Not often	Sometimes	Often	Almost always

5. I engage in at least one activity each day that is pleasurable to me.

1	2	3	4	5
Almost never	Not often	Sometimes	Often	Almost always

6. I prefer to watch other people do things rather than to do them myself.

5	4	3	2	1
Almost never	Not often	Sometimes	Often	Almost always

7. I make an effort to try new things on a regular basis.

1	2	3	4	5
Almost never	Not often	Sometimes	Often	Almost always

8. I stay in bed in the morning even when I have things I ought to be doing.

5	4	3	2	1
Almost never	Not often	Sometimes	Often	Almost always

Add up the points to all eight questions.

If you scored 33 to 40 points, you are behaviorally active and have good motivation!

If you scored 25 to 32 points, your level of activity is sufficient, but you could benefit from additional behavioral activation. Try adding two or three new pleasurable activities that involve physical activity to your weekly schedule.

If you scored fewer than 25 points, your level of physical activity is in the danger zone. Add at least one new activity that involves physical movement to your schedule each day. The more you force yourself to engage in activities, the more your motivation to be active will return.

Update on Taylor

Taylor, the college student we introduced earlier in the chapter, eventually realized that she was slipping into depression and went to her college counseling center for help. Her counselor immediately recognized that Taylor's slide into depression was fueled by inactivity caused by her embarrassment over weight gain. Because eating disorders are a big problem on campus, the counselor didn't recommend dieting but instead helped Taylor to become more active. She suggested that Taylor force herself to get dressed every day and go to class. She also recommended that Taylor join a hip-hop dance club on campus. As Taylor became more active, her depressive symptoms began to subside and she also began to shed the extra pounds. Taylor is now enjoying college more and is becoming more involved in campus life.

Update on Betty Ann

Betty Ann, whom we met earlier in this chapter, had become almost completely housebound and immobile when she saw a scene in a daytime TV show that changed her life. In the scene, two sisters were struggling to care for their elderly mother who could not care for herself. Betty Ann said that she realized she was becoming like the elderly woman in the show, and that scared her. She forced herself to get up and start moving again. She began by taking short walks around her complex. And she was surprised that almost immediately she began to feel better. Betty Ann now takes part in many of the activities at her local senior center and has even begun to take Spanish classes with the goal of going on a seniors' tour of Spain next year. "The world was always out there for me," she told us. "All it took to find it was putting one foot in front of the other."

. . .

Like Taylor and Betty Ann, you can enter the upward spiral out of almost depression by increasing your activity level—through both exercising and increasing the number of pleasurable activities you engage in each week. Here are some tips for getting started.

First, make a list of activities that you find pleasant and enjoyable. Pick activities that involve physical movement, such as gardening, dancing, going to yard sales, playing golf, or walking your dog. If you can't think of activities you currently find pleasant, that's okay. Remember that one of the signs of depression-spectrum disturbances is anhedonia, the loss of pleasure in activities. One way to get around this block is to think of activities that you *used* to enjoy. Another way is to ask someone close to you what you used to enjoy doing. Keep working at this list until you have between twelve and twenty items on it. And add new items as you remember them. We'll call this your Pleasurable Activities List.

Second, make a copy of the Daily Activities Calendar and, for the next week, fill in each square with the major activity you did during that two-hour window. (You can also download this calendar at www.AlmostDepressed.com.)

When you review your calendar after the week is through, we suspect you'll see that you haven't spent time either exercising or engaging in activities you find pleasurable.

Step three is to make another copy of the Daily Activities Calendar and, for the coming week, replace two to three of the activities you listed with physical activity—either exercise or an item from your Pleasurable Activities List. Then try your best to *follow through!* We know it's really hard to get going when you're feeling down, but you *can* do this! Push yourself to actually complete those activities and, when you do, congratulate yourself for your success. You can add two to three activities the following week, and you should soon see that the additional physical activity improves your mood and begins to lift the fog of almost depression. Please remember that adding physical activity into your weekly calendar is a process; like everything in life, there will be ups and downs. If or when you miss a day or a week of exercise, you may be tempted to get down on yourself; we encourage you to be kind and patient with yourself and

Table 6.
Daily Activities Calendar

Time	Monday	Tuesday	Wednesday	Thursday	Friday	Saturday	Sunday
8 am to 10 am							
10 am to Noon							
Noon to 2 pm							
2 pm to 4 pm							
4 pm to 6 pm							
6 pm to 8 pm							
8 pm to 10 pm							
10 pm to Midnight							

to recognize that at each juncture you can simply begin again. Remember that your commitment is to *you* and to helping yourself feel better. It's okay and even normal if you take a step backward occasionally.

If you look at your calendar and conclude that you just don't have time for exercise or pleasurable activities, you will not be alone. We have seen many clients and patients who believe they are too busy to indulge in exercise or pleasurable activities, even though these activities are crucial to their health and well-being (we've been guilty of this ourselves!). If "too busy" describes you, then ask yourself if you are functioning at your peak level. Ask yourself if you would be more effective and energetic if you were physically fit and happy. The answer is yes. Remember that even the president of the United States (arguably one of the busiest individuals on the planet) still makes time for golf, theater, and outings with his family. Making time for activity will help you achieve a physically active state of well-being, which will in turn make you *more* efficient and effective than you are while struggling with almost depression.

In this chapter, we have looked at how increasing your physical activity and positive movement (behavioral activation) can decrease the symptoms of almost depression. In the next two chapters, we'll look at other aspects of behavioral activation—value-based activity and creative activity—and how they, too, can transport you out of the gray zone of almost depression.

■ ◆ ■

6

Improving Your Mood through Meaning-Based Action

Ever more people today have the means to live,
but no meaning to live for.
—Viktor Frankl

In the last chapter, we saw that increasing physical activity and involvement in pleasurable and rewarding activities can help lift you out of being almost depressed. However, sometimes it isn't the *quantity* of the activity but its *quality* that is the most important aspect of behavioral activation. Even if you find an activity to be pleasant, you may not find it rewarding if it doesn't seem *meaningful.* If simply adding physical and pleasurable activities to your schedule doesn't improve your depressive symptoms, it may be because your activities are lacking a sense of meaning.[1]

Let's look at Blake's case. Blake was certainly physically active, but he was lacking a sense of purpose.

Blake's Story

Blake, age thirty-one, is an ex-Marine who served five tours of duty in Iraq and Afghanistan and who is now the manager of an auto parts store in North Carolina. He works out at his local gym each day before going to the shop, and on most evenings he goes for a six-mile run before dinner. Formerly, he would also spend a great deal of time keeping the family's modest yard mowed and green. Despite his level of fitness and physical activity, Blake feels that he is slipping into an almost depressed funk. His work at the auto parts shop seems trivial compared to his military duty. "In the Sand Box, everything you did was important," he says. "The people we dealt with—we were keeping their villages safe for them. And we used to go out on night patrol; one false move could mean the difference between life and death for you or your buddies. But here, what am I doing? Selling parts to yahoos who want tricked-out rides so they can show off to other yahoos?" Blake didn't see his job getting better in the future. "Even if I get promoted to regional manager, what's the use? I'm still just selling auto parts; I'm not really making the world a better place." Blake says he cut back on yard work because no one in the family appreciates it or offers to help. All they do, according to Blake, is keep pushing for a bigger house and bigger yard.

Blake feels he has a good marriage but says that his wife, a nurse, complains that he has been aloof and irritable lately and that he is too hard on the kids. He responds that the kids are sloppy, out of shape, and ungrateful. Blake feels that his life is lacking meaning, and he sees his future as a continuation of the same useless grind. In a perfect world, he says, he would own a chain of fitness centers rather than running an auto parts store. The only parts of his day he finds meaningful are his workouts at the gym and his evening runs. "Staying fit and able-bodied is important. Getting soft is not an option," he explains. Blake is almost depressed; he is still functioning at home and on the job, but he isn't finding meaning and purpose in his activities.

· · ·

One of the reasons people may lose interest in activities, as we have seen, is that their activities do not provide the pleasure that they once did. Another reason people lose interest is that the activities may no longer seem meaningful. Both pleasure and meaning turn on the reward centers of the brain, and this internal reward then provides the motivation to engage in more of the activities that provide pleasure or meaning. Clearly, when you are no longer motivated, you may drift into an almost depressed state, like Blake did, that can cause distress and potentially lead to deeper depression.

Let's look at another person, Loni, who also suffered from lack of meaning in her life that led to a state of almost depression.

Loni's Story

Loni is a divorced flight attendant in her early fifties. She has been working for the same airline since she was twenty-five years old, when she gave up her job as a dental assistant to "see the world." Her seniority now allows her to work the best trips, and she has been able to spend time in many of the world's great capitals. Lately, however, she has lost the excitement she used to feel in a foreign country. She also feels the airline industry has changed over the years and that her work isn't as important as it used to be. "I used to love to talk to passengers about why they were traveling and what kind of work they did. They really appreciated having someone pay attention to them and make the flight go by faster. However, now passengers have their laptops and the movie screens, and no one wants to be interrupted. We just do our service and hang out in the galley." She also says that the crews aren't as friendly as they used to be. With all the new regulations, everyone just does their own thing, and during layovers she is often left on her own.

During her thirties, Loni was married for seven years, but it didn't work out. She has always wanted children but she never met the right man, and she didn't think having a child without a father would be fair to the child. "If I had children and a husband, I know my life would be more meaningful and I would be happy," Loni laments. "But that seems pretty unlikely now. I guess I'll just be a 'glorified waitress' until I'm too old to do the job, then fade into the sunset."

Loni is almost depressed. Although she is doing her job, she doesn't find meaning in it anymore. The things that she feels *would* make her life meaningful seem out of reach for her.

• • •

Blake's and Loni's stories beg us to consider the question of what it is that actually makes life meaningful. This is a question that philosophers—from Plato to Thomas Aquinas to Kant to Charlie Brown—have pondered since the time of the ancient Greeks. Without going into the details, we find that these philosophical arguments share some consensus: people consider their lives meaningful (1) if they are emotionally engaged in their activities and (2) if they pursue aspirations that either make them a better person, help others, or make the world a better place—even in a small way. Loni and Blake seem to have become *disengaged* from their work and their activities, and they haven't replaced these with new goals or aspirations they would find personally meaningful.

The behavioral activation therapy that we discussed in the last chapter suggests that replacing activities we find dull and uninspiring with more pleasurable and meaningful activities will improve symptoms of depression. We have already discussed how to add pleasurable activities to your weekly schedule, but before you can add meaningful activities, you need to be clear on exactly what activities you might consider meaningful. In other words, you need to identify activities associated with worthy aspirations and goals. But there is a problem here. What if you don't have any goals and can't conceive of anything that would make your life more meaningful? The fact is that when you're depressed (or almost depressed) it may seem that nothing much has meaning. And if nothing seems worthwhile, how will you even go about setting goals that will help you feel better and make your life seem worthwhile? It's sort of a catch-22. Here's where I (Shelley) would like to tell a story of my own bout with almost depression.

Shelley's Story

In my late twenties, I began experiencing symptoms of almost depression. Even though it may have looked to the outside world like I was living a fabulous lifestyle (great apartment on the beach in Miami, good job, lots of friends, opportunities to travel around the world), I was beginning to feel doubt—even anguish—about the future. Beloved members of my family were having severe problems with health, addiction, alcoholism, and even legal issues, and I didn't know how to help them. At the same time, I was almost constantly preoccupied with the strong sense that I wasn't doing what I needed to be doing with my life. I had this heavy feeling that I was running out of time to make some important changes, but I didn't know what those changes were. Regardless of your age, you may be able to identify with the feeling of knowing that you need a change but not being able to put your finger on what you should do next.

After six years of living carefree on my own, I moved back home to help out until the family problems eased. It was good to be physically close to my loved ones again and to feel like I was contributing—even if only to give hugs or to be there to listen during late-night bouts of sleeplessness. What I discovered during that return to my parents' home was that I needed, as I feel we all do, to be involved in something greater than myself. The lifestyle I had been living in Miami was focused on self-indulgence; it was great fun but it wasn't enough. To be fulfilled, humans (most of us, anyway) benefit from a relationship with a larger purpose, whether that purpose is seen in terms of helping family or others in the community, patriotism, spiritual or religious activity, humanitarian causes, or "saving the earth."

After I moved back home and took the time to really reflect and think about my life, my purpose and intentions, as well as new goals and aspirations, slowly began to emerge. This didn't happen all at once, but rather over months and even years. During this time, I was able to do the important work of personal goal-setting that Jeff and I discuss in this chapter, and I found that it really helped. As my goals for the future became clearer, a sense of excitement and anticipation gradually uprooted my state of almost depression.

. . .

I (Shelley) found, and perhaps many of you will find as well, that while almost depression is painful, it can also be a sort of "call to action" to make a transition in your life or to change your circumstances. In fact, we encourage you to consider how the pain of almost depression might be a "growing pain." As we have discussed throughout this book, almost depression is a negative state that is distressing and, if untreated, can lead to more serious depression and suffering. It needs to be understood and addressed. Along the way, however, this negative state of almost depression may prompt us to commit to new goals and meaningful activity that will ultimately enrich our lives.

The Importance of Goals and Meaningful Activity

Research into the relationship between depression and life goals during the last few decades has produced three main findings. First, believing that you can *only* be happy if you attain certain goals (for example, "if only I can find the right person to marry, then I'll be happy") is related to depression and hopelessness. Second, holding on to unattainable goals is related to depression and hopelessness. Third, having specific and attainable goals is an important component of personal well-being and is an antidote to depression and hopelessness. New research has also found that being flexible enough to adjust your goals prevents depression from developing in response to negative life events.[2] Let's look at these findings more closely.

As we discussed in chapter 2, the way people perceive their

future can set them on a path to well-being or to depression. A negative view of the future is part of the depressive triad of beliefs (which include a negative view of oneself, the world, and the future) and is considered an important risk factor for depression and almost depression. Two different types of beliefs about the future may fall into this pessimistic category. First, you may believe, like Blake, that the future will be an endless continuation of your present circumstances—which you view as purposeless drudgery. Second, you may believe, like Loni, that a happy and meaningful life would be possible if you could just attain specific goals—but those goals are likely out of reach for you. Psychologists call this second pessimistic view of the future *conditional goal setting*, meaning that higher-order goals, such as being happy, are conditional upon attaining lower-order goals (in Loni's case, this includes having children and a husband) that are either impossible or that you *feel* are impossible to accomplish.[3] People who hold such beliefs have unwittingly set themselves up for depression; they believe that happiness will only come through circumstances that they feel are unlikely to occur.

Yet research shows that just the opposite is true. People who pursue personally meaningful goals that they believe are within their reach are less depressed and happier than people who pursue happiness per se, especially if they believe happiness is dependent upon achieving lesser, unfeasible goals. Indeed, people who have a set of goals that have personal meaning and who believe they *can achieve* these goals become motivated and energized.[4]

Since lack of motivation and energy are primary signs of almost depression, establishing personally meaningful goals is one of the paths you can take to feel better. On the other hand, if you are invested in goals that you *cannot achieve*, or if you are *not pur-*

suing your goals even though they are achievable, you are more likely to experience negative feelings and almost depression.

Achieving goals, or even making progress toward personal goals, also enhances your sense of self-efficacy (your belief in your own competence). Self-efficacy in and of itself is a protective factor against depression.[5]

Developing Specific and Achievable Life Goals

If you can't specify your life goals, or if you are "waiting" to be happy until you achieve some vague or likely unattainable goal(s), it will be more difficult for you to increase the amount of personally meaningful activities in your life. It will also be more difficult for you to overcome almost depression. But you *can* set specific and attainable goals to help direct meaningful behavior by following some simple steps.

First, look at this list of life value areas (table 7) and choose those that are most important to you at this time in your life. Start by rating the importance of each area on a scale from 1 to 5, with 1 being the most important. (Use the table, a sheet of paper, or download this exercise at www.AlmostDepressed .com.) It's imperative that you rate life values according to what's really important to *you*, not what you think others would want you to say is important and not what you feel you *should* find important. (For example, many people feel they *should* put "Helping others" as their highest priority, but they really value financial growth more at this point in their lives.) Remember that the priority you give to various life values can change over time, and you can always reassess your current values. For the purpose of setting your current goals, rate your choices based on what you honestly value *at this time*.

Table 7.

Life Values Assessment

Life Value	Rating	Life Value	Rating
Career growth	1 2 3 4 5	Helping others	1 2 3 4 5
Education	1 2 3 4 5	Hobbies and sports	1 2 3 4 5
Family	1 2 3 4 5	Personal growth	1 2 3 4 5
Friends/social contacts	1 2 3 4 5	Protecting the environment	1 2 3 4 5
Financial growth	1 2 3 4 5	Public service	1 2 3 4 5
Health and fitness	1 2 3 4 5	Spiritual growth	1 2 3 4 5

List your top three life value areas here.

1._____

2._____

3._____

Now think about a goal that you would like to accomplish in each of your top three life value areas. On a separate sheet, write your goals in the following form: "My goal is to . . . ." Make each goal a positive statement rather than a negative statement. A negative statement includes negative words such as "won't," "not," or "don't." New research shows that people who are depressed are more likely to write negative goals (which psychologists call *avoidance* goals), while positive statement goals (or *approach* goals) are associated with greater well-being.[6]

Check your goals to make sure they reflect *your* desires, not the wishes of someone close to you and not what you think society expects you to do. To achieve their full effectiveness, your goals have to come from within. They have to reflect something that is meaningful to *you*.

Make your goals as specific as possible. A recent study by Oxford researchers found that people who were able to formulate specific and achievable goals (for example, "sign up for a Pilates class next week at my local gym") were more likely to pursue their goals and experience a larger reduction in depression symptoms than people who had vague or nonspecific goals (for example, "get fit").[7] Certainly, specific goals can be part of larger and more comprehensive goals, but the value of goals in relieving depression is related to how specific and doable you can make them. So, for now, keep them specific.

> *Too general:* "My goal is to be a better person."
> *Better:* "My goal is to clean my apartment and organize my belongings so that I know where everything is."

> *Too general:* "My goal is to go back to school to become a doctor."
> *Better:* "My goal is to get a B or better in two premed courses this fall."

Finally, your goals should be attainable. Although it's true that you can accomplish almost anything you set out to do (and people are accomplishing seemingly unattainable goals every day!), if you are having issues with depression, the last thing you want to do is set yourself up to fail by choosing a near-impossible goal. Save doing the impossible for a time when you're on top of your game—not when you're down in the gray depths of almost depression.

Review your goals to see whether they are challenging but at the same time realistic for your current situation. If your goals are too difficult, you'll feel anxious and frustrated. If you fail to make progress toward your goals, you will lose self-esteem and sink deeper into depression. However, you also want your goals to be challenging—you want them to move you a little out of your comfort zone. If they are too easy to meet, you'll become bored and lose motivation. In short, you want your goals to be a stretch but not impossible.

When you have set your goals, choose the goal that is most important to you and determine what intermediate steps you can take to make your goal a reality. Do you need to do some research on the Web or at the library concerning your goal? Do you need to get training or more education? Do you need supplies or equipment? Do you need to save money or work some extra hours to fund the steps involved with meeting your goal? Make a list of these things and put them in the order you need to complete them. We know that this task can sound almost overwhelming if you're in a depressive state, but see if you can push yourself to do it. Just the act of filling out the form below will begin to activate your internal reward system!

You can use table 8 or a notebook page to create a tentative timetable for completing the steps. Fill out the chart for the goal in your highest priority life area. That will be your main focus. If you feel up to it, you can also fill out separate charts for the other two goals you have identified. (You can also download this chart at www.AlmostDepressed.com.) Be sure to schedule time for contingencies and setbacks. If you plan for snags ahead of time, you will not get more depressed when these hurdles inevitably occur.

Table 8.
Goal-Setting Chart

Description of goal:	Target date:	
Why this goal is important: 1. 2. 3.		
Intermediate steps to complete before I reach my goal:	Check	Date
1.		
2.		
3.		
4.		
5.		

CONTINUED ON NEXT PAGE

TABLE 8 CONTINUED

Activities associated with intermediate steps and my overall goal:

Once you have set specific and attainable goals, you can begin to incorporate more meaningful activities into your life. Make a list of activities you can do that will move you closer to each of your intermediate steps and to your overall goals. Try to come up with a list of at least ten to fifteen activities that are related to your goals.

Now, if you completed the Daily Activities Calendar in chapter 5, you can try to incorporate two goal-related activities into your weekly calendar for the coming week. Each week, try to add more activities related to your goals into your calendar. As you spend more time engaged in activities that are meaningful to your goals, your symptoms of almost depression should begin to resolve.

Update on Blake and Loni

We were able to work with both Blake and Loni (the people you met earlier in this chapter) and help them set goals that would add meaning to their lives. Recall that Blake wanted to own a chain of fitness centers because he felt that staying fit was an important aspect of life that too many Americans, including his own children, are ignoring (his exact words were that "we're soft!"). He could not quit his job running an auto parts store to pursue his dream because he needed to have a steady income to support his family. We were able to help him, however, to set a specific and attainable goal of getting certified as a fitness coach. After he accomplished that goal, he was able to take on clients at a local gym in the evenings and on weekends. He is currently saving the money he makes from coaching to buy into a franchise gym. Blake reported that as soon as he had a goal to work toward, he began to feel better about his auto parts job.

He now knew that there was something in his future that he could work toward.

Loni, the flight attendant in her early fifties, had wanted to meet the right man and have a family. However, that goal was vague and not specific enough for her to work toward. She decided instead to focus on finding a more rewarding career and was immediately drawn back to her original field, which was dentistry. She set a goal of returning to her local university night school to take the prerequisite courses in biology and chemistry that would prepare her to apply to a master's program in dental hygiene research. She reports that her depression symptoms began to dissolve as soon as she had a plan for a meaningful future. She feels her short foray into almost depression was instrumental in helping her to make a positive life change. She also has started dating a fellow student in her biology course who is also making a career change. "He may or may not be the *right* one," she told us recently. "Only time will tell. But in the meantime, we're having a lot of fun and learning a lot."

• • •

Two final words about goals: First, write down your goals and post them where you can review them daily. Reward yourself when you reach each of your intermediate goals. And when you complete your first goal, give yourself some time to savor your accomplishment. Then move on to your next goal. Second, during this process, revisit your goals and intentions on a regular basis and update what is really important to you. As Stephen Covey, author of *The Seven Habits of Highly Effective People*, said, "The main thing is to keep the main thing the main thing."

Through the act of thinking about your intentions, your behavior will stay connected to your goals. As you weave your goals and intentions into the fiber of your life, you'll find that your life takes on more purpose and meaning, and you'll be eager—like Blake and Loni—to take on even greater challenges.

In the next chapter, we'll discuss how you can use creative activity to reduce the symptoms of almost depression, as well as how you can use the negative mood associated with depression to produce original and creative work.

■ ◆ ■

| 7 |

Improving Your Mood through Creative Activity

Feeling and longing are the motive forces behind
all human endeavor and human creations.
—Albert Einstein

So far, you've seen how the behavioral pathway works to counter the symptoms of almost depression by increasing your level of activity in general and by increasing the time you devote to activity that is pleasurable and meaningful in your life. In this chapter, you'll see how you can use almost depression as a source of creative energy.

Many highly creative individuals—both past and present—have suffered from mood disorders ranging from almost depression to major depression. Many have experienced long bouts of irritability or loss of pleasure, yet they have found ways to use their state of negative emotion to enhance their creativity. One of us (Shelley) has done extensive research on the interface between depression and creativity and has found that negative mood can enhance creativity in two ways:

- Creative activity can be a way to cope with negative feelings associated with depression; it is a type of self-administered therapy.

- Negative feelings can serve as subject matter for creative work. Many famous paintings, poems, novels, and musical compositions have focused on a state of negative emotions.

Here is a look at how creative activity and work can help you cope with negative feelings and mood.

Creativity as a Coping Mechanism

Graham Greene, the British novelist, wrote: "Art is a form of therapy. Sometimes I wonder how all those who do not write, compose or paint can escape the madness, the melancholia, the panic inherent in the human situation."[1]

Negative, depressive mood states often seem to sap all of a person's energy and drive. Many people have described depression as a black hole, as though it is a vortex through which ambition, motivation, and joy are sucked into a colorless void. Therapist Brett Newcomb describes treating a person with depression like this: "You are pulled against your will into a place where there is no light, no energy and no solid foundation to stand against."[2] However, astronomers have discovered that black holes are not actually voids in the universe at all; rather, they are areas of compressed matter and energy with a gravitational pull so strong that no light can escape. If we further explore this metaphor of depression as a black hole, we can then imagine that depression—like the astronomical black hole—is actually full of dense and dark energy.

Freud, in fact, suggested the energy of negative emotions that is too dangerous or unacceptable to be expressed directly can be redirected into creative work that is more socially acceptable. This is a type of beneficial defense mechanism called "sublimation." According to Freud's theory, as an individual releases negative energy into the creative work, the negative emotions lose some of their power to cause distress and depression.

Numerous personal accounts of the power of creative expression to diminish negative feelings have appeared in biographies, on websites, and in personal diaries. Raymond is a carpenter whose personal experience with creativity and depression is a good illustration.

Raymond's Story

Raymond, a forty-two-year-old Colorado native, makes a living as a finish carpenter. He has been troubled by depressive symptoms since he was in high school and described his life as "a race to keep one step ahead of the black cloud that is always following me." Raymond had moved to the Boston area a few years ago so that his wife could be near her ailing and aging parents. Although he had no trouble finding work in his adopted city, he felt that the quality of his work was slipping. He blamed this lack of motivation to excel on depression and believed that homesickness for his beloved Rocky Mountains was contributing to his darkening mood.

After reading a blog about using creativity to combat negative emotions, Raymond invested in a beginner's kit of acrylic paints and brushes and began attempting to express his dark feelings on canvas. Even though he had no artistic training, Raymond reported that he has gained enormous satisfaction from filling a canvas with hues and shapes that match his mood. He describes how he began to feel excited anticipation at the end of each workday as he sped home to work on his paintings for an hour or so before dinner. "Suddenly I had something to look forward to again," he adds.

Raymond also reported that he is enjoying his carpentry work again. And he is beginning to explore Boston and develop a sense of belonging in the city rather than pining for his native Colorado. He is also starting to do some representational painting, spending time at the seashore trying to capture the light on the waves in his images. "Someday I'll go back home and paint the mountains," he says. "But for now, I'm pretty content. I was going down a slippery slope. I feel like learning to paint actually saved my life."

We'd like to share another powerful story about the healing power of creativity.

Sally's Story

Sally, a retired clinical psychologist, was enjoying her new career in art—painting, exhibiting, selling, teaching, and volunteering—when she was diagnosed with breast cancer. As far too many women have learned, this diagnosis can send you into an emotional upheaval. Sally described the stress of dealing with the diagnosis as a visceral roller coaster.

Fortunately, surgery was successful in removing the cancer, but Sally then faced a strong recommendation by her cancer care team for radiation therapy. She realized that during radiotherapy, she would likely experience more emotional turmoil, perhaps even feelings bordering on depression. So Sally devised a personal strategy that would provide a greater sense of self-control and balance as well as an outlet for strong emotions, especially ones for which she did not have adequate words. She decided to make a small, quick oil painting immediately after each of her thirty-three daily treatments.

"It was the process of painting per se," says Sally, "not the paintings themselves that helped steady me." But when her radiation therapy was over, she also had a pictorial record of her travel into the depths of anxiety, loneliness, and the gray landscape of almost depression as well as her gradual transition back into positive emotional territory. On the last day of treatment, Sally created a hopeful picture and a caption that speaks of a "surge of joy and anticipation of life ahead."

• • •

Sally's story is the only one in this book (other than our own!) in which we did not attempt to disguise the individual's identity. Sally Loughridge has personally approved of the inclusion of her story. Her artistic journey through radiation has been published in book form (*Rad Art: A Journey through Radiation Treatment*, American Cancer Society, 2012) and has already provided inspiration to many who face difficult health issues.

Like Raymond and Sally, you can use your negative energy as a motivator to do something creative. Expressing your depression or emotional distress through creative writing, journaling, painting, sketching, or making music can distract you from those destructive feelings and even help you find meaning in a painful event or situation.

You don't have to be a trained writer, musician, or artist to receive the benefits of creative activity. Personal expression of emotion is powerful, even for the untrained creator. There are many ways you can channel your negative feelings into creative work. Typical creative outlets include music (singing, playing an instrument, or composing a melody), writing (poetry, short stories, or writing a journal), art (drawing and sculpture), and drama. However, you can also creatively express yourself through photography, gardening, dancing, quilting, whittling, flower arranging, or cooking. The ways that you can creatively express depressive feelings and transform that negative emotion into something original and useful are virtually endless.

The experience of creative activity is such an effective way of coping with negative moods that dozens of creative therapies have sprung up to help individuals who suffer from depression. These include art, drama, writing, poetry, music, and dance therapies. The number of scientific studies attesting to the effectiveness of creative therapies for depression is growing. For example, in a recent study, Finnish researchers compared the improvement in depressed patients who were randomly assigned to receive standard care to those who received standard care augmented by music therapy. These patients created music by improvising on drums and mallet instruments, such as a xylophone, and then discussed their creations with a trained therapist. At follow-up testing three months after treatment, the music therapy patients had improved at a rate twice as great as those who received standard care alone.[3]

Just as you don't need to be a trained artist or musician (note that the patients in the Finnish study had no musical training), you likewise don't need guidance from a trained art therapist to receive the therapeutic benefit of creative work. A pen, a guitar, a computer keyboard, a set of colored pencils, or a drum will get you started. You can express your feelings through many creative media.

One of the most widely studied techniques for creative expression is called "expressive writing." The work of University of Texas psychologist James Pennebaker indicates that doing expressive writing for just twenty minutes a day for three or four days can significantly improve both physical and mental health, including depression.[4] A recent study conducted by researchers at Boston University found that undergraduates who engaged in expressive writing that was meaningful, personal, and revealing, cut their scores on a standard measure of depression in half. The expressive writing students maintained their improvement in depression for two months following the experiment.[5]

Expressive Writing Exercise to Reduce Depression

The goal of this exercise is to practice self-expression concerning an area of dissatisfaction in your life and to promote mental processing of this dissatisfaction state. The exercise should be done for twenty minutes on three consecutive days at roughly the same time each day. You can use either pen and paper or the word processor on your computer. The exercise, which is adapted from the work of Dr. James Pennebaker, has been tested on thousands of individuals and has shown to benefit both physical and mental health.

Find a quiet spot where you can write uninterrupted. Set the timer for twenty minutes and begin to write using the following guidelines:

For the next three days, write about your very deepest thoughts and feelings about an extremely important issue that has affected you and your life. In your writing, really let go and explore your very deepest emotions and thoughts. You might tie your topic to your relationships with others, including parents, lovers, friends, or relatives; to your past, your present, or your future; or to who you have been, who you would like to be, or who you are now. You may write about the same general issues or experiences on all days of writing or choose different topics each day. No one will see your writing but you. Don't worry about spelling, sentence structure, or grammar. The only rule is that once you begin writing, continue to do so until your time is up.[6]

When you have finished your writing for the day, put it aside and don't look at it again. When you start the next day's writing, don't review what you wrote on the previous day. The value of this exercise is in the actual writing. You never need to look at what you wrote, and you don't need to show it to anyone else to get the benefit of it.

Visual Arts Exercise to Reduce Depression

If you don't care to write, you can express your feelings visually, as Raymond and Sally did in our earlier examples. You can use paints, colored pencils, crayons, markers, or any medium that offers a variety of colors to work with. Before you begin, sit in a quiet place and allow yourself to just experience your current feelings. Then set a timer for ten minutes and depict your feelings on paper or canvas. Use whatever colors seem appropriate. Don't censor yourself; draw whatever comes to your mind. Your work can be abstract, representational, or anything in between, as long as it comes from your inner well. Try to draw for the entire ten minutes. When the timer sounds, look over your work. If you have more to add, continue to draw. When your picture is complete, look it over. Does it adequately depict what you're feeling? Did you learn anything about yourself from examining the picture? If you do this exercise on a regular basis, you will gain insight into your feelings and also develop your skills of self-expression.

Music Exercise to Reduce Depression

You can also use music for self-expression. Percussion instruments (such as drums) or mallet instruments (such as a xylophone), used by Finnish music therapists in the study described earlier, allow you to incorporate improvised rhythms, melodies, and volume to creatively express your mood. Singing also has therapeutic benefits. Swiss researchers who investigated the effects of singing on well-being found that after a thirty-minute singing lesson, amateurs who used singing as a method of self-expression reported increased joy, energy, and relaxation.[7] Singing may work to relieve depression by promoting relaxation and self expression, and through the release of endorphins—the brain's natural painkillers.[8]

Depression as Subject Matter for Creative Work

Although depressed feelings are unpleasant and distressing, they are also an aspect of the human experience. If you are almost depressed, you may have found some relief or comfort in music, poetry, or art that resonates with your melancholic mood. Explorations of negative feelings have been the subject matter for creative works since at least the time of the early Greeks.

The long history of depression and art was highlighted at a 2005 exhibition at the Paris Grand Palais titled "Melancholy:

Genius and Insanity in the West." The exhibition brought together 2,000 years of art and sculpture around the theme of depression. It included work from first-century BC Greek sculptors as well as pieces from artists such as Picasso, Rodin, van Gogh, Munch, Hopper, Goya, Delacroix, and Blake.

Here is a small sample of other work from creators who have used their depression as subject matter to connect with others and to share their mutual experience of the human condition. (This list first appeared in Shelley's book *Your Creative Brain: Seven Steps to Maximize Imagination, Productivity, and Innovation in Your Life*.)

- Emily Dickinson's famous poem "There's a Certain Slant of Light" describes depression on a winter's afternoon (perhaps an early description of seasonal affective disorder, or SAD).

- Edvard Munch's famous Expressionist painting *The Scream* portrays a state of high anxiety and depression.

- The entire genre of blues music is based on a negative feeling state. It gets its name from the term "blue devils," which the African American community has used for centuries to denote a state of melancholy and sadness.[9]

- Playwright Eugene O'Neill's masterpiece *Long Day's Journey into Night* portrays an entire family's dysfunction and melancholy. O'Neill won a Pulitzer Prize posthumously for this work.

- Tchaikovsky's Symphony no. 6 in B minor, *Pathétique*, is often referred to as the composer's suicide note (he died nine days after conducting its premier performance).

Author and musicologist Joseph Horowitz says "this is a work which cannot be listened to casually . . . here's a guy who's in an extreme personal crisis baring his soul."[10]

- J. D. Salinger's classic 1951 novel *The Catcher in the Rye* is the consummate description of almost depression and teenage angst.

Seeking out other works of art—works of literature, paintings and sculpture, popular or classical music—that express the feelings you may have trouble expressing yourself can give insight into your inner experience and offer comfort and even healing.

Narrative Story Exercise to Reduce Depression

You can also use your depressed mood as subject matter for your own creative work. One exercise that has been helpful to Shelley's clients (although not scientifically validated) involves writing a redemptive story. Your story should have a main character who has some of the same problems in life that you have. Describe this fictional character in detail. The plot of the story is a description of how your main character changes his or her own life so that the sources of dissatisfaction are alleviated. The events in your story should be realistic (no being saved by Captain Kirk and the starship *Enterprise* or a knight in shining armor!). The character must *earn* his or her way out of current misery to a better future. Along the way there should be some character development—your main character should experience personal change in some meaningful way. Force yourself to finish this story. Do not leave your character dangling in a depressed state! When you finish the story, read it over. You may learn something from your character's growth that could be useful in your own life. Sometimes your subconscious, after all, tells you what you need to do through creative sparks.

Again, you don't have to have training or innate talent to do this creative activity. Whether you believe it or not, you *are* creative! You can use the negative energy of your depression symptoms as motivation for creative work and also as subject matter for a variety of different creative activities. And in the process, you will reap the benefit of improving your negative mood through immersion in the creative process.

◆

| 8 |

Improving Your Mood by Reducing Stress

There's never enough time to do all the nothing you want.
—Calvin and Hobbes (by Bill Watterson)

Often, engaging in physical activity and exercise, meaningful activity, or creative work—as we saw in previous chapters—is enough to ward off the grays, translate negative emotions into positive feelings, and restore feelings of well-being. But what if you are still dealing with a boatload of stress? Exercise may not be enough to keep those inner demons of hopelessness and fatigue at bay. You may need to turn to other stress management strategies to help lift the gray veil of almost depression and put the color back in your life. Do you remember Pia, a doctor we introduced in chapter 3? We'll review her story here and then discuss the stress management strategies that can help individuals like Pia go from almost depressed to feeling good about themselves and their lives.

Pia's Story Recounted

Pia is an emergency department (ED) physician with two small children and a poorly trained cocker spaniel named Woo. Her husband, who is in the import/export business, travels for months at a time. Pia's mother-in-law has recently moved in to help with the kids while Pia works. Pia had originally joined a group of ED doctors with the expectation of a salaried position and a set number of shifts per week, which would allow her a good bit of family time. She liked the idea that she would not have to bring her work home with her or be awakened by late-night calls that her colleagues in private practice experienced. However, when one of the partners in her group had a heart attack, Pia began to take on more shifts and work longer hours to keep the ED covered. She feels guilty if she is called to do extra work and refuses. She also feels guilty about her role as a mother, expressing remorse that she is missing out on her children's milestones, but finding she has little patience for their daily problems when she does have so-called quality time with them. And she has no patience at all with her mother-in-law, whom she views as "taking over" her household. She feels mildly resentful of her husband for traveling and is somewhat short with him when he's at home. This shortness on her part leads to more guilt. In fact, everything from her job to taking care of her family is beginning to feel like one big hassle and guilt trip, and Pia sees no hope for things to improve. She is constantly fatigued and on edge. One night, when Woo had an accident on the expensive Chinese carpet, it seemed like the last straw, and Pia did something that as a physician she knew was irrational: she bought a package of cigarettes and lit up for the first time in seventeen years. Pia's stress level is leading her down a dangerous path. She is not enjoying either her work or her family: she is almost depressed.

Pia is confronting a variety of stressors from her professional and her family life, and she is experiencing a prolonged stress response. In chapter 3, we discussed how the stress response is determined by the seriousness of the stressor, the total weight of stress you are under (which could be coming from a variety of sources), and your perceived ability to handle that stress load. When the stress response is activated over extended periods, it can have a serious negative effect on your mood and behavior, as well as your health. Pia is experiencing guilt, resentment, feelings of hopelessness, and almost depression due to stress.

Figure 13.
The Stress Sequence

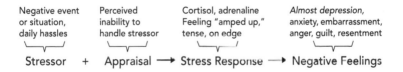

What strategies could Pia use to reduce stress and relieve her growing depression? According to extensive research on coping conducted by Charles Carver and his colleagues at the University of Miami, there are a number of common strategies people use to cope with stress.[1] Clearly, some strategies are more helpful and appropriate than others.

When we first met Pia, she was trying a *substance use* coping strategy. She was attempting to relieve her stress by smoking, a behavior that might bring temporary relief but would lead

Effective Strategies for Coping with Stress

- *Distraction.* This can include losing yourself in a good movie or novel, sleeping or daydreaming, going out to a party with friends, becoming involved in a favorite hobby or pastime.

- *Active coping.* This strategy involves taking direct action or active steps to try to remove the stressor or deal with it head-on.

- *Planning.* Rather than actually taking action to remove or defuse a stressful situation, this strategy involves making plans for dealing with the stressor. Often, stress can be diminished simply by realizing that you have options that you could implement, even if you don't actually implement them.

- *Emotional support.* This strategy allows you to reduce stress by discussing your emotional distress with others and crying on the shoulders of friends or loved ones. This can turn into an ineffective strategy if you become overly dependent on others and avoid learning coping skills to deal with stressors directly.

- *Instrumental support.* This strategy involves getting others on board to help you solve your problems. It could, for instance, include finding someone you know to provide a loan during a personal financial crisis, legal help in a case when someone is accusing you of wrongdoing, or a couch you can crash on for a few days if your apartment burns down. The difference between emotional support and instrumental support—both of which rely on the support of other people—is that one provides emotional comfort and the other provides practical assistance in dealing with a stressor.

- *Behavioral disengagement.* This strategy basically involves removing yourself from the source of stress or taking yourself out of the game, so to speak. For example, if you are stressed over whether you will be let go as your company downsizes, you simply submit your resignation, ending the suspense. This could become an ineffective strategy if it's done to avoid dealing directly with stressors.

- *Prayer or meditation.* This entails turning to religion or other sources of mental strength to find comfort.

- *Humor.* This strategy reduces the stress reaction by finding and focusing on the funny or ironic aspects of the stressful situation.

- *Positive reframing.* This strategy involves looking for the silver lining of the stressor or stressful situation and focusing on the benefits of having encountered the stressor. This can turn into an ineffective strategy, however, if it plays into denial or avoidance of the stressor.

- *Acceptance.* Using this strategy means making peace with the stressor's presence in your life and agreeing to coexist with it rather than trying to remove it or avoid it.

Ineffective Strategies for Coping with Stress

- *Denial or avoidance.* This strategy involves refusing to acknowledge that the stressor exists or that it is causing distress. You carry on as though there is no problem, carefully avoiding the elephant in the room.

- *Substance use.* This strategy consists of drowning your distress with alcohol or other psychoactive substances.

CONTINUED ON NEXT PAGE

CONTINUED FROM PREVIOUS PAGE

- *Rumination.* This strategy involves constant mental attention to the stressor, including worrying, obsessing over things you should have done to avoid the stressor, guilt, self-blame, and concern over how the stressor will negatively impact your future.

to addiction and other health problems in the future. Those problems, of course, would further *increase* her stress load over the long term. There were more effective ways that Pia could manage her stress problems.

Researchers who study coping habits generally divide coping strategies into two broad categories—referred to as *problem-focused* coping and *emotion-focused* coping. Problem-focused coping strategies center on efforts to remove the source of stress from your life by directly altering the stressor or your relationship to it. In other words, problem-focused responding intervenes in the stress process *before* the stress response occurs. Some of the problem-focused strategies listed earlier include active coping, planning, and getting instrumental support from others. Emotion-focused coping strategies attempt to reduce the negative emotional effects of the stress response on your life, either by reducing the physical effects of stress or by reducing your emotional distress. In other words, they intervene in the stress sequence *after* you have experienced the stress response. (See figure 14.)

Some of the emotion-focused strategies listed earlier include distraction, denial, substance use, humor, and seeking

Figure 14.

Coping Strategies and the Stress Sequence

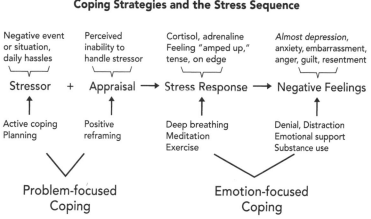

emotional support from friends. Each individual tends to use a general coping style that falls into either the problem-focused or emotion-focused category.

Table 9.

Your Coping Style

To get a feel for whether you tend to use a problem-focused or emotion-focused coping style, answer the following question: You are really stressed about an exam you have later this week in an important course you are taking. You respond to this stress by . . .

☐ scheduling extra time to study this week.

☐ forming a study group with others in the course.

☐ finding out what to expect from the test from someone who took it last year.

☐ going to a movie to distract yourself.

☐ having a few drinks.

☐ going for a long run or exercising another way.

☐ withdrawing from the course.

If you chose an answer from the left-hand column, you responded with a *problem-focused* coping strategy. All of the choices in the left-hand column are examples of directly coping with the stressor. That is, you decided to do something by directly confronting the cause of the stress. If you chose an answer from the right-hand column, you chose an *emotion-focused* coping strategy, and you decided to do something that would reduce the negative emotions associated with the stressor. The choices in the right-hand column include the coping strategies of distraction, substance use, and behavioral disengagement.

Of course, stress comes in many packages—all of which can make you more vulnerable to almost depression. And not all coping strategies are appropriate for dealing with *all* stressors or combinations of stressors. However, a large body of research has shown that, in general, using a problem-focused coping style is associated with a lower risk for depression, higher levels of resilience, and higher levels of well-being than using a general emotion-focused coping style. Identifying the source of stress and taking steps to directly reduce or eliminate that stress helps you lower your overall stress load. Emotion-focused and avoidant coping styles, on the other hand, work only to temporarily reduce your negative emotional response to stress. They do not reduce the overall stress load and have been associated with higher levels of depression, and even suicide.

For example, a 2011 study of adolescents conducted by researchers at the University of Michigan found that coping style was highly predictive of the number of depressive symptoms and suicidal thoughts these adolescents reported, with emotion-focused and avoidant coping strategies leading to higher depression scores.[2] The individual coping strategies that were related to both depression and suicidal thinking included denial, substance use, use of emotional support, behavioral disengagement, and rumination.

Recent studies of coping styles have linked problem-focused coping with greater psychological hardiness, better grades, higher life satisfaction, and positive feelings about school in high school students; greater resilience and well-being in the face of serious stressors; and more effective leadership skills in Air Force officers.[3] And a therapy that focuses on problem-focused solutions (aptly named problem-solving therapy or PST) is considered one of the most effective psychotherapies for treating mild to moderate depression, according to both a recent meta-analysis of psychotherapies and the Clinical Practice Guidelines published by the Department of Veterans Affairs.[4]

Why is it that a problem-focused coping style is so effective at helping you manage stress and reduce depression? There is a twofold benefit. By confronting and dealing directly with stressors, you not only eliminate or reduce the causes of stress in your life but also increase your confidence in your ability to deal with and control problems—a factor that may change your perceived ability to cope with stressors you encounter in the future. So problem-focused coping can reduce your stress response on two fronts: directly, by *reducing* the causes of your stress, and indirectly, by *increasing* your perceived ability to deal with stressors. Further, developing a problem-focused coping style will increase your resilience in the face of future adversity.

A Problem-Focused Approach: Nine Steps to Dealing with Stressors

You can deal directly with stressors as problems that should be, and can be, solved by using the following simple but effective steps. You'll also see how Pia, from our earlier example, employed them to reduce her stress load and move from almost depressed to living a satisfying life.

Step 1. Recognize the signs of stress.

Stress can creep up on you gradually. You may be so busy putting out the little fires in your life that you don't notice how heavy your stress burden has become. Then one day you wake up and realize that you're overwhelmed! You may also realize that you're losing interest in things that used to be fun or that you're feeling irritable, fatigued, or blue a lot of the time—sure signs of almost depression. Rather than getting sucked further into this downward spiral, as soon as you recognize your mood is slipping, use it as a wake-up call. In chapter 3, you learned to recognize the signs of stress, and you had the opportunity to create a personalized list of stress signs. Remember that the stress reaction is your brain and body preparing for action. When you feel stressed, it may signal that a problem needs to be addressed.

> *Pia:* "I felt frustrated, guilty, and resentful: getting through each day was a chore. But I didn't realize there was anything wrong with me—I thought it was the rest of the people I was dealing with that were the problem. I especially blamed my mother-in-law, when all she was trying to do was help out. Then when I found myself smoking, I realized that I was in a bad place. I didn't like the person I was becoming and I said "Whoa, I'm a bright person—I've got to figure out what's going on here."

Step 2: Define the problem.

Determine what the actual problem is and be specific about how it is triggering your stress reaction.

> *Pia:* "When I looked over all the causes of stress in my life, I realized that there was one stressor that

was actually causing all the other things in my life to seem like problems. The big source of my stress was my work. I was working too many shifts and feeling resentful about that. The family things were really only stressful because I didn't have enough time to take care of them due to my work."

Step 3: Set a goal.

Set a very specific goal for dealing with the stressor. Make sure that this goal is within your power to achieve.

> *Pia:* "My goal was to get out of doing extra shifts at the hospital—especially the night shifts. I really had to fight myself over setting this goal because it made me feel even guiltier. I think I felt it was *my* responsibility to keep the partnership going single-handedly. If I could give one piece of advice, especially to women who are under a lot of stress, it would be that you don't have to do everything yourself. Lots of times women feel responsible for making everything right, but when you allow others to help you, you will feel so much better."

Step 4: Brainstorm possible ways to meet your goal.

Brainstorm possible solutions to the problem that will satisfy the goal you set. Open your mind and get really creative about possible solutions. When you brainstorm, *do not judge* any of the solutions you come up with; just let them flow. Don't worry if some of your ideas seem ridiculous; just write them down without judging them.

> *Pia:* "My goal was to get out of doing extra shifts in the emergency department. I knew that if I could get

back to my regular hours, I would be fine. But the problem was how to staff the department when we were short two doctors. Here are some of the solutions I thought of without judging them: hire more doctors to cover the shifts; close the ED at night; get the other partners to do more shifts; have a self-service ED where patients could use our equipment to fix themselves; have a sign on the door that directs patients to another hospital after hours; make all the patients drink the cafeteria coffee—that ought to chase them away!"

Step 5: Evaluate possible solutions.
Make a list of the pros and cons for each of the possible solutions you developed in step 4.

Pia: "I actually set up a chart to look at the pros and cons. Hiring more docs, for example, the pros were that the new doctors could cover the extra shifts and relieve the extra stress on myself and my partners. If some of my partners wanted to do extra shifts, they could still do that. The cons were that we would have to do a search for suitable docs (and that would take time that none of us had) and that we would each have to take a hit in pay if we hired more staff."

Step 6: Choose the best solution based on pros and cons.
After you look over the pros and cons of all reasonable solutions, choose the best one. (Note: Problem-solving experts suggest giving special consideration to the solution with the *least cons* rather than the one with the most pros.)

Pia decided that hiring two more physicians was the best solution.

Step 7: Make a plan to implement the solution and try it!

You now need to create a specific plan to implement your solution. You may need to divide the plan into steps. Set a time and / or date for the completion of each step.

> *Pia:* "I had a plan with three steps. First I needed to present my solution to my partners and get them on board. Second, we would have to find qualified applicants for the new positions. I decided that I would take on doing the search and interviewing in exchange for two fewer shifts a week for the time being. Third, we would have to train the new docs on our procedures. I would make a plan for how to divide up the training among the partners."

Step 8: Assess success.

After giving your solution a fair try, the next step is to decide whether it worked. Did you meet your goal?

> *Pia:* "The whole thing was easier than I expected. My partners had thought I *enjoyed* working the extra shifts. I guess I had been playing the part of the totally together professional; no one at work knew I was so stressed. As soon as they saw I had a concrete plan for easing everyone's workload, they were delighted."

Step 9: If the first solution didn't work, try another!

If your solution worked, your stress should decline. Pia, for example, found that by spending less time at work, she could enjoy her family without feeling that every little glitch at home was a major crisis. Her mood began to improve, and she had more time to devote to her other interests. Not every problem will be solved as easily as Pia's, however. If your first solution does not work, you can always try the second and then the third solution from steps 4 and 5 until you find one that will work for you. Make sure to create a specific plan and give it adequate time to work.

Positive Reframing and Emotion-Focused Approaches

Earlier in the chapter, we mentioned that not all coping strategies are appropriate for dealing with *all* stressors or combinations of stressors. While active problem-focused coping (such as using the set of problem-solving steps we just presented) is generally considered the most helpful way to deal with stressors, there are times when direct problem-solving strategies may not be your best choice for relieving stress. Positive reframing of your stressor or even emotion-focused strategies may be more appropriate in some instances. For example, if you find yourself in a stressful situation where you cannot control (or choose not to control) the stressor, you will need to have some coping options so that you can deal with the effects of stress in an adaptive way. Let's look first at how positive reframing can be used to cope with difficult situations.

Rocco's Story

Rocco is a successful freelance writer who works out of his home in upstate New York. He has a history of depression but has been able to keep it under control with medication and exercise. He has established a daily routine that he feels is really important in maintaining his psychological health. However, after Hurricane Sandy devastated the East Coast in the fall of 2012, his routine was shattered. His wife's sister and her family, including two teenagers, lost their home in New Jersey and moved in temporarily with Rocco and his wife. Rocco's study (which had always served as his workplace and sanctuary) was converted into a makeshift bedroom for the kids.

At first, Rocco was happy to help his family members in need. But as time went on and it became evident that the relatives would not be able to return to their New Jersey home for months, Rocco felt himself slipping into almost depression. This was a dangerous sign because of his psychiatric history. His refuge had been taken over by teenagers, the house seemed in a constant state of frenzy, he wasn't able to sleep, and there was no place in the house where he could work in peace. To escape from the chaos of his own home, he began spending most of the day at a local bar where he could write in peace. Now he was starting to drink too much. "I can't take this invasion any longer," he complained. "I feel like a foreign country that has been overrun by Goths, and my stress level is through the roof."

Rocco's situation was indeed stressful and his reaction to it was leading him down a bad road. He felt trapped between two alternatives: if he kicked his relatives out, he would look like a monster, but if he suffered their presence in silence, his resentment would build until he either exploded or sank into a serious depression. With the help of a therapist, however, he was able to reframe his appraisal of the situation. Instead of seeing his relatives' presence as an unwelcome invasion, Rocco was encouraged to think about it as an opportunity to do writing research on teenagers (Rocco and his wife did not have children of their own). He could really get to know his niece and nephew and perhaps even have a hand in shaping their lives for a short period. And, as a bonus, he could use his experience as subject matter for a few writing pieces.

Once Rocco was able to make this perspective change, he took on his new role as mentor to his niece and nephew with enthusiasm. Instead of constantly trying to escape from the house, he began to see the situation as an opportunity to learn about teenagers and parenting. He began helping them with their homework (especially writing assignments), and in turn, they taught him to play some trendy video games. He also wrote some insightful articles that he was able to sell.

Rocco used positive reframing as a way to cope with a stressful situation. Although it sounds cliché, there is good evidence that when you can't really control a situation, you can reframe it to make the proverbial lemonade out of lemons. That said, there are cases where you may have already reframed the situation in a positive way, but you still need some relief from the stress. In such cases, it's a good idea to have a few emotion-focused strategies on hand to reduce the negative emotional impact of the stress.

Amella's Story

Amella is a forty-six-year-old piano teacher and mother of twin teenage girls. Recently, her father, who is a widower, had a stroke that left the right side of his body paralyzed. He is still mentally aware but needs round-the-clock physical care and assistance. Amella, who has no siblings, made a vow to herself after the stroke that she would personally care for her father and not let him languish in a nursing home. She feels strongly that "family should care for family" and that it is a privilege to give back something to the man who gave her life. She also feels that helping care for their grandfather is a good experience for her daughters. Despite in-home nursing care several hours each day, Amella has found that the burden of caring for her disabled father 24/7 has added a tremendous emotional and physical stress to her life. He has become more negative and difficult over the past year, and Amella has given up her piano students because her father can't rest "with all that noise" in the house. She has also given up most of her leisure activities to be available for her father because the family can't afford more nursing care. Amella has made these choices freely but still feels herself slipping into a low-grade depression.

Amella's situation is not uncommon. Many individuals—through choice or necessity—sacrifice their careers and/or their personal time to care for a disabled or ill family member. Constant caregiving of a family member is a noble undertaking, but depression in caregivers is a recognized problem. Although Amella has made a firm commitment to care for her father, she still needs breaks from the emotional stress that comes with caregiving if she is to stave off depression. Research indicates, for example, that the feeling-focused strategy of seeking emotional support from others is helpful in reducing caretaker stress. Other strategies can also provide much-needed respite from caregiving stress, including exercising and distraction techniques such as reading, watching a movie, or listening to music.

It's a good idea to have a few emotion-focused strategies in your mental toolbox to soothe frayed emotions when you're faced with a stressful situation you can't (or, as in Amella's case, choose not to) change. However, there are many maladaptive, unhealthy ways to cope with the emotions of stress. Here are some strategies to avoid:

- drinking alcohol
- using recreational drugs
- smoking (or smoking more) cigarettes
- overeating
- driving fast
- risky behavior
- gambling
- unsafe sex
- starting a fight

To avoid falling into one of these maladaptive strategies for coping with stress, keep a ready list of more positive ways to deal with the negative emotions surrounding stress. Look at the following list of emotionally focused strategies. Using table 10 or a sheet of paper, note those that appeal to you, then keep the list handy to remind you of positive ways you can "take a break" from negative emotions and stress. (You can also download this checklist at www.AlmostDepressed.com.)

Table 10.
Emotionally Focused Strategies for Coping with Stress

☐ Listen to music.
☐ Read a good book or watch a movie.
☐ Take a hot shower, steam bath, or sauna.
☐ Get together with a friend.

☐ Enjoy humor (jokes or funny movies).

☐ Exercise.

☐ Write in a journal or diary.

☐ Pray or engage in other spiritual activity.

☐ Work in a garden.

☐ Paint or draw.

☐ Practice yoga.

☐ Meditate.

☐ Take a nap.

☐ Work on a hobby.

☐ Play a video game.

☐ Other: _____

In this chapter, you've seen some coping strategies for managing the stress that the world may throw at you. You've learned a procedure for directly dealing with stressors through step-by-step problem solving. You've also seen examples of positive reframing and some emotion-focused ways to deal with stress. In the next chapter, we'll focus on how you can further develop the skill of positive reframing. While it is a valuable coping mechanism for stress management, reframing can also provide even broader benefits by helping you challenge negative beliefs that can lead to depression.

■ ◆ ■

TAKING THE
Psychological Pathway

| 9 |

Challenging and Reframing Your Depressive Thoughts

The greatest weapon against stress is our ability to
choose one thought over another.
—William James

In chapter 8 we discussed helpful ways you can cope with stress to reduce symptoms of almost depression. Problem-focused coping (that is, dealing with problems head-on rather than trying to avoid them) is associated with positive and effective results and is a protective factor against depression. Positive reframing (reappraising the way you look at a stressful situation) is also a positive and adaptive coping strategy. In this chapter, we'll broaden the discussion of reframing and explore how your ability to reframe your thoughts influences both your emotions and your behavior. How you choose to think about situations and events can keep you stuck in an almost depressed state—or it can lift you to a state of emotional well-being and personal effectiveness.

Reframing Threats into Challenges

You've already learned how your *appraisal* of an event or situation determines the extent of your stress response. If you appraise a situation as being quite threatening, your brain and body will go into action and release a flood of adrenaline and cortisol, and you will experience the fight-or-flight response. However, one person's threat is another person's challenge. And you can *choose* whether you appraise a situation as threatening or challenging. Remember: You always have a *choice* about how you view things!

When you perceive potential stressors as challenging rather than threatening (in other words, when you view them as something you can handle), you will still feel stress but it is invigorating rather than anxiety-provoking.[1] In fact, the way you perceive stressors (challenging rather than threatening) actually changes your body's response to stress. As we mentioned in chapter 3, appraising a situation as a challenge prompts the stress system to function in a healthier way than when a situation is appraised as a threat. Instead of leading to anxiety and depressive symptoms, the bodily changes you experience with a *challenge* appraisal are interpreted as increased alertness, attention to your goal, and extra energy to help you perform. The result is that you feel engaged with the challenges in your life rather than wanting to avoid them.

Jason's Story

Jason, a college senior, was scheduled to graduate in May and had lined up a good job in a large New York investment firm. However, several months before graduation, Jason's girlfriend, whom he had been dating since his senior year of high school, broke up with him. Jason had chosen this college in part to be close to her and had always assumed they would get married. Now he felt his whole life had been pulled out from under him. To make matters worse, his former girlfriend became engaged to one of Jason's fraternity brothers. At first, Jason was angry and distraught. However, he then slipped into an almost depressed state and began having trouble sleeping, eating, and studying. Although he had major exams coming up, he claimed he couldn't concentrate on anything but his former girlfriend and his lost dreams of life with her. If he did poorly on the exams, he was in danger of not passing his courses or graduating. And if he didn't graduate, he would lose his coveted position with the New York investment firm.

Jason needed to focus on his studies *immediately*. He didn't have the luxury of using problem-focused coping to work out his relationship problems right then. If Jason didn't pull himself together, he risked sabotaging his college career and losing his great job opportunity. How could he best deal with his stress? Jason was actually taking a psychology course that covered the research on threat and challenge appraisals, but he hadn't thought of applying this knowledge to his own situation. A teaching fellow he had confided in pointed out that if Jason could reframe his appraisal of the situation with his former girlfriend as challenging rather than threatening, he could channel some of the negative energy that was fueling his depressive symptoms into more positive activity, such as studying. Here's how Jason reframed this situation.

Table 11.

Jason's Reframing of His Appraisal

Threat Appraisal	Challenge Appraisal
"I just can't concentrate on my exams right now, not when my future and my life are ruined. What's the point?"	"I'm upset, sure. But I'll be darned if I'll let this ruin my last semester in college! I have the opportunity to show everybody I can do a great job on my exams even when I've taken a blow to the gut in my personal life."

Fortunately, Jason was able to adopt this challenge appraisal of his situation, which helped energize him to finish his college work. Rather than feeling like a victim whose life was irreparably damaged, he was able to use his situation as a challenge to action rather than as the route to almost depression. Jason graduated, took his position with the firm in New York, and seems to have moved on very nicely from his "lost dreams."

Positive and realistic reframing takes work and practice, but, as Jason's case demonstrates, it's very effective in reducing depressive symptoms and countering stress. Viktor E. Frankl, the eminent psychiatrist who survived life in a Nazi concentration camp, is quoted as saying, "Between stimulus and response there is a space. In that space is our power to choose our response. In our response lies our growth and our freedom." Jason has a choice about how to interpret situations and events, and so do the rest of us. Our interpretation determines how well we will cope with our stressors.

Think about Dr. Frankl's words again: we have the "power to choose our response." Sometimes, during an emotional event or situation, it's easy to forget that we *do* have choices. Even if we can't control the actual event, we *can* control how we respond to it. And one way we can do that is to choose how we appraise (or reappraise) the event or situation.

Identifying, Challenging, and Reframing Depressive Thoughts and Beliefs

Reappraisal and reframing (we use these terms interchangeably) can be an effective coping strategy for dealing with stressful situations, as we've seen; however, reframing is not only related to stress reduction, but is also directly connected to emotions, actions, and relief from depressive symptoms. Indeed, it's so effective and so crucial to good mental health that an entire evidence-based treatment for depression (cognitive therapy) is based on it.[2] We'll examine this therapeutic model and explore the concepts of developing an internal "locus of control" and "realistic optimism" as ways to challenge and reframe our depressive thoughts and beliefs.

Challenging Negative Self-Talk with Cognitive Techniques

Everyone has a constant stream of thoughts running through their minds—this is called self-talk. These thoughts are often *automatic*. Automatic thoughts don't happen because you consciously try to have a particular thought; they tend to just pop into your head. These thoughts reflect your beliefs and attitudes about the world, other people, and yourself. So *listening to what you say to yourself* can be a key to understanding your core beliefs about yourself and the world. In chapter 2, we noted that a specific set of core beliefs—namely, negative thoughts about yourself, the world, and the future—are often referred to as the cognitive triad, and they are a serious risk factor for depression. Because this pessimistic cognitive triad tends to form early in life—generally in childhood or adolescence—this way of thinking becomes automatic over time, and you don't even notice that your negative thoughts are poisoning your outlook on life. If you listen to your self-talk, you'll begin to see whether this negative triad is an issue for you.

Many people mistakenly believe that what happens to them in life dictates their happiness or their misery. But if that were the case, then the people who have suffered the most traumatic events and the most misfortune would be the most depressed, while those who have been blessed with good health, wealth, and a life of ease would be the happiest. However, both empirical research and the stories of resilient people (for example, Helen Keller, Lou Gehrig, and Maya Angelou) tell us that this is not the case. Some of the happiest and most grateful people we have worked with in our professional lives have suffered great misfortune. They include severely injured service members, some of whom live near the poverty level and have dealt with amputations and painful disfiguring burns. Conversely, some of the most depressed and unhappy individuals we have worked with are privileged, bright young people who would appear to have everything.

In a classic study of lottery winners, researcher Phillip Brickman and his colleagues found that major lottery winners were no happier than people who'd been paralyzed in an accident, and that they actually experienced less pleasure in everyday events.[3] More recent research by psychologist Dan Gilbert indicates that all of us consistently overrate how happy or how miserable specific events or situations will make us. As an example, Dr. Gilbert found that most people believed they would be miserable if they were forced to live as conjoined twins. Yet studies of conjoined twins indicate that they are not any more miserable than the average person.[4] Indeed, it is not what has happened to you that makes you happy or depressed; rather, it is how you interpret or appraise what has happened to you (in other words, your *beliefs* about what has happened) that determines your emotional reaction and your behavioral responses.

Psychologist Albert Ellis, who developed an early version of cognitive therapy called "rational emotive behavior therapy" in the late 1950s, captured this relationship between thoughts, emotions, and behavior in his influential ABC model.[5] It goes like this:

A = activating event (or adverse event)

B = beliefs about the event (your appraisal of what happened)

C = consequences (emotional and behavioral) of the event

A occurs. But it is **B** (*not* **A**) that leads to **C**.

We'll demonstrate with a hypothetical example. Rory and Jessica are driving separately to work on the Southeast Expressway in Boston. There is a fender bender ahead that ties up the highway for miles. Traffic is at a standstill and both Rory and Jessica will be late for work. Now let's look at their individual thoughts and reactions to the event.

Table 12.

Examples of the ABC Model

	Rory	Jessica
A = Activating Event	Stuck in traffic; late for work.	Stuck in traffic; late for work.
B = Beliefs	"The day is ruined. Why does this always happen to me? I can't catch a break. Some idiot up there can't drive and now I'll never get a parking place, I'll be late for my meeting, and I can forget about that big deal I've been working on. The client will think I'm totally incompetent. This is disastrous!"	"Well, this is certainly inconvenient. But it could be worse—*I* could have been the one involved in the accident. I guess I'm pretty lucky. I'll use my cell phone to let the client know what's happening. And this traffic will give me some extra time to listen to the new playlist I made last night."
C = Consequences	Takes out frustration on coworkers, then fumes and sulks during what's left of the big meeting. Doesn't make good impression on client. Downward spiral of negative emotion.	Arrives at office late but cheerful. Apologizes to client and seals the deal over lunch. Makes pact with herself to leave earlier for work in the future.

Even though this is a minor example of how beliefs influence behavior and emotions, it is clear that Jessica's beliefs will lead to a better outcome and a better day for her all around. The interesting thing is that neither Rory nor Jessica is aware that they are making a choice about how to respond to the activating event. That's because their self-talk (all those stream-of-consciousness thoughts that ran through their heads while they were driving) was an automatic response to their core beliefs about themselves, the world, and the future.

The premise of cognitive therapy is that if you can change your self-talk to reflect a more positive and realistic set of core beliefs, you can change both your negative emotional responses and the maladaptive behaviors that often lead to negative consequences. Forty years of scientific evidence support this premise. Meta-analytic studies consistently show that changing the way you appraise events and situations to reflect a positive and realistic point of view reduces symptoms of dysthymia, as well as mild to moderate depression, and also reduces the chance of having a relapse to such symptoms.[6]

"Locus of Control" and Almost Depression

Researchers have known for several decades that a person's sense of control is related to both mood and physical health. People who feel that they have control over their lives are said to have an *internal* locus of control (they feel control comes from within), while people who feel that events in their lives are controlled by others or by chance have an *external* locus of control (they feel that events in their lives are dictated primarily by forces outside themselves). Recent research found that external locus of control is associated with dysthymia and chronic low-level mood.[7] Earlier research found that having an internal locus of control predicted better immune functioning, lymphocyte proliferation, and natural killer cell activity in people with depressive symptoms.[8] Developing an internal locus of control is a protective factor that promotes better mood and immune system health.

One way to develop an internal sense of control is to replace the language of *being* controlled with the language of *having* control. Remember that outside forces, such as other people or circumstances, can exert pressure on you—or *invite* you—to feel or act a certain way, but you ultimately control whether you accept that invitation. Psychologist Charles P. Bosmajian suggests that you replace the "language of powerlessness" with the "language of invitation."[9] Then you can choose to say yes or no to that invitation. Here are some examples from Dr. Bosmajian.

Table 13.

The Language of Powerlessness vs. the Language of Invitation

Language of Powerlessness	Language of Invitation
"Everything she says just *pulls me down*."	"When we talk, she often invites me to feel bad about myself."
"She really *made me* mad when she said that."	"When she said that, she was inviting me to get angry."
"It seems I'm always being *taken advantage of*."	"It seems I'm often being invited to do things that are against my own best interests."
"Every time I talk to him he *puts me on* a guilt trip."	"When I talk to him he often invites me to feel guilty about my decisions."
"I'm always *getting shoved around* at work."	"I'm regularly being invited to do things I don't want to do at work."
"When we were talking, he kept *dumping on me*."	"When we were talking, he kept inviting me to believe I was worthless."

Notice how you are the object of someone else's actions or intentions when you speak in the language of powerlessness. By listening for that language of powerlessness in your speech and your self-talk, and replacing it with the language of invitation, you can remind yourself that you have a choice: you can decide to be the willing object of outside influences or to take the reins and respond in a manner that gives *you* the power over your feelings and actions.

Developing Realistic Optimism

The tendency to think optimistically (in other words, to naturally appraise events and situations in a positive and realistic manner) has been associated with lower risk for depression, higher levels of resilience, better relationships, and greater psychological well-being. Although your genes have something to do with this trait, psychologist Martin Seligman (who is often called the father of positive psychology) has shown that realistic optimism is also a skill that can be *learned*.[10] For the rest of this chapter, we'll talk about three steps you can take to develop a more positive and realistic attitude, and thereby reduce almost depression symptoms. Here are the three steps:

1. Recognize and identify pessimistic or distorted thinking.

2. Challenge maladaptive thoughts.

3. Reframe thoughts to be more positive and realistic.

The steps may seem easy. However, remember that developing realistic optimism is a skill—and like all skills, it improves with practice. Just as you cannot get better at shooting hoops by simply reading a book about it, you can't develop optimism without practicing the skill-building steps. It is not enough simply to know *how* to build a skill; you need to practice that skill until it becomes second nature. This process may seem tedious, especially if you're already suffering from depressive symptoms. And while developing an appraisal style that is both realistic and optimistic takes practice, the results really are worth the effort!

1. Recognize and identify pessimistic or distorted thinking.

Since your self-talk is an indicator of your deep beliefs about yourself, the world, and the future (and since these beliefs strongly affect your tendency to be depressed or happy), re-shaping your self-talk should produce dramatic improvements in your mood. Before you can reshape your self-talk, however, you need to know what it is. One major step you can take to develop a positive and realistic appraisal style is to become aware of your thoughts and how you are actually talking to yourself and others. This takes effort because, as you've seen, your thoughts are largely automatic; that is, you are not con-sciously choosing the words you say to yourself. You need to become a self-talk detective.

Whenever you notice that you are feeling depressed or ex-periencing some other negative emotion, such as guilt, embar-rassment, shame, anger, anxiety, or hopelessness, write down what was going on at the time, what the negative emotion was, and what you were saying to yourself. This procedure is called "self-monitoring." You can copy the chart on the next page onto paper or download it from www.AlmostDepressed.com to track your thoughts. Try to do this for a week, then look over the record of what you have written.

As you examine your thought chart, check your self-talk for evidence of pessimistic or distorted thinking. Some common indicators are words like *always, never, everyone, nobody, should have, should not, if only, worst, terrible,* or *awful.* These words often accompany distorted thinking patterns, which psychologists call cognitive distortions.

ALL-OR-NOTHING THINKING

The most common of these is *all-or-nothing thinking* (in which you judge things as either all good or all bad, right or wrong, successful or unsuccessful, depending upon some arbitrary rule

Table 14.
Self-Monitoring Chart

Date		Time of day
What emotion were you feeling?	☐ sadness ☐ shame ☐ guilt ☐ anger ☐ embarrassment	☐ anxiety ☐ helplessness ☐ hopelessness ☐ frustration ☐ self-consciousness
What was happening at the time?		
What were you saying to yourself? (your self-talk)		

you have set up). Here are two examples of all-or-nothing think-ing that contributed to almost depression:

Tim told us, "I didn't get into an Ivy League law school; I might as well go back home and live in my parents' basement." Tim believed that either he got into a particular school or he was a failure. So he chose to think of himself as a "failure" rather than as a bright and talented young man with a promising fu-ture (which was a more realistic view).

Adrian was feeling depressed and insecure about her mar-riage when she told us, "If he really loved me, he wouldn't go on that business trip." In her mind, her husband's interest in his business meant he didn't love her. She didn't see how he could love her and not want to be with her all the time. This all-or-nothing thinking was making Adrian miserable and was also affecting her marriage.

The irony in both Tim's and Adrian's cases is that their dis-torted thinking might actually bring about the result they feared by evolving into a self-fulfilling prophesy.

OVERGENERALIZATION

Another common cognitive distortion is *overgeneralization*, or drawing sweeping conclusions about yourself or the world based on a single incident. For example, Tony came to us with symp-toms of almost depression. He said that women just didn't find him attractive and he doubted he would ever find someone to date. When asked for evidence, Tony said that he had asked his coworker Gretchen to go to a concert with him. She said she couldn't go, claiming she already had plans for that night. On the basis of this incident, Tony had concluded that women didn't find him attractive—a gross overgeneralization.

EXAGGERATION

Another type of cognitive distortion associated with depression is *exaggeration*. This is sometimes called "catastrophizing," because many exaggerations involve interpreting minor events as major catastrophes. For example, if you encounter an unexpected traffic jam and say to yourself, "Great! Now the whole day is ruined!" you have made a catastrophe out of a minor everyday event.

"SHOULD" THINKING

Yet another type of distorted thinking that often afflicts people with depressive symptoms is called *"should" thinking*, in which people hold themselves and others to impossible or unrealistic standards. When these standards aren't met, one is inevitably let down and almost depression rears its head. Clues that you are using this type of distorted thinking include saying things such as "I should have . . ." or "If only I had . . ." or "He shouldn't have . . ." For example, Jocelyn told us that she "should have" canceled her trip to Aruba last winter so her pipes would not have frozen and her antique piano would not have been ruined. In Jocelyn's mind, she "should have known" that disaster would befall her piano if she took a vacation. She has been carrying around inappropriate and unrealistic guilt over this event, and it has led her to conclude that she can't trust herself to make decisions. All-or-nothing thinking, overgeneralization, exaggeration, and "should" thinking are just a few of the common cognitive distortions that are associated with depression. Additional cognitive distortions are described in appendix C: Negative Thinking Patterns Associated with Depression. You can examine your own self-talk for these patterns and also ask people who are close to you to listen for negative words and patterns in your daily speech.

2. Challenge maladaptive thoughts.

When you recognize pessimistic patterns or cognitive distortions, either in the self-talk you recorded on your self-monitoring charts or in your daily speech, challenge these maladaptive thoughts by asking yourself the following questions:

> Am I using all-or-nothing thinking?
> Am I catastrophizing the situation?
> Do my thoughts contain the telltale words *always,*
> *never, everyone,* or *no one?*

Are my thoughts and beliefs based on emotions rather than facts? (For example, if your thought is "I'm worthless," and your reason for thinking this is that you're *feeling* inadequate, then you're basing your thoughts on the way you feel rather than on facts.)

Finally, ask yourself: What is the evidence for and against this negative thought? The most effective strategy for challenging your thoughts is to look carefully for evidence that either supports or disproves your negative self-talk. Review concrete details and information that would and would *not* support your negative thoughts. For example, Tim, whom we mentioned earlier, believed that he was a failure because he didn't get into a specific law school. We asked Tim to make a list of evidence for or against his thought that he was a failure. See table 15 for part of Tim's list.

Table 15.
Tim's Evidence of Negative Thoughts

Evidence That I'm a Failure	Evidence That I am NOT a Failure
• didn't get into my top choice for law school	• got into three top-tier law schools
	• graduated with honors from college
	• worked on state senator's reelection campaign during my junior year and was offered a full-time position on senator's staff
	• learned to speak Japanese fluently

The list of evidence against Tim being a failure was very long. (The same thing happened, by the way, when we asked Adrian to list evidence for and against her thought that her husband didn't love her.)

When you challenge your automatic thoughts and self-talk, you will likely see how unrealistic and negative they are. These maladaptive thoughts may be fueling a pessimistic view of yourself, the world, and the future. In short, they may be driving your feelings of depression. (Of course, there are times when your negative and pessimistic thoughts may have some basis in fact. In these situations, the list of evidence supporting your negative automatic thought might be longer than your evidence against it. When that's the case, it's time to implement one of the positive coping strategies we discussed in chapter 8 and see what you can do to improve the negative situation.)

3. Reframe thoughts to be more positive and realistic.

When you have identified maladaptive automatic thoughts and self-talk, take a moment to consider how you could have reframed the thought and used more positive and realistic words. Let's return to our examples of negative thinking and see how they could be reframed in ways that could lead to improved mood and better outcomes.

Table 16.

Examples of Reframing Negative Thinking

	Original Distorted Thought	Reframed Thought
Tim	"I didn't get into an Ivy League law school; I might as well go back home and live in my parents' basement."	"I'm disappointed that I didn't get into my top choices of schools, but I do have other good schools to choose from. I know I can do well in law school and I look forward to learning the legal profession."
Adrian	"If he really loved me, he wouldn't go on that business trip."	"I'll miss my husband while he's gone, but I know he loves me and I'm glad he's passionate about his work."
Tony	"Gretchen wouldn't go out with me. Women just don't find me attractive."	"Gretchen had plans for that night. I'll ask her out again in a couple of weeks. Since she can't go to the concert, I'll see if someone else is available."
Jocelyn	"I shouldn't have gone on vacation. Something was bound to go wrong."	"I'm sad about the damage to the piano. But I have insurance, and next time I'll make arrangements to have the house checked while I'm gone."

Every situation has a silver lining and presents opportunities to learn and grow. The more you focus on these aspects, the more control you'll have over your life and the more satisfaction you'll feel. Again, this process of reframing takes a lot of practice before it becomes second nature. However, once you master the process and begin thinking more optimistically and realistically, you'll likely be surprised that changing the way you frame your thoughts can change your life. You can use the Cognitive Reframing Form below to practice this important task; it can also be downloaded at www.AlmostDepressed.com.

Table 17.

Cognitive Reframing Form

Date_____

Fill out the following whenever you experience negative feelings about yourself or a situation.

1. Where were you?	
2. What happened?	
3. What were you saying to yourself (self-talk)?	
4. What were the emotional consequences? (How did you feel?)	
5. What were the action consequences? (How did your thoughts affect what happened?)	
6. Was your self-talk positive and realistic or negative?	☐ Self-talk was positive ☐ Self-talk was negative

CONTINUED ON NEXT PAGE

TABLE 17 CONTINUED

7. What is the evidence for and against your self-talk?	Evidence for:	Evidence against:
8. How could you have used more positive and realistic self-talk to mentally reframe this experience?		
9. How would an attitude of realistic optimism have changed the consequences?		

In this chapter, we've discussed how thoughts influence emotions. Negative and pessimistic thoughts can lead to negative mood states and depression. Positive yet realistic thoughts protect against mood disturbances and increase your well-being and effectiveness. In the next chapter, you'll see how learning to think and act mindfully is another pathway out of the gray world of almost depression.

■ ◆ ■

| 10 |

Improving Your Mood by Applying Mindfulness Strategies

The range of what we think and do
is limited by what we fail to notice.
And because we fail to notice that we fail to notice,
there is little we can do to change, until we notice
how failing to notice shapes our thoughts and deeds.
—R. D. Laing, Scottish scholar and psychiatrist

Mindfulness is, in essence, the practice of noticing. It is the practice of opening your mind in a nonjudgmental way to becoming aware of your experience and the world around you. In a state of mindfulness, experience is not seen as good or bad or neutral (although you may, through mindfulness practice, *choose* to see it as any or all of these simultaneously); rather, it is the acceptance of what is. This serene attitude of acceptance can be very powerful in dealing with symptoms of depression.

Sarah's Story

Sarah, age thirty-six, is busy: she's the mother of three (a twelve-year-old and nine-year-old fraternal twins). To make ends meet, she works full time as an administrative assistant to the president of an auto parts supplier. She is separated from her husband, Gary, but she sees the separation as a case of "addition by subtraction."

Before the separation, Gary had been out of work for several years following a back injury. Several operations were not helpful, and he endured significant chronic pain. Although Sarah says that he's always been a "great guy," over time Gary became depressed and then addicted (or addicted and then depressed—it's still not clear). To take his mind off his troubles, Gary started betting on football games. Soon enough, he'd lost a significant amount of the family savings. The last straw occurred for Sarah when Gary gambled away the twins' First Communion money. Sarah insisted he leave and go live with his mother. She has refused to answer his phone calls or let him spend time with the children since then.

Sarah receives support from her mother and two sisters who live nearby. She counts on them for helping with the kids but declines their offers of financial assistance. Most of the time, she's exhausted, feeling as if there is too much to do and not enough time. Fortunately, her job pays well enough to cover the rent payments, but everything else is tight. She feels more like a "human doing" than a "human being." She can't remember the last time she relaxed, and even though she's exhausted, she has trouble falling asleep at night.

When she finally sleeps, she often wakes up, wondering what's next. She thinks and thinks, but things remain the same. The morning comes too soon and she drags herself out of bed, gets ready to face the day, and drinks a cup or two of strong coffee. Although back at it, her body aches with tension, her head aches, and she craves a cinnamon roll. The commute is a total drag, and she asks herself, "How come I am the only one who knows how to drive?" At work, she puts on a front. If she runs into her colleague Robert, she smiles and greets him cheerfully but looks at his bow tie and thinks, "How could such a successful company hire such a loser?" And she always has a kind word for her boss, Cindy, but under her breath she mutters, "If she asks me to do this for her one more time, I might punch her in the face." At some time during the day she thinks of Gary, her husband, and wonders, "How could he do this to us? Doesn't he realize the position he put me in?" One day, Sarah looks over on the waiting room table and sees a copy of an old *Time* magazine featuring the serene face of a woman meditating. She thinks, "The closest I'll get to feeling like that is watching a vintage 'Calgon, take me away' commercial." Sarah is almost depressed, but she is about to pick up that magazine and change her life. For the first time, she will read about a living role model of mindfulness.

The Eastern Tradition of Mindfulness

Health is more than treating and preventing disease. Health consists of your ability to promote physical, mental, and social well-being. These qualities generate a sense of wholeness and coherence out of which you may live a balanced and fulfilling life in line with your values. About 2,500 years ago, the Buddha described mindfulness as a way to heal suffering. While all the world's religions include some form of contemplative practice, it is important to realize that mindfulness is not a religion. Nor is it a strategy, philosophy, or just a good idea. Mindfulness is a way of being and has been called the "art of conscious living." Dr. Jon Kabat-Zinn describes mindfulness as "paying attention, on purpose, moment to moment, nonjudgmentally" as if your life depends on it, because it might.[1]

The ability to live "in the moment" can be cultivated, over-coming your mind's natural tendency to wander. Mind-wandering tends to be associated with dysphoria. Often, when your mind wanders, it wanders to areas of life where you are feeling anxiety, uncertainty, or regret. Using a smartphone application to gather data, psychologists Matthew Killingsworth and Daniel Gilbert recently showed that almost half the time people aren't thinking about what they are actually doing (the exception was making love) and that when their minds wandered, they were less happy.[2] Moreover, mind-wandering seemed to be the cause—and not the consequence—of unhappiness.

In 1979, at the University of Massachusetts Medical Center, Dr. Kabat-Zinn developed the Mindfulness Based Stress Reduction (MBSR) program. MBSR is an eight-week experience in mindfulness that is now taught around the world in various forms. Research since the 1980s demonstrated that mindfulness training has a supportive role in the management of medical conditions (such as chronic pain, cancer, psoriasis, fibromyalgia, and multiple sclerosis) and psychiatric conditions (such as anxiety, post-traumatic stress disorder, emotional dysregulation, and depression), as well as stress reduction in "healthy" individuals.

For individuals with three or more episodes of clinical depression, a variant of MBSR, mindfulness-based cognitive therapy (MBCT), has been shown to reduce relapse by 50 percent.[3]

Participants in MBCT are taught to become aware of body sensations, emotions, and thoughts without trying to change or act on them. This training appears to support disengagement from negative, ruminative thoughts and emotions, therefore reducing the risk of relapse. Mindfulness training is believed to enhance access to internal resources that promote health. And mindfulness practices are now a fundamental part of newer proven therapies, such as dialectical behavioral therapy (DBT) and acceptance and commitment therapy (ACT), both of which fall under the umbrella of cognitive-behavioral treatments.

Mindfulness training also appears to support neuroplasticity (the brain's ability to reorganize its structure, function, and connectivity). You don't have to be an expert meditator or train for 10,000 hours to benefit from this practice. Just eight weeks of MBSR has been shown to increase the thickness of the cortex, to increase gray matter, to enhance intrinsic connections between brain regions, and to aid the neural regulation of brain waves.[4] I (Jeff) would like to share with you how mindfulness training and practice changed my life and helped me cope with the symptoms of depression.

Jeff's Story

It began about nine years after I started working in child psychiatry. The excitement of busily working in a field I loved was beginning to wear off, and I was beginning to feel like I was drowning in work. There were never enough resources for the kids, their families, and the clinic, and I felt like I was trying to bail out a sinking boat with a bucket—no matter how hard I worked, I felt squeezed by all the administrative and financial realities of trying to sustain work in this area. I was also traveling to give talks (again, that had been exciting in the beginning but was now feeling like a drag). I wasn't always there for my family, either. I felt like I could never do enough; there was always something "out there" missing. I felt helpless and like I couldn't control things. I became irritable, drank too much wine, and ate too much pizza. At the same time, my brother was struggling with alcohol issues but refused to go into treatment. He lost his home and moved back in with our parents. Having an alcoholic family member who is bringing down the rest of the family is draining. I could only do so much to help, and it wasn't enough. This made me feel even more stressed and helpless. I was almost depressed and heading down a dangerous road.

Fortunately, my wife recognized the signs of impending depression in me and helped me realize that my life was "out of balance." That's when I made several changes: I cut down my travel, started to help coach my kids' sports teams, and went back to playing pickup basketball (that glorious thing called physical exercise!). I changed the way I ate and backed off on drinking. However, the thing that really changed my life at that time happened when a friend introduced me to the work of Thich Nhat Hanh. I listened to an audiotape of *The Art of Mindful Living*, and this led me to the work of other mindfulness experts, such as Jon Kabat-Zinn. I took to mindfulness and yoga like a fish to water, and I began to feel and accept the flowing, changing nature of life. Through the practice of mindfulness, I was able to let go of my drive to control everything (myself, my surroundings, and others). Practicing yoga and mindfulness has kept me present, grounded, and literally in touch with life. For me it was lifesaving. I am now more available to my family and my work. I found the practice of mindfulness so beneficial in my own life that I began to incorporate it into my work with both adolescents and adults. If you have not yet been introduced to mindfulness, I would like to share some of its very basic principles in hope that you will be able to practice mindfulness, as I did, in your journey away from depression.

Foundations of Mindfulness

Mindfulness is the deliberate practice of aiming attention to your moment-to-moment experience with a certain attitude. This attitude embodies several important components, including these:[5]

Nonjudging: Being an eyewitness to your own experience; becoming aware of your constant stream of judging and reacting to inner and outer experiences; learning to step back, not to change or stop your experience, but just to be aware that it is happening.

Patience: Being completely open to each moment; accepting it in its fullness; realizing that things unfold over time.

Beginner's mind: Being willing to see everything as if "for the first time."

Trust: Learning to trust your own intuition and your own basic wisdom and goodness; because you cannot become someone else, your best hope is to become more fully you.

Nonstriving: Not trying to accomplish anything other than to just "be here now"; trying less and being more.

Acceptance: Seeing things as they actually are. Usually we struggle with how things are, but the experience of struggle is a sign that we aren't open to something important.

Through intentionally cultivating acceptance, you are creating the preconditions for healing. Acceptance does not mean you like what may be going on or approve of it, but rather that you are willing to see things as they are; receiving each moment as it comes, being with it fully, as it is.

Letting go: Refusing to categorize objects or situations; we often view our experience through the dualistic lens of pain/pleasure, good/bad, gain/loss, praise/blame. While categorization has its uses, for now just "be with" what is here without putting it onto one or the other pole of a continuum.

Discipline: To take root, mindfulness requires active participation and practice. Note that you are already disciplined. You already get up and do what needs to be done, most likely for others. Now you need to give yourself the same kind of attention, not in a selfish or narcissistic way but in a gentle, caring, and self-accepting way. The commitment is to practice mindfulness every day, with the knowledge that you can make that practice as short as it has to be for that day.

The Role of Perception

When you were born, your first source of wisdom came from your body. At that point, all you had was the information that arrived through your bodily senses. However, over the course of time, life gets busier, your thoughts become more abstract, and you get disconnected from awareness of your body (just like James Joyce's character Mr. Duffy in *Dubliners*, who "lived a short distance from his body").[6] Still, perceptual awareness and body awareness are key to a tranquil mind. As the thirteenth-century Sufi poet Rumi asks, "Do you make regular visits to yourself?" Understanding perception is important to the training and practice of mindfulness. Psychologist Mihaly Csikszentmihalyi agrees. In his influential book *Flow: The Psychology of Optimal Experience,* he states, "The information we allow into consciousness becomes extremely important; it is, in fact, what determines the content and quality of life."[7]

The usual way your mind works is by taking a small amount of information and making it into a story (cognitive psychologists call these stories "schemas"). Your perceptions may be "primed" so that you see only what you're expecting to see. For instance, Sarah (whom you met at the beginning of this chapter) saw her coworker Robert's bow tie and concluded he was a "loser." She was now closed to seeing the war veteran; the kind, loving father; the accomplished violinist; the competent manager; and the excellent weekend chef that existed behind that bow tie. We see what we "decide" to see.

Try this: mentally investigate a particular situation in your life that is currently bothering you. How much of all the available information coming in from your senses did you actually notice about this situation? What information did you "decide" to focus on? What meaning did you add to it? What assumptions did you make? What conclusions did you jump to? Did you mistake your own opinions for facts? This exercise is helpful in reminding you to notice more and assume less. Some situations, objects, and people—like Robert in Sarah's story—are more than you are allowing yourself to see.

Mindfulness Practices

In mindfulness there are two types of practice, formal and informal. The formal practices occur during a chosen daily time and usually involve some of the following: awareness of the breath, body scan meditation, mindful movements (such as yoga), sitting meditation, and/or walking meditation. The informal practices, as the saying goes, are the rest of your life. These are moments of mindfulness that arise in common daily activities (such as eating, brushing your teeth, washing dishes, and having conversations). Of course, the formal practices are intended to develop the informal practices so that mindfulness becomes a way of life. In this section, we'll describe three formal meditations that are associated with positive mood outcomes when practiced regularly: mindful eating, diaphragmatic breathing, and sitting meditation.

In mindfulness-based stress reduction, we usually begin with an eating meditation. Traditionally, this is taught with a raisin, but we have used clementines, grapes, and Starburst candies. Really, anything will do; what's most important is the attention you bring to the practice.

Mindful Eating Exercise

The goal is to eat one object as if you were a scientist form Mars. Investigate the object using all of your senses:

- *Holding:* Taking the object in hand, holding it between your thumb and index finger, imagine you've never seen an object like this before.

- *Seeing:* Taking time to really see it, gaze at the object, inviting your eyes to explore every part of it. Notice how the light shines on its surfaces, the darker hollows, the folds, the ridges, the asymmetries and unique features.

- *Touching:* Turn the object over between your fingers, exploring its texture, maybe closing your eyes to enhance your sense of touch.

- *Smelling:* Holding the object beneath your nose, with each inhalation drink in any smell or aroma or fragrance, noticing as you do this anything interesting that may be happening in your mouth or stomach.

- *Placing:* Now slowly bring the object up to your lips, noticing how your hand and arm know exactly how and where to position it. Gently place the object in your mouth, without chewing, noticing how it gets into your mouth in the first place. Spend a few moments exploring the sensations of having it in your mouth, exploring it with your tongue.

- *Tasting:* When you are ready, prepare to chew the object, noticing how and where it needs to be for chewing. Then, very conspicuously, bite into it one or two times, noticing what happens in the aftermath, experiencing any waves of taste that emanate from it as you continue chewing. Without swallowing yet, notice the bare sensations of taste and texture in your mouth and how they may change over time, moment to moment, as well as any changes in the object as you chew it.

- *Swallowing:* When you are ready, see if you can notice the intention to swallow as it comes up, so you experience the intention before you actually swallow.

- *Following:* See if you can feel what is left of the object moving down into your stomach, sensing how your body as a whole is feeling now.

Diaphragmatic Breathing Exercise

The next step in the formal practice is to choose an object of awareness. In MBSR we generally start with awareness of the breath. Begin by just witnessing your everyday breath, which is usually taken for granted. Thich Nhat Hanh, the influential Vietnamese Buddhist monk and poet, speaks of the breath as the intersection of the mind and the body. Breathing is an act in which the whole being participates.

Pranayama is a compound word meaning *science of breath regulation.* Yoga teacher and author Richard Rosen provides the following information on Pranayama:

> On average we breathe about 15 times per minute or about 21,600 times per day. Women breathe significantly more often, about 29,000 times daily, than men. How often do you breathe? You can't answer this question because as soon as you start to observe your own breath it begins to slow down and is no longer our true everyday breath. This process is akin in physics to the "observer effect" that says that by witnessing something we change it. Also notice that as you slow the breath you calm the brain, which in turn slows the breath, thus calming the brain further. This cycle allows you to witness your breath more clearly.[8]

After you have learned to observe your everyday breath, the next step is to practice deep (or diaphragmatic) breathing. This type of breathing reduces sympathetic nervous system activation by reducing the release of adrenaline. It calms the body and the brain, while renewing energy reserves. Here are the guidelines:

1. You may practice diaphragmatic breathing in several positions, and it's wise to try different ones. First, wear loose clothing that does not restrict your breathing and

practice at a time when you won't be interrupted. Start by practicing for two to three minutes once or twice daily, and if you like it, increasing each session by one to two minutes, until you discover the "right" amount of time for you.

2. Select a preferred position in which to practice:
   ○ Arrange to lie down on a flat surface in a way that is comfortable. You may support your head, neck, back, and/or knees using rolled-up blankets, towels, or pillows. Your legs may be extended, with your feet lying next to one another, or you may bring the souls of your feet together, touching, and allow your knees to fall away from each other.
   ○ Or you may lean back against a wall with your feet on the floor and your knees bent.
   ○ Whichever position you choose, make sure you feel well supported.

3. Place one hand on your sternum (also known as the breast bone) and one hand just below the rib cage. With the lower hand, you'll be able to feel the diaphragm as it constricts (moving down and forcing the lower abdomen to move out) and as it releases (moving up as the lower abdomen moves inward).

4. Gently close your mouth, allowing the jaw to relax. Your tongue may rest on the floor of your mouth, or the tip of your tongue may lightly press against your upper teeth. You may either gently close your eyes or allow them to be slightly open. If you choose to let them remain open, focus on one spot.

5. For two or three cycles, just breathe naturally through your nostrils, not changing the rhythm. Then, slowly inhale through the nostrils, allowing the lower abdomen to fully expand. Your hand on the lower belly will also move out while your hand on the sternum remains relatively still.

6. At the top of the in-breath, pause briefly and then allow the abdomen to gently fall inward as the breath flows out. Try not to push the breath away; just let go, allowing it to leave. You may try two ways for the breath to flow out; either through the nostrils or through "puckered-up" lips (shaping your lips as if you were going to blow out through a straw or blow out birthday candles).

7. Toward the bottom of the out breath, try tightening your stomach muscles and pausing briefly at the bottom. After a moment, allow the next breath to flow in.

Try to practice diaphragmatic breathing at least once a day for two weeks. That's how long it often takes people to become comfortable with breathing with their stomach instead of the shallower chest breathing. By the end of two weeks, you should experience a calming effect from this exercise, and you will notice that you automatically begin to slip into diaphragmatic breathing whenever you start to get agitated, stressed, or irritable.

Sitting Meditation Exercise

To begin the regular practice of meditation—of looking into yourself—arrange to spend this time on a regular basis, in a place where you can comfortably still the body, and at a time when you will not be interrupted. Allow this to be a time in which you set aside the usual mode of operation, that of pursuing action and activity (the mode of "doing"), and switch to a mode of non-doing, a mode of simply "being." This, of course, will tend to slow time down. Sit in an erect and dignified posture, either on a straight-back chair or on the floor on a cushion. Allow the body to become still, just bringing your attention to the fact that you are breathing. Become aware of the movement of the breath as it comes into your body through the nostrils and as it leaves your body through the nostrils, not manipulating the breathing in any way or trying to change it, simply being aware of it and of the feelings associated with breathing. And if you feel comfortable with it, observe your breathing deep down in your belly, feeling the abdominal wall as it expands gently on the in-breath and as it falls back toward your spine on the out-breath. Simply allow yourself to be totally here in each moment, with each breath—not trying to do anything, not trying to get any place, simply being with your breathing.

Try to stay in this mode for at least five minutes in the beginning. You can lengthen the time as you become more adept at remaining in the "being" mode. As you finish your session, recognize that you have spent this time intentionally nourishing yourself by dwelling in this state of non-doing, of being. You have made time for yourself to be who you are without judgment. Congratulate yourself for making the time and taking the energy to do this. This meditation, when practiced on a regular basis, will promote calmness and quiet energy, which will gradually expand into the active expression of your life in every domain as it continues to unfold.

These exercises are just a small sample of the meditations that can enhance mindfulness and reduce depressive symptoms.

We have provided additional meditations, including a body scan meditation in which you observe different parts of the body, on this book's website (www.AlmostDepressed.com). In addition to meditations, we suggest that you incorporate mindful movements, such as yoga, into your life. Before practicing any mindful movements, please consult with your health care professional to make sure this is a wise time for you to start this practice. If it is, you may access from the website a guided movement practice for both standing and lying down.

The Cognitive Theory of Mindfulness

Social psychologist Ellen Langer has a somewhat different conceptualization of mindfulness than the Eastern Zen-based concept we have been describing in this chapter. Dr. Langer developed her theory of mindfulness based on scientific findings from her extensive research on perceived control, decision making, and health. Her version of mindfulness has been influential in cognitive science. While there are distinct differences, both types of mindfulness share some principles and both have the power to improve well-being.[9]

Langer's cognitive theory of mindfulness (or mindfulness-without-meditation) is a flexible state of mind that results from drawing novel distinctions about your situation and the environment.[10] When you are in a *mindful* state, you are actively engaged in the present, noticing new things, and sensitive to both context (the situation in which these "new things" are couched) and perspective (seeing from a different or novel point of view).

On the other hand, mind*less*ness is a state of rigid thinking in which a person adheres unwavering to a single perspective and acts like an automaton. People in the mindless state cannot see alternate perspectives and pigeonhole their experiences of the world into rigid categories of "good" or "bad."

When you are in a state of mindfulness, you realize that you can make choices about how you think of your experience. This is called "cognitive flexibility." Further, you can change the way you think about the same experience as often as you want to suit the context. For example, in a study conducted by a senior honors student under my (Shelley's) supervision, we tested Dr. Langer's theory by surveying more than seventy Massachusetts breast cancer survivors. They filled out questionnaires about their quality of life, depression and anxiety symptoms, and personalities. They also reported on the severity of their cancer and how long they had been cancer-free. Then we asked one crucial question: "Do you consider yourself 'in remission' or 'cured'?" Even though they reported similar levels of cancer severity and time since treatment, the survivors who considered themselves cured reported a higher quality of life, less pain, more marital satisfaction, and fewer depressive or anxiety symptoms. They were just as likely as those who thought of themselves as "in remission" to believe their cancer could return, and they were also just as likely to feel nervous before their checkups. However, *choosing* to think of themselves as "cured" during their daily life allowed them to go about the business of living with more happiness and confidence than if they had chosen to think that they were in the midst of an illness that was currently (or temporarily) in remission.[11]

Like the breast cancer survivors in this study, you have a choice about how you view even the most serious situations in your life. Likewise, you can choose how to view yourself. Although others may call you stubborn, you can choose to think of yourself as persistent. You can choose to think of yourself as conscientious rather than obsessive, or courageous rather than foolhardy. When you think mindfully, choices in perspective can have huge implications for your self-esteem, as well as your depressive symptoms.

Sarah's Story (continued)

Earlier in this chapter we met Sarah, a harried mother of three who was separated from her husband and who was almost depressed. Fortunately, she was introduced to the benefits of mindfulness in a magazine article. Several weeks later, Sarah signed up for free mindfulness meditation training at a local wellness clinic. As she learned the principles and techniques of mindfulness, she began to realize that she was in the habit of making rapid judgments (usually negative) about events and people in her life.

With training, Sarah was able to appreciate present moments more often and found less need to judge everyone around her. As a result, her relationships with her coworkers and her family members improved. She is less anxious now and her sleep is improving. She is even considering reconciliation with her husband, whom she had previously written off as a deadbeat. "I still have plenty of problems," Sarah says. "But I accept them and am grateful to have family, a job, and good health. I don't feel the need to criticize everything anymore, and I'm much more serene."

• • •

In this chapter we have introduced two different conceptions of mindfulness, including an overview of the roots of mindfulness, the foundations of mindfulness practice, and a few of the core practices. If these practices resonated with you, consider exploring the many terrific resources available for learning more advanced mindfulness techniques, including teachers, CDs, audiotapes, DVDs, conferences, and retreats. We encourage at least some guidance from a certified teacher as a basis from which to make the practice your own. You can find useful suggestions on this book's website (www.AlmostDepressed.com).

❖

| 11 |

Using Mindfulness to Diminish Shame and Foster Self-Acceptance

My mind is like a bad neighborhood—I try not to go there alone.
—Anne Lamott, American writer

Shame is a powerful negative experience that may lead to symptoms of depression. People tend to respond to shame either by excessive self-criticism ("I am an unworthy person") or by anger toward others ("You need to pay for making me feel so bad about myself"). Shame generates a good deal of negative energy, but understanding the nature of shame can help you develop healthy ways to work with it, and perhaps even harness its energies for good.[1]

Shame is often rooted in early experiences, perhaps moments when a parent, teacher, or other authority figure expressed disappointment in you or berated your actions or performance. Because we humans have such a strong craving to belong and be respected by others, attempts by early-life authority figures to manipulate our behavior using shame are often very effective. Mara's story is an example.

Mara's Story

Mara is a thirty-two-year-old editor for an online magazine, who is described by her boss as "bright and conscientious." Mara was recently promoted to a new editorial position in her company that requires her to write weekly blog posts for the magazine website. Although she was comfortable staying behind the scenes and editing other people's material, Mara doesn't feel that her own thoughts are worthy enough to be out there on the Internet. She is ashamed and embarrassed of her posts, even though she anguishes for days over them and her boss seems satisfied with her writing.

Mara claimed she had been going slowly downhill since her promotion. Sleep became difficult and she was feeling sad a lot of the time. She had started to withdraw from her friends and spent most of her time at home alone, worrying about her work. Mara was almost depressed. She insisted that she was a detriment to her company and was leaning toward quitting her job, adding that when she had had the same feelings during a previous job, quitting had made her feel better.

Mara believed that her feelings of shame stemmed from an incident when she was in junior high school. Her mother had thought that Mara had a lovely voice and had encouraged her to take the singing lessons that were offered at her school. While Mara loved singing for her teacher, when the time came for the end-of-year recital, Mara had frozen on the stage. To her horror, her father had stood up, apologized to the other parents for his daughter's unacceptable behavior, and left the auditorium in disgust. Later, when Mara was crying in her room, her father had come in. Instead of comforting her, he had told her that her performance had "brought shame to the family." She has not sung since then and has shrunk from any situation that calls for her to do work that would be evaluated in front of others, a problem that has severely limited her career choices.

. . .

Many people, like Mara, have experienced situations in which they were made to feel embarrassed or ashamed. The unfortunate thing is that shame is often the gift that keeps on giving. Not only do people feel embarrassed and distressed at the time of the shame-related incidents, but they may develop self-defeating tendencies that color their actions in the future. A nagging inner voice that says they are unworthy grows louder, and people begin to avoid situations where they see the possibility of being shamed again. An early experience of shame can lead to significant loss of self-esteem and a pattern of underachievement as the person avoids trying new activities or learning new skills in which they could disappoint themselves or be judged negatively by others. The feelings of personal inadequacy created through shame can also be a risk factor for developing depressive symptoms, and can affect the way you organize and make sense of your current and future relationships.[2]

Shame, like guilt, is considered to be a "self-conscious" emotion. That is, it develops during childhood in response to social interactions rather than coming prepackaged (as do the emotions of fear, anger, sadness, and joy) in the neural hardware of the brain.[3] Although shame and guilt are often viewed as interchangeable, there are several important distinctions between these two emotions. Guilt is an emotional response to an action that either hurt another person or violated a social norm; shame is an emotional response to a public or private exposure of personal inadequacies, which may be exaggerated or entirely manufactured. While guilt involves negative self-judgment of a behavior, shame involves negative self-judgment of the whole self. You can understand a fundamental difference between the two experiences this way: guilt says, "You made a mistake" whereas shame says, "You *are* a mistake." A recent meta-analysis of more than 100 research studies found that shame has significantly stronger associations with depressive symptoms than guilt does.[4]

Shame and Perfectionism

Perfectionism is defined as the tendency to set demanding goals and standards for oneself and to believe that failing to achieve these goals is a sign of personal unworthiness. Perfectionism can be a positive thing if it motivates you to do better work and to try harder to achieve your goals. However, it can also be a negative trait that is associated with shame and depression.[5]

For example, Aaron, an accountant in his early thirties, decided to run a marathon. To qualify, he had to join a charitable team and pledge to raise at least $2,500 for the charity. Aaron pledged to raise a lofty $10,000 and worked really hard to train for the race. Despite finishing the marathon (a great life achievement!) and raising $6,095 for his charity, Aaron felt like a failure. He had fallen short of his $10,000 pledge goal and insisted on making up the difference out of his own checkbook (a gesture that he really couldn't afford). Months after the marathon, Aaron still felt shame and was beginning to show signs of depression as he berated his "poor effort" and failings concerning the marathon.

Researchers have divided perfectionism into two categories: *Normal* perfectionism (which is associated with healthy and adaptive behavior) is the tendency to set high but realistic standards and to aspire to meet these standards. *Neurotic* perfectionism is the tendency to set unrealistically high standards and to see any deviation (real or perceived) from those standards as a personal failure.[6] Aaron displayed this neurotic type of perfectionism. One aspect of Aaron's problem is what psychologists call "conditional self-worth," meaning that neurotic perfectionists believe they are worthy only if they perform or achieve at an almost unattainably high level. By aspiring to meet impossible standards, neurotic perfectionists set themselves up to fail and to experience shame and feelings of worthlessness.

There are three expectations that perfectionists may have regarding unrealistic goals and standards: First, they may expect themselves to meet unrealistic standards they have set for themselves ("self-oriented"). Second, they may expect themselves to meet unrealistic standards that others set for them ("socially prescribed"). And third, they may expect others to meet unrealistic standards that they (the perfectionists) have prescribed ("other-oriented"). Perfectionists, especially the "self-oriented" or "socially prescribed" types, tend to be at greatest risk for depression. The self-oriented type of perfectionism is also linked to the subclinical levels of depression (what we are calling almost depression).[7]

If you believe that you or someone you love might be perfectionistic, here are some questions to consider:

- If you don't complete a task perfectly, do you feel like a failure?

- Are you not satisfied until every little detail of a project or task is dealt with?

- Do people tell you that you're too much of a perfectionist?

- Did your parents punish you when you made a mistake?

- Do you feel that people will think less of you if you make a mistake?

- Even when you've done something well, do you feel your performance wasn't good enough?

- Do you take an unusually long time to complete tasks to make sure they're done "right"?

- Do you feel that you never quite live up to other people's expectations?

If you answered yes to two or more of these questions, then perfectionism may be contributing to your depressive symptoms. One way to work on reducing your perfectionistic tendencies is to use the thought reframing techniques we discussed in chapter 9 to restructure your perfectionistic thinking. You can also use the mindfulness techniques in this chapter that focus on self-acceptance and self-forgiveness.

Shame Can Be "Unlearned"

If shame is part of your depressive profile, you likely feel dominated by your "inner critic," the internalized voice of those experiences that taught you to feel unworthy.[8] If you have perfectionistic tendencies, this is the voice that punishes you for not meeting unrealistic standards and goals. Your inner critic may have gained strength over time. Because shame tends to generalize or spread, you may be devoting a large percentage of your time and resources to making sure you do not do anything that will cause further shame. You may try to avoid more and more actions that might cause shame. However, avoiding action actually leads to more areas of perceived incompetence that can strengthen your inner critic's message that you are "not enough."

The good news is that, just as you *learned* to feel shame as a child, you can *unlearn* the shame response now that you are a competent adult with many emotional and cognitive strengths to help you out. An attitude of mindfulness will help you realize that you have a choice about how to view both yourself and the negative experiences that have happened in your past. Philosopher Jean-Paul Sartre captured the essence of this choice when he said, "Freedom is what you do with what's been done to you."

The first step in unlearning the shame response is to realize that feeling shame is a judgmental action. You are judging yourself to be unworthy or inadequate in some fundamental area of your life. A healthy solution involves balancing self-criticism and harsh self-judgment with self-compassion. A kinder, more accepting attitude toward yourself will gradually diminish feelings of shame and improve self-acceptance and self-esteem.

Self-Compassion

We often don't realize how well-developed our "inner critic" has become or how much we are feeding and maintaining our inner critic by blindly accepting its negative pronouncements.

Initially, you may be resistant to directing compassionate feelings towards yourself (your inner critic may block such efforts by reminding you that you don't deserve compassion or by generating feelings of numbness). However, if you continue to practice self-compassionate behaviors, your inner critic will soften over time. One exercise, suggested by Buddhist author and teacher Pema Chödrön, is called "Receiving Practice" and consists of allowing yourself to receive compassionate strength by focusing on those who appreciate and recognize you.[9]

Receiving Meditation

Start by placing yourself in a quiet space; while sitting (or, alternately, standing, lying down, or even walking), establish a posture that facilitates easy breathing. Direct your attention to the sensations of the flow of the in-breath and the out-breath for one to two minutes. Now, gently slide the awareness of your breath to the background and bring to mind someone (this could be a person or even an animal such as a pet) who has made you feel loved ("loved" means the sensation of warmth, appreciation, recognition). Focus on this experience of being loved and experience it in the body, nonverbally; continue to breathe and to "receive love" (warmth, appreciation, recognition, understanding, or whatever other word is genuine for you), remembering that it is normal to feel blocked or numb at first. It may be helpful to call to mind the experience of sunshine on your skin or to see yourself as a small child without an inner critic. Practice receiving love for one to two minutes each day for two weeks, gradually building to longer periods of meditation. You can also give yourself a "receiving love snack" during the course of a busy day.

Loving-Kindness

The Buddhist mindfulness meditation of loving-kindness, or metta, promotes concern, tenderness, loving-kindness, and a feeling of warmth for oneself and others.[10] The practice of this meditation opens you to deep feelings of connection and kindness toward yourself and others that do not depend on whether you "deserve" them or not. When you become adept at this meditation, you can include not only friends and family in your meditations, but all living beings. Metta does not depend on relationships, on how another person feels about you or vice versa. The process is first one of breaking down barriers that we have constructed to protect ourselves from experiencing pain but that also keep us from experiencing warmth. We must first dissolve the barriers that keep us from loving ourselves and then those that we feel toward others.

Guided Loving-Kindness Meditation

Sit down in a comfortable position. Start by taking a few deep breaths to relax the body, allowing the breath to become natural, without trying to force it or control it; feel that sense of breath being your connection to life . . . Let your mind settle on the experience of this breath, very gently . . . See if you can move the breath from wherever you are accustomed to watching it to the heart center, which is in the center of the chest . . . As you focus your attention in this area, see if you can formulate the things that you wish the very most for yourself, not just for the day or the week but your deepest aspirations in life, the things you wish for the most for yourself.

Express these wishes into phrases and gently begin to repeat them over and over, silently to yourself or aloud in a gentle voice, along with awareness of the breath as it moves in and out of the heart center . . . Settle your mind on one phrase at a time . . . You don't need to rush through . . . It's as if you are cherishing it, as if you are holding something very precious . . . and you don't want to hold it too tight because it will damage it . . . and you don't want to hold it casually because you might lose it; just one phrase at a time, just very fully . . .

> May I be peaceful
> May I be happy
> May I be safe and free from danger
> May I have ease and well-being

Then add phrases for whatever it is *you* wish for most deeply:

> May I . . . [add a personal wish]

Repeat these phrases several times, generating the feel of loving care and acceptance, remembering that the Buddha said, "You can search the entire universe for someone more deserving of your love and affection than yourself and that person is not to be found anywhere." . . . Continue to generate kindness and care and warmth toward yourself, keeping your mind focused on the repetition of the phrases and the breathing in and out of the heart center . . .

Now, think of somebody whom you feel a lot of gratitude toward, someone who's helped you a lot in some way, and direct the feeling of loving care toward that person . . . wishing for him or her just what you have wished for yourself . . .

Just as I want to be peaceful, so may you be peaceful
May you be happy
May you be safe and free from danger
May you have ease and well-being

Again, repeat these phrases several times, generating the feel of loving care and deep gratitude.

Try to complete this mediation at least once a day. You may initially begin with a meditation of five minutes, adding two or three minutes each week. As you become adept at the meditation, add other objects to your loving-kindness focus:

Add a good friend, someone you love and care about, wishing for him or her just what you wished for yourself.

Add a neutral person, someone from your life whom you don't have a particularly strong feeling about, liking or disliking, wishing for him or her just what you have wished for yourself.

And add someone you have difficulty with, somebody who is angry with you, somebody you feel anger toward, somebody with whom you have conflict or tension. Recognize that people you have difficulty with also play a very important role in your life. When you feel able, wish for them just what you have wished for yourself, regardless of their behaviors or actions, just by the virtue that they are alive and that they also want to be happy. Generate this feeling of loving-kindness toward them, very gently repeating the phrases and breathing in and out of the heart center. Do not allow your mind to dwell on the things they have done that might have harmed you; see if you can find even one good quality about them, and if you can't, then recollect the universal wish to be happy, to be free of suffering.

Later, you may expand these wishes further and further outward—through the building, the town, the state, the country, the planet, the universe; those beings near and far, known to us and not known to us; those visible and those invisible; those we like and those we don't; those being born and those who are dying; those who are happy; those who are suffering and those who are causing suffering; those who have wisdom; and all beings.[11]

. . .

If you have difficulty feeling loving-kindness and compassion, you are not alone! This is common and normal, especially at the start of practice.[12] Your internal conversation might go something like this: "If I feel excited, then I might lose control" or "If I let my guard down, something bad will happen" or "If I feel close to others, then I am open to mistreatment/abuse" or "If I feel compassionate and forgiving, then I am weak and permissive; I don't want to be a doormat." These thoughts are conditioned emotional responses that reflect undigested feelings of being "not enough."

Many years ago the influential psychiatrist John Bowlby noted that when he was kind to patients, sometimes they became anxious, irritable, or even stopped coming to see him.[13] Dr. Bowlby understood that receiving, feeling, and offering kindness activates your attachment system, and when you do this, you will activate whatever is in that system. If you have a history of negative attachment, a potentially positive signal can become toxic—meaning that feelings associated with warmth and compassion are actually experienced as a threat.

Your work then is to detoxify your system by proceeding slowly with the meditation. Direct it toward yourself and those for whom you feel gratitude. Branch out to others only when you are comfortable with the experience of loving-kindness. With practice, you should notice changes in your habitual reactive pattern of shame, opening you to experiences of kindness and self-compassion in the way they are intended.[14] This practice may be simple, but it's not easy.

Update on Mara's Story

When Mara first arrived for counseling, she was ready to quit her job as an online magazine editor because she was ashamed and anxious over writing weekly blogs. She was beginning to feel depressed. Her treatment consisted of three parts: First, her therapist helped her to "sit with" the feelings of shame she experienced whenever she thought of blogging. Mara was instructed to read her blogs over and over until they quit producing shame or anxiety for her. Second, she was instructed to read all the comments that people wrote in response to each blog and count both the positive and negative comments. Although some comments were negative, the response to Mara's blog posts was overwhelmingly positive. This helped Mara to frame her writing in a more positive light. Finally, mindfulness techniques were added to Mara's therapy, and she began practicing the loving-kindness meditation, focusing on herself and her father, whom she had blamed for most of her shame and depression problems.

Within a month, Mara was feeling much more confident about her blogs. Her depression symptoms had lifted, and she was actually considering taking singing lessons again.

Mindfulness Theory and Self-Acceptance

Self-acceptance is the opposite of shame and is crucial to mental health. The absence of ability to unconditionally accept yourself can lead to a variety of emotional difficulties, including depression.[15] Just as the Eastern-influenced meditation of loving-kindness can nullify shame, the cognitive theory of mindfulness (introduced in the last chapter) can foster self-acceptance. The following summary of the principles and techniques of mindfulness theory as it relates to self-acceptance are drawn from work that I (Shelley) published with Dr. Langer in 2006.[16]

Mindfulness and Authenticity

One aspect of self-acceptance is feeling authentic. Many people who are ruled by shame reveal that they feel like a "phony," or they worry others will eventually see them "for who they truly are." However, if you are fully engaged with the environment and noticing novel aspects of each situation, you will not have the time or attention to devote to trying to win the approval of others or to bolstering your fragile self-esteem. Mindless people act the way they think others want them to behave in a given situation in the hopes of receiving approval; however, they end up distancing themselves from their honest feelings and their ability to be in the moment simply enjoying the situation. Acting in ways that are not authentic to who you are in an effort to impress others can alienate you from yourself.

Yet, there are situations where manipulating self-presentation can be mindful and beneficial. For instance, you can mindfully act as a role model for yourself. By purposely acting "as if" you are somehow different from how you actually are—say, by acting as if you have a personality trait that you aspire to have—you can promote self-improvement. This can be a very beneficial technique for changing a bad habit as well.

Mindfulness and Self-Evaluation

You have the ability to decide how to view each of your own traits. For instance, rather than branding yourself as impulsive, you can choose to evaluate yourself as spontaneous. You may choose to see yourself as serious rather than grim or as flexible rather than unpredictable.[17]

You also have a choice about how you view your actions and experiences. Rather than being ashamed that you broke your diet by eating a piece of chocolate cake, for example, you can choose to think of it as a beneficial decision you made to treat yourself when you needed a psychological lift. Each behavior made sense to you at the time it occurred or you wouldn't have done it—even if it seems like a bad decision in retrospect. You don't have to be hard on yourself when you remember that you had reasons for your actions at the time. (This is not to say that you should make a habit of justifying inappropriate or outrageous behavior, but rather that you should remember there are multiple perspectives from which to view any act.) You can decide how you evaluate yourself and your actions; whether you choose to see yourself in a positive or negative light is a choice that *you* make.

Mindfulness and Mistakes

One of the main roadblocks to self-acceptance is the inability to accept past mistakes, real or perceived. However, each mistake can be viewed from either a positive or negative perspective. Positive mistakes are those from which you learn something of value. Bad mistakes are those that you avoid thinking about because they make you feel ashamed. It's important to realize that every mistake offers a lesson and a potential for growth when examined from the appropriate perspective. Thomas Edison made literally thousands of mistakes as he worked to create a practical electric lightbulb. The Wright brothers, likewise, had many failures in their attempt to build a working airplane. Each mistake was a learning experience. Going off course does not have to be a negative experience, and it can present you with possibilities for future growth that may not have otherwise been recognized.

Strategies for Mindfully Enhancing Self-Acceptance

Here are six strategies that use the cognitive theory of mindfulness to enhance self-acceptance.

Strategy 1: Spend more time looking nonjudgmentally for novel aspects of your surroundings.

Actively observe your environment in a nonjudgmental way. The act of observing new distinctions increases positive emotions and interest in the event, object, behavior, or situation. Actively noticing new things in your environment (or actively noticing new aspects of things previously taken for granted) is a hallmark of mindful thinking. As nonjudgmental, active mental exploration becomes a way of life, it becomes easier to explore those aspects of self that have previously been kept hidden or avoided.

Strategy 2: Think of yourself as a "work in progress."

When you think of yourself in rigid and static terms (for instance, "I am not attractive" or "I'm no good at tennis"), you pave the way for self-fulfilling prophesy and you feed your inner critic.

Noticing New Aspects Exercise

(from Shelley's book *Your Creative Brain*)[18]

In order to notice new aspects of your environment, begin with what you see:

- Look for colors and notice how subtly or drastically the colors change where there are shadows or where sunlight or artificial light strikes the walls, floors, and ceiling. Look closely and see how the color of fabrics or paint may vary where it has faded.

- Look for angles and notice the variety of angles in your environment. Look at the angle of the door frame to the ceiling. Notice the angles made by furnishings in your environment. Also notice the angles of incidental items in the environment, say a newspaper tossed on a table, a jacket draped over a chair, or a piece of trash left in the corner of a subway car. If you can see out a window, notice the angles made by objects outside—the angle of a tree or a bush to the window sill, or the angle of rain falling.

- Notice movement in your environment. Is there a fire flickering in a fireplace? Are curtains moving gently in the breeze? Is a fly flitting around the room? Are people in motion around you? If so, notice the patterns of their movement. If you are in a vehicle, notice the movement of the landscape streaming by the window (of course, do *not* perform this exercise while you are actually driving).

- Now pay attention to what you can hear. First, listen to the foreground noises in your environment. Is there a television or radio turned on? Are other people talking? Rather than listening to words that are spoken, listen to the tonal

CONTINUED ON NEXT PAGE

CONTINUED FROM PREVIOUS PAGE

qualities and the modulation of the voices. Do the voices remind you of angry thunder or of a babbling brook?

- Can you hear music? If so, listen to its qualities. Is the rhythm fast or slow? Constant or varied? Is the music in a major or minor scale? Can you hear more than one instrument? Are the different instruments playing different melodies and harmonies?

- Can you hear a dog barking, water running, a toilet flushing, someone coughing? Listen to the variations in all of these sounds. Listen for other outside noises—the buzz of traffic, a lawn mower, a distant siren.

- Listen for background noises. Notice the hum of an air conditioner, a furnace, or a refrigerator. If you hear rain, listen carefully for variations in its sound. Rain makes a different noise when it hits the lawn, the road, trees, or a metal roof.

- Next, pay attention to what you can feel. Become aware of the air around you. Is it moist or dry? Warm or cool? Can you feel movement in the air, like a gentle breeze? Be perfectly still for a moment and see if you can detect variations in the temperature of the air.

- Next, pay attention to the odors and fragrances in your environment. Can you detect any food smells? Any floral smells? Resist the temptation to judge what you smell . . . just notice the different odors and fragrances of this place.

No matter where you are, your environment is infinitely interesting. Focusing on it in a nonjudgmental way will teach you to appreciate and accept the present state of things, including yourself.

Whenever you catch yourself thinking in these rigid terms about yourself, replace the "certainty" words with "possibility" words such as "could be" or "can be" ("I can be attractive" and "I could be good at tennis"). These changes acknowledge that you are not currently where you want to be and that the potential exists to attain that personal place.

Strategy 3: View your situation from multiple perspectives.

Whenever you hear the inner critic rearing its belittling voice, look at your current situation or actions from multiple points of view. How would your dentist view this situation, or your cocker spaniel, or a Martian looking down from outer space? Chances are, when you see the situation from other perspectives, it will look much more benign than the way your inner critic is telling you to view it.

Strategy 4: Keep a catalog of personal accomplishments.

This can be in the form of a journal or diary or a file on your computer. Whenever you catch yourself doing something that works out well, no matter how small (such as cooking a good meal, comforting a friend, getting to the gym, or completing a report for work), write it down. Read through your catalog at least once a week to remind yourself (and your inner critic!) of how competent and worthwhile you really are.

Strategy 5: Look for the lesson in your mistakes.

Whenever you make a so-called mistake or do something embarrassing, force yourself to find a positive aspect of your action. You may prefer to avoid thinking about the action because it evokes the feelings of embarrassment and shame all over again. Even so, force yourself to sit with the thought of what you've done until you can see what it taught you. Write a short description of the "mistake." Then write down different ways you could view it in a positive light. Remember that each mistake presents an opportunity to discover new knowledge or motivation for change or is an opportunity to teach yourself or others a valuable lesson. As you practice reframing your mistakes as opportunities, you will gradually come to accept your actions, past and present, as positive life-shaping events.

Strategy 6: Start a "mindfulness" journal.

End each day by writing down the significant events of the day. Look back on the events with the purpose of nonjudgmentally observing new things and new perspectives about them. Mindfully viewing events and situations in retrospect will enhance your ability to mindfully experience events and situations at the time they occur. Keeping a mindfulness journal will also preserve a record of your own continuity and growth, enhancing self-acceptance.

• • •

In this chapter, we took a look at shame and self-acceptance from the perspective of mindfulness. Mindful practices can help you tame your inner critic and learn to accept yourself. In fact, when you practice mindfulness, you may be able to use shame as it was meant to be used—as a motivator for positive personal growth and change. As Frederick Nietzsche said, "Everyone needs a sense of shame, but no one needs to feel ashamed."

■ ◆ ■

TAKING THE
Social Pathway

| 12 |

Increasing Your Social Engagement and Support

A true friend never gets in your way unless
you happen to be going down.
—Arnold H. Glasow, American humorist

You may have seen this commercial: four women are in a car and one has just been "dumped" by her boyfriend. The others are consoling her with statements about how he wasn't good enough for her anyway and how she's better off without him. Before the ad is over, the woman is laughing through her tears as the foursome head out for a fun evening. This ad is so effective because it pairs its product with one of the most important and basic of human needs: an available social support system.

Your social support system is the sum of all the people you can count on to help you when things start to get rocky in your life. Having a strong social support system is a protective factor against both clinical and subclinical depression, and indeed against most other mental disorders as well. It is also important in combating depression that already exists, as well as in preventing relapses.[1] In fact, the importance of social support in dealing with all stages of depression is one of the most robust findings in psychiatric research. There are also biological reasons to keep your social support system strong. Low levels of social support have been linked with increases in a person's reactivity to stress and with higher blood pressure and resting heart rate. In laboratory studies where people were given stressful tasks to complete (such as public speaking), those who had social support exhibited much lower heart rates and lower production of the stress hormone cortisol than people without social support. Other studies have found that lonely people have higher cortisol levels and stress system reactivity. Moreover, low levels of social support predict all manner of health problems—leading prominent Stanford University biologist Robert Sapolsky to conclude that social support affects one's life expectancy almost as much as obesity, smoking, or physical exercise.[2]

Clearly, your relationships with others are an important factor in your mental and physical health. For all these reasons, it's crucial to have positive social relationships and a solid social support system.

Mapping Your Social Support System

Social support is measured by both the quantity of your relationships and the quality of those relationships—especially their ability to provide support when you need it. Support is not a measure of how much you love and respect a person or how much they love or respect you. In fact, some of the people you are closest to may not be able to provide support for you for various reasons. For example, if you have a parent who has Alzheimer's or some other form of dementia, he or she may not be in a position to provide support to you. Likewise, if you have a brother who has been deployed to a war zone, he may not be able to provide much support at this time. So, when mapping your overall support, it's important to determine not only how many people are there to support you but how able they are currently to do so.

To determine your support system, copy the diagram below into a notebook and write the names of people on whom you can depend into one of the concentric circles. (You can also download this diagram at www.AlmostDepressed.com.) You can use initials rather than names to make more room on the diagram. Each name or set of initials should be followed by a number from 0 to 5, with 5 representing the highest amount of support you believe that person can provide and 0 representing the lowest amount. Place the names closer to or farther from the center depending upon how close you are to each person.

Self = you (place your name here).

Intimate = the person with whom you are most intimate. This is the person with whom you can share your innermost authentic feelings. This is often a spouse, partner, or significant other, but it could also be a sibling or best friend.

Family/Close friends = your "inner circle." These are people who know you well and are very close to you.

Friends = people you count as friends but who are not in your inner circle. These may be people with whom you spend time and whose company you enjoy.

CONTINUED ON NEXT PAGE

CONTINUED FROM PREVIOUS PAGE

Professional colleagues = people you know professionally. You may spend a lot of time with them and have a good working relationship with them.

Group members = people you may know from groups to which you belong, such as a golf or tennis club, your place of worship, or a community organization, whom you might count on for help.

Others who could help = people you may see often in a non-professional setting. They may be neighbors, acquaintances, distant relatives, or friends of friends.

Instrumental support = people who may help you in a practical way. These could include your doctor, lawyer, banker, baby-sitter, clergy member, social worker, or therapist.

Figure 15.
Social Support System Map

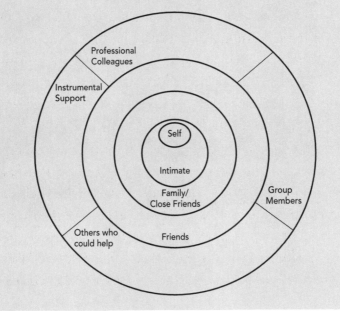

After you have completed your Social Support System Map (figure 15), check for any areas where you need to improve your relationships. Ideally, you should have a number of entries followed by 4s and 5s. If most of your social contacts are 2s or if you have areas where there are no names, it is time to beef up your social support system.

Social support can come in many forms. A person does not need to purposely help you to provide support. Sometimes, just being in the presence of a friend or loved one is supportive. Sometimes a smile or verbal greeting from an acquaintance provides support. These gestures can be *perceived* as increasing your overall connection to humanity. In fact, research shows that low *perceived* social support (how much you subjectively believe that people will support you in a time of need) may be more of a risk factor for depression than actual *received* social support (the amount of help that people actually give you). A recent Danish study of more than 40,000 depressed men and women between twenty and eighty-nine years of age found that perceived social support predicted the severity of their depression.[3]

The distinction between perceived and received social support may be important as you work your way out of low-grade depression. When you are depressed, you tend to see things in a negative light, and you may be underestimating the support that is available to you. Look at the ratings of potential support you assigned to social contacts in your Social Support System Map. Are there any low ratings that you need to challenge and upgrade?

Psychologists have also classified social support by the *type* of support that is provided.

Emotional social support includes all the people around you who can provide caring, empathy, love, and stroking when you are in the doldrums of almost depression. This includes listening to your problems or offering a shoulder to cry on when you're in pain.

Instrumental or *tangible* social support includes all the people who can help you in a practical way when you're in need, whether it's the banker who will lend you money to make your mortgage payment or the neighbor who will watch your kids so you can go to your doctor's appointment. These social contacts provide tangible goods and services to help you.

Companion support includes all the people in your system with whom you can share activities and whose company can distract you from your woes.

Informational support includes all the people you know who can provide advice, guidance, or suggestions. Any person in your support system may provide more than one type of support to you, and all types of support are helpful when you're almost depressed.

Using Your Social Support System

You can use your Social Support System Map to remind yourself that there are many people you can count on for some kind of support. When you are feeling blue, rather than withdrawing from others, make contact with someone in your circle of friends. The goal is not to bare your soul but to distract yourself from your blues by having fun or focusing on another person rather than your own problems. If you created a Daily

Activities Calendar in chapter 5, try to add two new activities this week that involve getting together with friends who can lend companion support.

As you begin to feel better, add the following exercise to your Daily Activities Calendar: contact one person every two weeks or so from your outer circle of acquaintances whom you would like to get to know better. You can email the person, call on the phone, or get together for coffee. In this way, you can gradually move people you really enjoy and respect closer to the center of your map.

People often ask us how much of their almost depression problems they should disclose to others. This is your personal choice, but here are some suggested guidelines:

- Do not try to "hide" your mood from those who are closest to you. While you may want to put on a brighter face in front of people in your outer social support circles, your intimate partner and those in your inner circle should know that you are struggling with depression issues. Reassure your loved ones (especially children) that your withdrawal and/or anger is not their fault. A few words will go a long way toward clearing up any misunderstandings that result from your depressive symptoms. Here are a few ideas for what you could say:
  - "I want you to know that when I'm keeping to myself, it's not your fault and it's not because of anything you've done. I love you very much."
  - "I know I've been grumpy lately. I want you to know that when this happens, it's not your fault. I'm sorry if I hurt your feelings."

○ "I sometimes get sad or need to be by myself lately. When this happens, it doesn't mean I don't love you."

• Sit down with those closest to you and describe the symptoms you're having. Let them know what they can do to support you.

• Let those close to you know if your symptoms worsen. They may be able to determine whether you are in personal crisis better than you can yourself.

• If you don't feel that you have anyone in your inner circle you can talk to about your symptoms, contact your doctor, clergy member, or therapist. You should definitely inform someone whom you trust that you are going through a hard time.

• Monitor your actions so that you don't take your misery out on those you care about.

Meeting New People

Once people realize the value of their social support system, they are usually eager to increase their circles of friends and acquaintances. Even if you have a large social support network right now, you can benefit from meeting new people who might provide companion, informational, or instrumental support to you. And you, in turn, may be able to provide support to them as well. One question we are often asked is where a person can go to make high-quality acquaintances. We know that it's difficult to exert the effort to meet new people if you're feeling depressed. It's likely that you feel more like withdrawing from others rather than seeking out new support. Nevertheless, keep this in mind: increasing your social support and spending time

Social Support from "Man's Best Friend"

Having a pet has been associated with better physical health and psychological well-being.[4] However, you may wonder if pets can act as social support in the face of depression. The latest research shows that pets can have both positive and negative effects on emotional health. In general, the positive effects of pets include their companionship and unconditional affection. Pets can also act as "social facilitators" (for instance, walking your dog in the park may give you an opportunity to meet other dog owners). Exercising your pet may also provide you with the benefits of exercise (see chapter 5 for more on the advantages of exercise for depression). The negative effects include the strain of caring for a pet and using pets as a substitute for human companionship. Further, the benefits of pet ownership on depression may depend on several factors—such as your other sources of social support, your gender, your marital status, and how emotionally attached you are to your pet.

In a recent University of Missouri study of dog ownership and depression, researchers found that dog ownership in general did not affect a person's level of depression. However, dogs were more helpful for depression levels in single people than in married people. Women, and single women in particular, seemed to experience greater well-being from owning a dog.[5]

Another recent study, conducted by researchers from Columbia University using an Internet-based survey, found that single women who owned a dog or cat had fewer depressive symptoms compared with women who did not own a pet or single men who owned a pet. In fact, they found that single men who owned a pet had the most depressive symptoms of anyone in their survey![6] Perhaps women, who tend to enjoy nurturing others, found the strains of dog ownership more enjoyable, while

CONTINUED ON NEXT PAGE

CONTINUED FROM PREVIOUS PAGE

the men who owned dogs perceived pet care as an additional burden.

Yet another study of pet ownership and depression in those living alone (including unmarried and elderly people) found that people who had a pet as well as a strong human support system had fewer depression symptoms than those who did not have a pet. Further, being overly attached to a pet was associated with increased depression symptoms.

Taken together, these findings make it clear that owning a pet offers additional social support if you're depressed (especially if you are single and female), but pets are not substitutes for human support. If you are considering getting a pet for companionship, be sure to weigh the strains of pet care and ownership against the companionship of man's best friend (or should we say "woman's best friend"!).

with people who support you will make you feel better in the long run, even if you don't feel like it right now.

One way to meet new people who share your interests is to take up a new hobby or renew your interest in an old one. You may be able to find clubs or organizations in your community revolving around many of the following hobbies and activities. Try searching for such organizations online or check with your local community center or town hall. If your community does not offer an organization that supports an activity or hobby that appeals to you, consider starting one yourself. Suggestions for hobbies that involve meeting other people include these:

- acting
- adult education course
- auto detailing
- backgammon
- bird watching
- book club
- bowling
- building models
- checkers or chess
- cooking
- dog breeding
- dog training
- dog walking
- flying lessons
- foreign language classes
- gardening
- going to the beach or gym
- historical reenactments
- juggling
- karaoke
- martial arts
- paintball
- painting
- photography
- playing bridge or poker

- playing a musical instrument
- pottery
- quilting
- shooting range
- singing in a group
- team sports
- traveling
- visiting a museum

In addition to participating in hobbies, getting involved in your community is a great way to meet new people and build your social support. Robert Putnam's book *Bowling Alone: The Collapse and Revival of American Community* provides evidence that the decline in participation in civic and community organizations has been detrimental to both the individual and to society as a whole.[7] By participating in civic and community activities, you can improve your depression symptoms and have an impact on the greater world. The following list of community involvement ideas was adapted from the University of Pennsylvania Collaborative on Community Integration.[8]

- *Attend town meetings.* Most communities hold public meetings at least once a year where you can learn about your town's issues. Check your local newspaper or your town hall for dates.

- *Volunteer your skills.* Many organizations could use your help, and you may learn new skills and help others at the same time. Check online or at your local community center for opportunities.

- *Mentor a child.* Many young people lack a supportive adult in their lives. Mentoring is a chance to share your life skills with a young person. Think about becoming a Big Brother or Big Sister.

- *Work with the elderly.* Most communities have senior citizen centers that rely on volunteers to lead activities, provide rides, deliver meals, and act as companions.

- *Volunteer for emergency services.* A number of communities rely on volunteer fire departments or other emergency services, and they provide training. Your community may also need volunteers to answer crisis phone lines, supporting people with issues including suicide risk, domestic abuse, or animal rescue.

- *Work at an animal shelter.* Many communities rely on volunteers to work in animal shelters and care for stray or abandoned pets. If you love animals, this is an excellent way to get involved in your community. Contact your local Humane Society or town hall for more information.

- *Participate on a sports team.* Check with your community recreation department to find sporting activities and adult leagues in your area. If you have some experience in sports, you might also volunteer to be a coach or assistant coach for a local youth team.

- *Get involved with your child's school.* Most school districts have parent/teacher organizations (PTOs). Many schools encourage parents to volunteer in the classrooms and to help with school activities such as sports or fund-raisers.

- *Volunteer at a hospital.* Contact your community hospital to inquire about volunteer positions.

- *Get involved with your local faith-based organization.* Your local church, synagogue, or other spiritual center likely offers opportunities such as singing in a choir, helping with fund-raisers, or teaching.

- *Get involved with a local civic organization.* Most cities and towns have a number of civic associations that provide community services as well as social opportunities. To find out about civic organizations in your area, contact your town hall or look on the website of your town or city.

- *Participate in a community garden.* Gardening with others offers exercise, recreation, companionship, and the opportunity to add beauty to your community. You can find out about the community garden closest to you, or how to start one, by contacting the American Community Gardening Association (www.communitygarden.org).

- *Get involved in a political organization.* If you have strong feelings about political issues, you can make an impact at the grassroots level that may be heard in Washington, DC. Contact your local or state Republican, Democrat, or third-party headquarters for information on how to get involved.

- *Volunteer at your local library.* Your community library may offer a variety of volunteer opportunities, including reading to others, restacking books, and working at the circulation desk. Contact your public library for information.

- *Get involved with local veterans.* If your community has a VA hospital, you can provide a wonderful service by volunteering there. Veterans groups are organized at state, county, and local levels, and they welcome volunteers. If you have been helped by a veteran's group during your convalescence, consider volunteering for that same group as you reintegrate into the community.

However you decide to do it, meeting new people and spending more time in positive social engagements can help you avoid isolation, boost your mood, and build your self-esteem. In the next chapter, you'll learn some skills that will help you interact with others in ways that are rewarding and positive.

▪ ◆ ▪

| 13 |

Improving Your Social Skills

The most important single ingredient in the formula of success
is knowing how to get along with people.
—Theodore Roosevelt

Despite all the evidence pointing to the importance of social support during a depressed state, people who are depressed often begin withdrawing from friends and family or they act in ways that are off-putting to others. In effect, depressed people often undermine the very social support that they desperately need.

Elena's Story

Elena is a twenty-year-old college student of Hispanic descent. When she went off to a small liberal arts college as a freshman, it was the first time she had ever been away from home. Because she was on a scholarship, she wanted to do very well, so she threw herself into her studies. However, she found that many of the liberal and progressive concepts she was exposed to in her courses were at odds with her upbringing and her deep Catholic faith. She became confused about some of her core beliefs, and she was homesick and began to feel out of place.

When she reluctantly returned to school as a sophomore, she again began to sink into a mildly depressed state. Her roommates noticed that she was feeling low and tried to console her by including her in their activities. On one outing she went with her roommates to a beach party. Elena found the experience almost unbearable, as she sat on a towel by herself and watched everyone else playing volleyball and running in the surf. Their fun seemed frivolous to her in light of her own inner turmoil. Occasionally someone would come over and try to coax her off the towel, but she rebuffed their efforts. Eventually, they left her alone to brood, and she overheard one of the partygoers asking, "Who brought Debbie Downer to the party?"

After that incident, Elena's roommates spent less and less time with her. They rarely asked her to join them when they went out. In fact, they seemed to stay away from the dorm room as much as possible when Elena was there. Although she knew that somehow she was driving them away, she nevertheless felt rejected. Instead of trying to improve her relationship with her roommates, she concluded they were better off without her. With no one else to reach out to, Elena finally sought help at her college counseling center.

• • •

Elena's story illustrates a common progression with people who are becoming depressed. Psychologist James Coyne has labeled this the "interactional model" of depression.[1] According to Coyne's theory, this is how the interactional model plays out:

Initially, the depressed person elicits sympathy and concern from others. After all, no one wants to see a friend or family member feeling distressed. However, the depressed person simultaneously rebuffs the concerned efforts of others while continually seeking more reassurance from them. Eventually, others tire of offering reassurance only to have it refused. They become irritated with, or begin to avoid, the depressed person. Either way, the depressed person feels rejected and sinks further into the downward cycle of depression. This is exactly what happened to Elena. Her roommates attempted to give her social support, which she repeatedly repelled, ultimately leading to deeper depression.

What can you do to stop this spiral in which you may be alienating the very people you need? The first step is to notice how you are acting around people and then practice social skills that will attract people to you rather than causing them to avoid you. While a person in the depths of depression may need help to implement these skills, if you are almost depressed you can likely learn and practice these skills successfully on your own.

Extensive research on depression and social skills has found that depressed people are perceived as having poorer social skills than those who are not depressed. This doesn't mean that all people who are almost depressed are lacking in social skills. However, low mood can make a person *appear* less sociable. Moreover, depressed people themselves rate their social skills as lacking.[2] These social skills problems may have existed before the person became depressed (and are thus a risk factor for depression), or the problems may develop as a result of the depression itself. In other words, as the person becomes more depressed, he or she may begin acting in ways that others view as unsociable. Either way, social skill deficits can lead to negative interactions with others. The good news is that social skills can be practiced and developed and, when practiced regularly, they are effective in reducing symptoms of depression and preventing relapses.[3]

Improving Your Social Skills

While there are many different kinds of social skills, the strategies we present here will help you initiate, participate in, and conclude conversations with other people using an assertive communication style. People who are depressed may come across as negative, insecure, self-absorbed, and uninterested in the other person, or they may even seem hostile. By practicing a few simple strategies, you can change the image you project and interact more effectively with others to strengthen your social support.

Projecting an Assertive Style

There are three major styles of communication.

- The *aggressive* communication style involves threatening or intimidating words or gestures. It sends the message "My way or the highway." Aggressive communication damages relationships and makes others feel resentful. People who are depressed may be projecting aggression without intending to. They may come across as superior, arrogant, or hostile to cover up feelings of insecurity and inadequacy.

- The *passive* communication style involves shrinking away from conflict or disagreement. It sends the message "My needs are not important." Being too passive can also be destructive to social relationships. It signals insecurity and a lack of self-esteem. People who are depressed often project this "I am not worthy" style. However, if you do not hold yourself in high esteem, then others are not likely to do so either.

- The third style, *assertive* communication, sends the message that, while you respect the feelings and opinions of others, you also respect your own feelings, needs, and opinions, and you expect others to do so as well. Assertive communication projects a "win-win" attitude and makes conversations and social interactions go more smoothly.

What is interesting is that you project one of these three styles through your nonverbal body language as well as your verbal communication. People will form a first impression of you based on your posture, facial expression, gaze, and hand gestures before you even open your mouth. Because first impressions are difficult to overcome, it's important to project a positive nonverbal image.

Using nonverbal expression.

The *aggressive* style of communication includes an upright rigid posture with strained muscles and a tight jaw. Aggressive people often lean toward the person they are talking to in a menacing way. They may glare at others in an intimidating manner. They may engage in finger jabbing, fist clenching, or finger drumming. Alternately, they may fold their arms tightly across their chests and look down their noses at others, almost as though they are daring others to talk to them.

Passive communicators have slumped shoulders, lowered heads, and a general posture of defeat. They tend to avoid eye contact and either look down at the floor or focus on something else in the room instead of the person they are talking to. They often touch their faces or fiddle with their hair, gestures that send a message of insecurity and low self-confidence. People who are depressed often display these nonverbal signals.

Assertive communicators square their shoulders; have an erect but not a rigid posture, an uplifted face, and relaxed muscles; and they display a sense of calmness and control. They make nonthreatening eye contact with others. They look at people when they speak to them or when the others are speaking to them. They have relaxed arms and hands, and they don't make either intimidating or self-effacing gestures.

You can practice assertive nonverbal skills by role-playing in front of a mirror. Pretend that you are walking into a room filled with other people or holding a conversation with someone. Practice using these nonverbal skills until they feel natural and comfortable.

- *Posture:* Stand or sit tall with your head up.
- *Facial expression:* Appear relaxed but interested; smile.
- *Gaze:* Make nonthreatening eye contact.
- *Gestures:* Use relaxed, slightly open hands to make gestures; don't touch your face or hair.

Making assertive requests.

At times you will need to call on someone from your social support system to give you assistance. However, the way you ask for help may determine whether people will honor your requests or not. Consider how you would respond to each of the following requests. Which one would you be most likely to agree to?

Aggressive: "You'll have to cancel your plans for tomorrow so that I can use your car to go out."

Passive: "I know it's really short notice and I guess I shouldn't even ask . . . It's just that I don't have a car right now. Oh, never mind, I don't really need to go out tomorrow."

Assertive: "I have some things I need to take care of tomorrow, but my car is still in the shop. Would it be possible for me to use your car for a while tomorrow afternoon?"

Most people don't respond well to the aggressive style because they don't like to be told what to do. When you use the aggressive style, your message sounds more like a demand than a request. However, the self-effacing nature of the passive style often sounds like whining. The best way to get people to respond positively to your requests is to communicate in a straightforward, respectful, and assertive way.

An assertive request has three parts.

1. State your needs directly. (Example: "I have some things I need to take care of tomorrow, but my car is still in the shop.")

2. Make your request. Directly state what you want from the other person. (Example: "Would it be possible for me to use your car for a while tomorrow afternoon?")

3. Positively acknowledge the person's response. Whether or not they can help, thank them. (Example: "Thank you so much. This is really a big help to me!" or "I totally understand. Thanks anyway.") Ending on a positive note increases the probability that others will consider helping you the next time you make a request.

Negative Social Support

Not all people in your social support system may have your best interests at heart. Some relationships (either intentionally or unintentionally) are verbally, emotionally, or physically abusive. Some people may act like they are trying to help you, but are actually enabling you to continue behaviors that are harmful to you. Being in an abusive or enabling relationship is a risk factor for depression. Abusers or enablers often play on your insecurities to have control over you or your behavior. They may try to isolate you from others or convince you that you are incapable of handling your own affairs. Dealing with abusive and enabling relationships is beyond the scope of this book. However, if you feel that you are being abused or enabled by another person, you need more than an assertive approach to protect yourself. Contact someone you trust (a counselor, therapist, physician, or clergyperson) to help you assess the situation and take appropriate action. The longer you remain in an abusive or enabling relationship, the more difficult it will be for you to recover your self-esteem and emotional health.

Aim for "win-win" rather than an "I-win, you-lose" communication. You're more likely to get positive results if the other person feels respected than if he or she feels intimidated or annoyed by your request. In the ideal assertive request, you communicate your needs openly without making the other person feel obligated to you.

Starting a conversation.

Initiating a conversation can be very difficult if you're feeling depressed. Indeed, you may want to do just the opposite and avoid speaking to people, as Elena did in our earlier example. However, as we've seen with other techniques in this book, pushing yourself to step outside your comfort zone is the best way to begin feeling better. So how do you start a conversation?

Experts on conversation suggest that you start with small talk. Although small talk sometimes gets a bad rap, it is like oil that lubricates social interactions. Debra Fine, author of *The Fine Art of Small Talk*, suggests that you begin in the simplest way possible: by introducing yourself.[4] Try following these steps:

1. Make eye contact with someone you'd like to talk to and smile.

2. Offer your name first. "Hi! I'm [your name]. What's your name?"

3. Be sure to listen carefully to their name. Ask them to repeat it if you didn't get it the first time. And use their name periodically in the conversation. Being called by name makes people feel important. Using a person's name is a valuable social skill.

After introductions (or if you're talking to someone whom you have already met), you can use the *statement-question* technique to break the ice. This technique is simple. First, you make a statement (either a positive statement about something you've observed about the other person or about some aspect of the environment—say, the weather) and you follow it up with an open-ended question. Open-ended questions cannot be answered with just yes or no, so they help you learn something about the other person that you can then build a conversation around. Here are some examples:

Statement: "It's been such a hot summer! But it's great for the beach." *Question:* "What do *you* like to do in this type of weather?"

Statement: "That's an interesting tie (pin, hat, necklace) you're wearing. It looks like it has an interesting history." *Question:* "Where did you get it?"

Statement: "Your garden always looks so beautiful." *Question:* "How did you learn to grow so many different types of flowers?"

Statement: "You seem to know a lot about cars (computers, airplanes)." *Question:* "Where did you learn so much about them?"

A key part of being a good conversationalist is focusing your attention on the other person rather than talking about yourself. However, you may find this to be difficult if you're depressed. Peter Lewinsohn, a noted expert on depression from the University of Oregon, has conducted in-depth studies on the conversations of depressed people. He found that, compared to people who are not depressed, depressed people tend to talk more about themselves and their own pain. They also self-disclose more (they tend to say inappropriately personal things about themselves and their personal history). Further, people who are depressed express more negativity and pessimism in their conversations.[5] These issues make other people feel uncomfortable and even hostile toward the depressed person. If you are almost depressed, make a purposeful effort to monitor your thoughts for negative and critical statements before you say them out loud to others. Additionally, try to focus your attention on the other person during a conversation, even if it feels uncomfortable to you.

One way to focus on others is to express empathy. Put yourself in the other person's shoes and try to understand his or her point of view rather than expressing how you feel or how you would respond to a particular event or situation. A recent study indicated that people who are depressed have difficulty expressing empathy, even though they may be able to recognize when others are experiencing negative emotions.[6] To increase expressions of empathy in your conversations with others, try this: Imagine that the person you are talking to is the most interesting person in the world. Without prying, ask questions about the person's hobbies, family, and work. At first, you may feel that it's "fake" or "phony" to express interest in others when you don't really feel it. However, the more you practice trying to see and respond to the other person's perspective, the easier it will be to slip out of your own almost-depressed perspective and genuinely connect with other people.

Here are some other guidelines for having good conversations:

1. Focus on the other person and what may be of interest to him or her.

2. Limit the information you share about yourself, especially if it's negative information.

3. Keep the conversation upbeat and positive. Resist the urge to complain.

4. Keep focused on the conversation. Don't let your mind wander.

5. Use the other person's name several times during the conversation.

6. Practice *active* listening.

Active listening.

We often think of listening as a passive activity. However, listening is an important skill that can be very active and can help you develop rapport with others. When you really listen to others, it shows that you are interested in them and that you value what they have to say. Here are some guidelines for active listening:[7]

1. *Use a posture of involvement.* Squarely face the person who is talking to you. (Turning away from someone who is talking to you is the origin of the phrase "he gave me the cold shoulder.") Keep your arms uncrossed and make eye contact.

2. *Give your full attention.* Don't look around the room, send texts on your cell phone, read the paper, or watch TV while someone is talking to you. Don't zone out or plan what you're going to say next instead of listening.

3. *Provide indications that you hear and understand the other person.* Nod occasionally (nodding doesn't mean you agree with what the person is saying; it just means that you are following him or her). Alternately, make comments such as "I hear you," "I'm with you," or "I understand."

4. *Reflect what the other person is saying.* Periodically, check in with the other person to make sure you understood him or her by repeating the main points in your own

words. You can say, for instance, "What I hear you saying is . . . " or "You feel that . . . . Is that right?"

Ending a conversation.

Knowing how and when to end a conversation is another social skill. If you're experiencing symptoms of depression, it is best for *you* to end a conversation before the other person does. Leave the person while he or she is still enjoying your company. That way, the person will be more likely to seek out your company in the future, and you won't feel rejected because he or she ended the conversation first.

One effective "exit strategy" is the *statement-arrow-statement* combination. This is a three-sentence technique that includes a positive statement about the other person, an exit statement (indicating that the conversation is over), followed by another positive statement. Here's an example:

Positive statement: "It was great to catch up with you."

Exit statement: "I have to get going now."

Positive statement: "I hope we get a chance to talk again soon."

Note that it is not necessary to give an excuse or reason for ending the conversation (although you can give a reason as long as you keep it short). Once you have delivered your exit statements, be sure to actually leave the conversation. (Remember the title of the Dan Hicks song, "How Can I Miss You When You Won't Go Away?")

Now that you have some tips for social skills, it's time to put the skills to work. The ultimate goal is to have positive conversations with people you would like to get to know better. However, you can practice conversation, listening, and assertiveness skills anywhere—standing in the checkout line at the grocery store, on the subway, or in the barbershop. Make a goal to have at least two conversations with someone you don't know (or don't know well) each week. If you do this on a regular basis, you will dramatically improve your ability to communicate and you'll enlarge your social support network.

Inez's Story: A Follow-Up

In chapter 2, you met Inez, a young and troubled college professor. She is a good example of how learning and using social skills can turn an almost-depressed situation into a personal growth event. Here is her story again, complete with its happy ending.

Inez is a young college math professor. All through college and graduate school, she was a serious, diligent student who always did more than expected. She was also shy and spent most of her time at home alone, studying. When she landed the job she really wanted, as an assistant professor at a liberal arts college, she quickly became overwhelmed. Her skills as a student were now liabilities. Instead of spending hours diligently studying in her room or the library, she was now expected to step up and be a leader, to mentor students and contribute as an equal at department meetings. These expectations went against her natural inclinations of shyness and compliance with the directions of others. Now she was expected to initiate direction herself. Her reaction was to retreat and put on an arrogant, indifferent front to hide her fear and sense of inadequacy.

Each day, she fled from the university as quickly as she could, feeling self-conscious and awkward at campus activities or faculty social events. In her student days she could always lose herself in the elegance of mathematical calculations and equations; however, Inez was concerned that she was starting to lose interest in math, a pursuit which had formerly filled her with wonder. She spent her evenings worried that she would lose her position, and she began to have trouble sleeping. She realized that the arrogant demeanor she was projecting was not a reflection of her true self, and that made her feel false and guilty. However, she believed that if she let her colleagues know how awkward and self-conscious she felt in her new leadership position, she would lose stature in their eyes. Inez was almost depressed. She knew she needed to make some changes, but she was unsure of how to begin.

When she came for help, it was evident that she was hiding behind a veneer of arrogance and coldness to conceal her lack of social skills. She embarked on a program of social skills training that included assertive communication skills. After learning and practicing these techniques in coaching sessions, she decided to contact one of her senior faculty colleagues. She invited him to have coffee with her, during which she confessed her insecurities about teaching. It was a pivotal moment for Inez. Instead of shunning her, the colleague congratulated her for her honesty and then related stories about his own insecurities when he first began to teach. He became a mentor and confidant for Inez.

Over the next year, Inez's confidence in her abilities to teach and lead others grew. She attributes her recent teaching award to social skills training and the mentorship of the professor she reached out to. Currently, her career and her mental health are flourishing.

• • •

Humans are fundamentally social creatures. Human contact benefits both physical and psychological health. Positive human contact reduces stress hormones and elevates your mood. As you reach out to more and more people, like Inez, you should also feel the fog of almost depression begin to lift.

▪◆▪

TAKING THE
Biological Pathway

| 14 |

Improving Your Sleep and Diet

The worst thing in the world is to try to sleep and not to.
—F. Scott Fitzgerald

Sleep is vital to clear thinking, emotional balance, productivity, and health. But why do we sleep? What goes on during sleep that is so important? Although no one knows exactly, we do know that all known animals require a "quiet, restful time." Scientists suggest that sleep helps you on a cellular level by removing toxic materials, rebuilding tissues, restoring neurotransmitters, and strengthening synaptic connections to consolidate memories and solidify learning.[1]

Sleeping Well to Prevent Almost Depression

How'd you sleep last night? Insomnia occurs in up to 33 percent of the general population and is associated with tiredness, impaired thinking (attention and memory), irritability, difficulties in interpersonal relationships, and decreased quality of life.

Insomnia occurs more often in women than men, and symptoms generally increase with age.[2] Insomnia is also a risk factor for depression. People with depression are four times more likely to suffer insomnia as people without depression. They often complain of the inability to fall asleep, waking in the middle of the night and not being able to fall back to sleep, or waking early in the morning without feeling rested. Likewise, having insomnia doubles your risk of depression.[3]

What can you do about fitful sleep? While medication treatments are commonly used and often immediately helpful, recent research shows that cognitive-behavioral therapy for insomnia (CBT-I) and brief behavioral interventions are just as effective as prescription medication at relieving chronic insomnia in the short term and may be more effective in the long term.[4]

Putting CBT-I into Practice

CBT-I is a nonpharmacologic approach to treating insomnia. CBT-I aims to address the factors in your life that interfere with sleep and maintain insomnia. These usually include some combination of a dysregulated sleep cycle (such as feeling drowsy during the day but unable to rest at night), sleep-related anxiety, and sleep-interfering behaviors (such as napping during the day to "catch up" on missed sleep). While CBT-I is usually delivered by a therapist over four to eight weeks during thirty- to sixty-minute sessions, let's employ its principles and adapt them here for you. There are four primary steps involved in putting CBT-I into practice.

Monitor Sleep Patterns

The first step is to take a look at your pattern of sleep. While this can be accomplished in a variety of ways, we recommend keeping a sleep diary for the next two weeks. Although you can make your own using a notebook, a typical one looks like the one in table 18. (You can download this diary at www.AlmostDepressed.com.)

Other factors to consider:

- what/when you ate and drank
- what emotion or stress you had
- what drugs or medications you took

Healthy Sleep Hygiene

The second step in addressing insomnia is to practice healthy sleep hygiene. Here are some guidelines:

- Use the bed only for sleeping or sex.
- Sleep only as much as necessary to feel rested and then get out of bed.
- Maintain a regular sleep schedule (same bedtime and wake time every day).
- Minimize caffeinated beverages after lunch.
- Minimize alcohol near bedtime.
- Minimize tobacco (particularly during the evening).
- Have a small "bedtime" snack.
- Set the stage, creating a bedroom environment (light, noise, temperature) that is warm, comfortable, and inviting.
- In a different location, deliberately process worries before going to bed. Make a list of things to work on for the next day so anxiety may be reduced at night.

Table 18.
Sleep Diary

	Mon.	Tues.	Wed.	Thurs.	Fri.	Sat.	Sun.	Average or total
Bedtime								
Wake time								
Total sleep time								
Number of times you woke up								
Quality of sleep								
Caffeinated beverages								
Alcoholic beverages								

- Exercise regularly, preferably four or more hours *before* bedtime.

Techniques to Improve Your Sleep

If you are still having difficulty sleeping, the third step is to implement some additional techniques to improve your ability to sleep.

SLEEP RESTRICTION

Although you may expect that staying in bed a lot will help you fall asleep and feel restored, ironically spending less time in bed fosters more restful and healthier sleep. The foundation of this technique is to set a firm time to wake up, let's say 7:30 a.m. Sleep experts suggest aiming for six hours of sleep at first. This translates to staying awake, no matter what, until 1:30 a.m. and then retiring to bed. Once you sleep well for these six hours, you increase the time you sleep by fifteen or thirty minutes until you reach a "healthy amount" of sleep (seven to nine hours per night) and feel restored. If you know that you have a family history of bipolar disorder, then please consult with your health care provider before using sleep restriction.

RECONDITIONING YOUR RELATIONSHIP WITH THE
BEDROOM AND SLEEP

Not sleeping is really difficult and frustrating. Often the harder you try to sleep, the less rest you get and the more irritated you become. This "reconditioning" technique combines the elements of sleep hygiene that we discussed in step 2 and "stimulus control therapy."

Stimulus control therapy is based on the idea that you have learned to associate the bedroom with staying awake rather than sleeping. To change this association, follow these steps:

1. Spend no more than twenty minutes lying in bed trying to fall asleep.

2. If you cannot fall asleep within twenty minutes, get up, go to another room, and read or find another relaxing activity to do until you feel sleepy again. Activities such as eating, balancing your checkbook, doing housework, watching TV, or studying for a test, which "reward" you for staying awake, should be avoided.

3. When you start to feel sleepy, return to bed. If you cannot fall asleep in another twenty minutes, repeat the process.

4. Set an alarm clock and get up at the same time every day, including weekends. Do not take a nap during the day.

RELAXATION TECHNIQUES

Initially described in the 1920s by psychologist Edmund Jacobson, progressive muscle relaxation helps to soften your muscles from the scalp down through the toes. Beginning with the muscles in your face, squeeze (contract) your muscles gently for several seconds and then relax. Try tightening and letting go with the same muscle group several times before moving on. Using the same technique, move to other muscle groups, usually in the following sequence: jaw and neck, shoulders, upper arms, lower arms, fingers, chest, abdomen, buttocks, thighs, calves, and feet. Start by moving through all the muscle groups in five minutes; then increase the total time by two to three minutes every two to three nights. Repeat this cycle for as long as you like. The practice often helps your body let go of the day's stress, resulting in restfulness and sleep.

Relapse Prevention

The fourth step to better sleep is relapse prevention. Once you have learned to sleep well, you don't want to return to your old insomniac patterns. Make time each day or every few days to review the causes of insomnia and the changes you made to address it.

You will face challenges when implementing this CBT-I program. During the first few weeks of treatment, you may actually sleep less, and this may make you feel groggy and even more fatigued than normal—but stick with it. Improvements are usually not seen until you have practiced this approach for three to four weeks. One of the big advantages of implementing CBT-I is that it will reduce your exposure to sleep medications and supplements. This, in turn, reduces the possibility of drug dependence and of relapse once you discontinue the medications. Also, once in place, the program has staying power. Both the American Academy of Sleep Medicine and the National Institutes of Health recommend treating insomnia with this type of brief cognitive-behavioral intervention before resorting to sleep medication(s).

Using the Supplement Melatonin

If these techniques are not helpful enough, then consider supplements or medications to enhance your sleep. Your daily sleep-wake cycle is one of many bodily processes that make up circadian rhythms. The term *circadian* is derived from the Latin words *circa*, meaning "around" and *diem* meaning "day." The suprachiasmatic nucleus (SCN) in the brain orchestrates the daily fluctuations of blood pressure, hormone secretion, and body temperature. Disturbances in circadian rhythms share many symptoms with depression, including a delayed onset of sleep, early morning awakening, and daytime fatigue. People with depression take longer to get to sleep and wake frequently during the night. The goal of treating depression is to restore the sleep-wake cycle and resynchronize circadian rhythms.

Although antidepressants may improve symptoms of depression, they do not necessarily restore circadian rhythms. However, there are several effective strategies to accomplish this goal. The first tactic is to restore a healthy sleep-wake cycle with CBT-I. A second strategy involves melatonin. Synthesized in the pineal gland from the amino acid tryptophan, melatonin acts to promote and maintain the drive to sleep. Melatonin levels decline with age; however, a recent trial in more than 700 patients found that 2 mg (milligrams) of extended-release melatonin was effective in treating insomnia in patients fifty-five years and older over a six-month period.[5] In this study, as well as in many others, melatonin was well tolerated (not associated with side effects such as cognitive problems or rebound insomnia).

Melatonin can be thought of as the "chemical signal for darkness," and very little melatonin is secreted during the daytime. Melatonin levels begin to rise around dusk and bind to receptors in the brain, making you feel sleepy, cool, and less alert.[6] The U.S. Dietary Supplement Health and Education Act of 1994 allows melatonin to be sold as a dietary supplement, but it is not evaluated, controlled, or approved by the Food and Drug Administration (FDA) in the same way medications are. Melatonin is available as a supplement in the United States, and an extended-release form of it is available as a prescription in Europe. Melatonin has been used in doses ranging from 0.25 mg to 20 mg and is available in pills, capsules, disintegrating tablets that melt under the tongue, a liquid, and as a nasal spray. No one preparation is preferred. Since it is sold as a supplement, it is not intended to treat any medical condition. With that in mind, patients often use melatonin to alleviate insomnia associated with depression. It is reasonable to start with a dose of 1 to 2 mg (Jeff usually suggests the sublingual form), taken about thirty minutes before usual bedtime between 7 p.m. and midnight. It is often used along with antidepressant medications and, although it has not been formally studied for safety or efficacy, most patients report that they tolerate it well and find it helpful. Several patients have developed headaches or experienced vivid scary dreams while using it, both of which ended after stopping the melatonin. A variety of melatonin analogues (or substitutes) are available as medications, including ramelteon (marketed as Rozerem in the United States) and agomelatine (marketed as Melitor in Europe). If you are having trouble sleeping after trying the techniques outlined in this chapter, you may want to discuss using melatonin with your health care professional.

Eating Well to Prevent Almost Depression

It's true that you are what you eat. Recent evidence from around the world describes the relationship between the quality of your diet and depression.[7]

Your diet and nutrition directly affect your physiology, immune system, energy storage and utilization, brain plasticity, and the function of the stress-response system. In turn, the health of these processes either increases or decreases your vulnerability to depression. A Mediterranean-style diet—eating a lot of fruits, vegetables, nuts, whole grains, fish, and unsaturated fat (common in olive and other plant oils)—appears to make it about one-third less likely that you will develop depression compared to people who consume a lot of red meat and dairy. Likewise, consuming polyunsaturated fatty acids (found in nuts, seeds, fish, and leafy green vegetables) and/or monounsaturated fatty acids (found in olive oil, avocados, and nuts) decreases the risk for depression, whereas eating trans fats (found in many processed foods and "fast foods") increases this risk.[8]

Does this mean that you should never eat red meat? A recent Australian study found that eating *nonprocessed* red meats did *not* increase the risk for depression. These same researchers studied the effects of three different dietary patterns on depression and anxiety. They discovered that a *Western* pattern of eating was linked to an increased risk for depression in women and an increased risk for anxiety in men. The two other dietary patterns, *healthy* and *traditional Norwegian*, were not associated with an increased risk.[9] Here are the basic foods of these dietary patterns, with foods listed according to the quantity consumed:

1. *Western* consists of meat and liver, processed meats, pizza, salty snacks, chocolates, sugar and sweets, soft drinks, margarine, mayonnaise and other dressings, french fries, beer, coffee, cake, and ice cream.

2. *Healthy* consists of vegetables, salads, fruits, rice, pasta, cereals, fish, wine, and nonprocessed meats.

3. *Traditional Norwegian* consists of fish and shellfish, potatoes, fruits, vegetables, butter and margarine, milk and yogurt, bread, pasta, rice, meat, meat spreads, legumes, and eggs.

The Importance of Omega-3 Fatty Acids

In the last few years, there has been a lot of interest in omega-3 fatty acids for physical health and in relation to depression. Omega-3 fatty acids are called "essential" because your body can't manufacture them and, therefore, you must get them from your diet. In a "typical" American diet, you are likely to consume too many omega-6 fatty acids (usually in the form of linoleic acid found in sunflower, safflower, cottonseed, and corn oils) and not enough omega-3 fatty acids (oily, cold-water fish, such as salmon, herring, and mackerel, have the highest omega-3 levels). Two forms of omega-3 fatty acids include eicosapentaenoic acid (EPA) and docosahexaenoic acid (DHA). The bulk of research on omega-3s and mood symptoms, including a recent study of over 54,000 nurses and a large meta-analysis of past studies,[10] demonstrates that omega-3 fatty acids help prevent and relieve depression.

Omega-3 fatty acids are also healthy for your cardiovascular system. The American Heart Association notes that omega-3s reduce abnormal heart rhythms, reduce atherosclerosis, and may lower blood pressure.[11] This information is important because of the common overlap between depression and cardiovascular disease. The American Psychiatric Association currently recommends that people with depression take in at least 1 gram daily of EPA and DHA omega-3s.

Because of the recent concern about high mercury levels in the deep-ocean fish that are one of the best sources of omega-3s, it is recommended that pregnant women and children avoid swordfish, shark, king mackerel, and tilefish; you can substitute supplements of fish oil or flaxseed capsules for eating fish. Most studies on omega-3s have investigated dosages between 1 and

9 grams daily, and have shown benefit in doses between 1 and 3 grams daily.[12] (Please note that "more" isn't necessarily "better" when using this or any other supplement. In doses over 3 grams daily, you should be aware that there is a potential for bleeding more easily, especially if you are taking blood-thinning medication. Your health care provider can advise you of any potential drug interactions.) While most studies found the greatest benefit from a higher intake of the EPA form of omega-3s (at least 60 percent coming from EPAs), more research is needed before we can say with certainty what ratio of EPA to DHA works "best." Note: consider storing omega-3 supplements in the refrigerator or freezer to lessen the smell and fishy taste.

The Importance of Vitamin D

Vitamin D regulates various processes in the body, including gene transcription, and may decrease risk of cancers, autoimmune diseases, infectious diseases, and cardiovascular diseases. Early in life, low levels of vitamin D may lead to slower-than-normal growth and deformities in the skeletal bones; later in life, vitamin D deficiencies are associated with osteoporosis (porous bones) and fractures,[13] as well as depressive symptoms. Our primary sources of vitamin D are exposure to sunlight, diet (for example, oily fish, shiitake mushrooms, and egg yolks), and dietary supplements. When your skin is exposed to ultraviolet B (UVB) radiation in sunlight, your body converts a chemical compound in the skin into vitamin D. (Note: while sunlight can cause other damage, you cannot overdose on vitamin D by overexposure to the sun.)

It's estimated that 1 billion people worldwide have vitamin D deficiency or insufficiency. This deficiency may be due to various factors, including having darker skin (absorbs more UVB and slows the production of vitamin D), liver or kidney disease, or decreased exposure to sunlight (too much time indoors). Supplements come in the form of D2 (from plants) or D3 (from animals and is three times stronger). In 2010, the Institute of Medicine of the National Academies recommended that children and adults under seventy receive 600 International Units (IUs) and adults over seventy years receive 800 IUs daily.

The brain possesses vitamin D receptors, which has generated a lot of interest. Studies have found conflicting associations between vitamin D levels and depression. However, recently, the largest study to date of 12,594 adults found a significant link between low levels of vitamin D and depression.[14] In this study, the strongest association occurred in people with a history of depression. Therefore, if you have a history of any form of depression, we recommend that you talk to your health care provider about checking your vitamin D level. If needed, there are several safe ways to supplement your vitamin D. First, remember, more is not necessarily better. Vitamin D is fat-soluble, easily stored in the body, and when there is too much, it can be toxic. If you live outside of the tropics (or you spend most of your time indoors), you may want to supplement your diet with vitamin D, especially during winter months. Jeff recommends 1,000 to 2,000 IUs daily. However, you should check with your health care provider before adding any supplement to your diet.

The Importance of Probiotics

The gastrointestinal (GI) tract contains more than 100 million neurons and is the meeting place for nerves, bacteria, and the immune system. The term *probiotic* is derived from the Greek phrase *pro bios,* meaning "for life." In 1908, Nobel laureate Ilya Metchnikoff observed that people from a certain region in Bulgaria lived longer, which he attributed to their regular drinking of a fermented milk product. Patients with depression (and many with almost depression as well) have overly active stress-response systems that release high levels of cortisol into the body. When depression is successfully treated with medications, this unhealthy response is corrected. In animal models of depression, giving the bacterium *bifidobacterium infantis,* which is common in the gut of infants and in probiotic supplements, can reverse this hyper-response. In two recent studies, subjects taking probiotics (either in the form of capsules or in yogurt) experienced reduced symptoms of distress and urinary cortisol and improved mood.[15]

In 1930, dermatologists John H. Stokes and Donald M. Pillsbury proposed a GI mechanism to explain the relationship between depression, anxiety, and acne. In 2011, dermatologists Whitney Bowe and Alan Logan revisited this relationship, suggesting that psychological distress, alone or in combination with a diet rich in processed foods and trans fats and devoid of fiber led to changes in gut motility and the GI flora. These authors suggest that the loss of your normal gut flora (and *bifidobacterium* in particular) makes the intestines more permeable, allowing toxins to circulate. These toxins stress the body, leading to inflammatory reactions, thus increasing your vulnerability to acne and additional psychological distress. Through interactions with the immune system, probiotics (and antibiotics) may play a role in breaking this cycle.[16]

The bottom line is that when fighting off almost depression, either eating yogurt regularly or taking probiotics appears helpful. I (Jeff) usually suggest that patients who are experiencing depressive symptoms take a probiotic supplement containing a mixed flora of at least 5 million per dose.

Alcohol in Moderation?

Alcohol is frequently used to relieve stress and anxiety, and to enhance mood. Some studies suggest that moderate use of alcohol may decrease symptoms of depression/anxiety and increase positive mood, sociability, and subjective health.[17] Please note that "moderate alcohol use" is defined as no more than one standard drink per day for healthy nonpregnant women and no more than two standard drinks per day for healthy men.[18] However, a recent large national sample found that, after controlling for health and socioeconomic factors, moderate drinking did not reduce the risk of depression.[19] If you drink moderately, there is likely no harm—and possibly a mild benefit—from low levels of alcohol consumption. However, because there is a definite link between alcohol *abuse* and the onset of depression, you must exercise caution if you choose to drink while suffering from almost depression; be sure to limit yourself to moderate intake. If you find yourself drinking to excess as a way of "medicating" your depression, it's probably best to abstain from drinking altogether until your depressive symptoms are stabilized. If, at any time, you find it difficult to stop or to cut down on your drinking, you may have a substance abuse problem. If you feel that your drinking is a problem, consider getting an assessment. It is important to address substance abuse before it gets further out of hand.

Coffee for Almost Depression

The world's most widely used stimulant might do more than just wake you up. In a new study that looked at depression and coffee consumption, women who drank two to three cups of coffee per day reduced their risk for depression by 15 percent compared to those who drank less than one cup of java per week. Women who drank four cups or more per day had the lowest risk for depression, decreasing their risk by 20 percent.[20] Likewise, Finnish men who drank about eight cups of coffee per day were found to have significantly less risk of depression compared to abstainers, light, and moderate drinkers.[21] Curiously, drinking tea was not protective. As long as you don't feel jittery, go ahead and indulge in that cup of joe. It might perk up your mood as well as your energy.

. . .

In this chapter we've taken a look at how sleep and diet are crucial in your battle with almost depression. Now let's look at the help that medications and supplements may provide.

■ ◆ ■

| 15 |

When You Need More
Medications, Supplements, and Light

Take a medication if it helps, but don't do only that.
You also need to train your mind.
—Daniel Goleman, author of *Emotional Intelligence*

If you are almost depressed, should you take antidepressants?
This is a somewhat controversial topic.

The Role of Antidepressants in Almost Depression

A recent Canadian study found that many people who are not
clinically depressed report taking antidepressant medications
to deal with subclinical depressive symptoms, including stress,
sleep problems, anxiety, or headache. Likewise, a European
study found that people were more likely to be taking antidepressants to deal with a specific emotional problem than for a
formal diagnosis of major depression.[1]

Findings like these have led experts to wonder whether

antidepressants are being overprescribed. They suggest that people who are not clinically depressed should not be medicated. Indeed, conventional wisdom has suggested that treating subclinical depression or dysthymia (in other words, almost depression) with antidepressant medications was not necessary or helpful, and could even be inappropriate.

There is some evidence to support this view. Researchers in Europe reviewed six studies of more than 500 patients and found there was little benefit of medication treatment over placebo for patients with minor depression. This study indicated that the effectiveness of treatment with antidepressants increased with the severity of the depression symptoms, so having fewer or milder depressive symptoms was associated with less drug effectiveness.[2] Similarly, a recent report in the *Journal of the American Medical Association (JAMA)* reviewed six previously published studies and found that, for the more than 700 patients involved in these studies, the response to antidepressants was related to severity of current depressive symptoms.[3] The authors of the *JAMA* study concluded that while antidepressants can have a substantial effect on more severe depressions, there is little evidence to support their use with less severe depressive symptoms.

This is only one side of the story, however. Let's look at Kallista's case before examining the evidence supporting the use of antidepressants for low-grade depression.

Kallista's Story

Kallista is a thirty-four-year-old woman of Greek descent. She and her husband run a popular pizza and sub shop that her father had started in the 1960s. Kallista and her husband have two young children who "help out" at the pizza shop and who were recently featured in the local newspaper under the headline "Pint-Size Pizza Makers Delight Customers." Kallista is active in the local chamber of commerce, and she sings with a small band (her husband plays saxophone) that performs at weddings and other special occasions.

Despite her full and active life, Kallista feels an undercurrent of sadness that has been with her since childhood. As long as she keeps busy, she can keep the sadness at bay, but when she is alone, the sadness threatens to overwhelm her. She doesn't know where it comes from but says she can't remember a time when it wasn't "lurking in the background of her soul."

Her mother died when Kallista was five years old, after years of struggling with an illness that no one has ever really explained to Kallista. She suspects that her mother may have been mentally ill and perhaps even committed suicide, although Kallista was too young to remember the details, and relatives just say that her mother was "ill." Kallista and her younger brother were sent back to the old country to be raised by their maternal grandparents. When Kallista was sixteen, she and her brother returned to the States to live with their beloved Papa and help out with the pizza shop. Kallista is close to all her family members and feels blessed to have so many good people in her life.

The sadness she feels does not interfere with her work or her relationships. Even so, she occasionally cries for no reason and is not sure she really understands what happiness is. "Sometimes I see my husband laughing with the children, and I see something in his face that I know I have never felt," she says. Kallista is almost depressed, but is functioning well.

She was a good candidate for antidepressant medication, as her underlying feelings of sadness had a biological feel to them, perhaps related to a family history of depression rather than to negative life events or stress. She was already active, highly social, and had a positive and grateful attitude, but she needed something more to help with the undercurrent of depressed mood. After two months on a low dose of an antidepressant, Kallista reports that she feels "lifted up." She knows the dark sadness is still inside her somewhere, but she can now feel moments of actual joy and, when alone, she often catches herself smiling instead of crying.

• • •

Clearly, antidepressants helped Kallista. And new studies are now supporting the use of antidepressants for the treatment of subclinical depression like Kallista's. For instance, a recent meta-analysis of more than 190 studies examined the effectiveness of antidepressants for the treatment of dysthymia. In this meta-analysis, the authors found that dysthymic patients treated with antidepressants were significantly more likely to improve compared to those treated with a placebo.[4] In another study, researchers analyzed six placebo-controlled studies including 1,440 patients with "non-severe depression." Their results showed that patients with mild to moderate depressive symptoms can benefit from treatment with antidepressants.[5]

Most recently, researchers published the follow-up results of a collaborative, multi-site study from across the United States involving nearly 10,000 people in all age groups who participated in controlled trials of the antidepressants fluoxetine (Prozac) and venlafaxine (Effexor). Their results do *not* support previous findings that antidepressants show little benefit except for severe depression. Rather, this study concluded that antidepressants were helpful for people with mild as well as severe depressive symptoms in all age groups, although more so in youth and adults compared with geriatric patients.[6]

The bottom line is that antidepressants can be a part of the solution even when you suffer with dysthymia or almost depression. Moreover, if you are almost depressed, it is important that you address your symptoms so they don't worsen. If the techniques that we've discussed in other parts of this book haven't helped you, then you—like Kallista—may benefit from an antidepressant medication. Remember, however, that all drugs carry side effects and the possibility of relapse when the medication is discontinued.

Taking an Antidepressant Medication

There are several different classes of antidepressants, each of which targets the neurotransmitters involved in depression in a different way. The most widely prescribed class is called selective serotonin uptake inhibitors (SSRIs). These drugs work by primarily regulating the amount of serotonin available in the synapses between neurons in the brain, and likely regulating the number and sensitivity of serotonin receptors as well. Another new class of antidepressant drugs, serotonin-norepinephrine reuptake inhibitors (SNRIs), affects both the serotonin and norepinephrine transmitter systems, and new medications are being introduced all the time.

If you decide to begin treatment with an antidepressant, you and your health care provider will choose a medication based on your medical history, your symptoms, and your lifestyle.

Here are some important points to remember if you decide to take an antidepressant:

- Make sure to tell your doctor about all prescription and over-the-counter medications you are currently taking or have taken in the past month. Drug interactions need to be carefully monitored for your safety.

- Do not be discouraged if you don't see improvement right away. Antidepressants may take as long as six to eight weeks to be fully effective.

- Many of the negative side effects of antidepressant drugs—including drowsiness, headache, diarrhea, dry mouth, and insomnia—should begin to decrease within weeks of starting medication treatment. Be sure to let your doctor know if these side effects do not diminish. However, two common side effects will likely persist during treatment, including weight gain and sexual dysfunction (see the sidebar "Sexual Side Effects of Antidepressant Medications").

- Do not be discouraged if the first medication you try is not helpful. Each antidepressant works in a slightly different way and has different side effects. If one doesn't help you, work with your doctor to adjust the dosage, add another medication, or switch to another antidepressant.

- Be aware that all SSRIs contain a "black box" warning that indicates they may increase suicidal thinking or behavior. Be sure to tell your health care professional if you have an increase in thoughts of suicide while on the medication. This is most likely to occur shortly after starting a new medication or when changing the dosage of your medication.

- *Do not* discontinue your medication on your own. If you are having serious side effects, contact your doctor for instructions on how to discontinue the drug or reduce the dosage. Doing so on your own could be dangerous and could lead to antidepressant discontinuation syndrome. Some of the common symptoms of this syndrome include dizziness, tingling, muscle pains, electric shocks, tremor, ataxia, visual changes, nausea, vomiting, diarrhea, decreased appetite, anxiety, depressed mood, intensification of self-destructive thoughts/feelings/behaviors, irritability, impulsivity, sweating, flushing, insomnia, vivid dreams, fatigue, and chills.

Antidepressant discontinuation syndrome can occasionally develop in patients who for years have been taking a name-brand formulation of a medication and then switch to a generic brand. The U.S. Food and Drug Administration (FDA) states, "Any generic drug modeled after a single, brand name drug (the reference) must perform *approximately* the same in the body as the brand name drug. There will always be a *slight*, but not medically important, level of natural variability."[7] The FDA permits a variability of 80 to 125 percent between a generic and the original formulation. Practically speaking, that means if you are taking 20 mg of a name-brand product, the FDA considers the generic to be equivalent if it falls in a range between 16 to 25 mg. As you can imagine, this change can make a big difference. Be sure to note if any abrupt changes in symptoms or side effects occur when you receive a refill; this may be due to a change in the generic drug that your pharmacy is providing.

Sexual Side Effects of Antidepressant Medications

A recent study summarizing data from eighteen epidemiological studies worldwide reported that sexual problems occur in 20 to 30 percent of men and 40 to 45 percent of women who are taking antidepressants.[8] As you can imagine, these problems are detrimental to self-esteem, mood, and interpersonal relationships. The two most common sexual problems are a loss of interest in sex, occurring in both men and women, and male erectile dysfunction. A significant, but too often unspoken, challenge with antidepressant treatment is the impact on sexuality. Sexual side effects are common, occur with all classes of antidepressants, and may diminish sexual interest, arousal, and orgasm. One study reported that 96 percent of women taking antidepressants report at least one sexual side effect.[9] Although there are lots of options for dealing with these effects, their success has been modest. The usual medical approach involves switching antidepressants, augmenting with various compounds, or adding a medication for erectile dysfunction. Two recent approaches are interesting and may provide an alternative.

- Maca root (Lepidium meyenii) is an Andean plant of the brassica (mustard) family thought to be an aphrodisiac. A 2010 review of four randomized controlled trials found that many, but not all, patients using maca root experienced an increase in sexual desire; in men there were positive effects on erections.[10] Our colleagues at Massachusetts General Hospital are conducting a study on this herb. Preliminarily anecdotal experience suggests that treatment with doses between 1.5 and 3 grams daily may improve sexual interest and orgasm. Again, we warn that you should not take a supplement without first consulting your health care professional.

- Exercise: A 2012 study found that for women treated with antidepressants, twenty minutes of aerobic exercise prior to sexual stimulation significantly enhanced genital arousal. Women with the most difficulties at baseline derived the greatest benefit.[11]

The Role of Supplements in Almost Depression

In the last chapter you learned about the importance of several food-related supplements, including omega-3 fatty acids, vitamin D, and probiotics. In addition to these helpful supplements, there are other substances that have been associated with mood improvement. Many of these have been known for centuries to herbalists but have only recently been tested for effectiveness in randomized controlled trials. You may find some of them help reduce symptoms of almost depression, but remember that there could be interactions with any prescription or over-the-counter medications you are taking. *It is important to check with your health care provider before taking a supplement or using a light box.* Discuss the risks and benefits of these treatments, just as you would for any medical treatments. Just because something is sold in a vitamin store doesn't make it healthy or safe.

Here are some of the common supplements used in treating depression.

St. John's Wort

St. John's wort *(Hypericum perforatum)* is derived from a yellow-flowering perennial herb found in temperate zones worldwide. Its earliest recorded medicinal use was in ancient Greece, and it has been widely used to treat depression since the 1980s, particularly in Germany. While the exact way it works is unclear, we do know that it inhibits serotonin reuptake and alters levels of dopamine, norepinephrine, and another neurotransmitter, gamma-aminobutyric acid (GABA). The safety and effectiveness of St. John's wort are well established. A recent meta-analysis examined twenty-nine double-blind randomized controlled trials that compared it with a placebo in over 3,000 cases and with standard antidepressant medications in over 2,800 cases.[12] Doses varied from 500 to 1,200 mg daily and appeared generally well tolerated. In these short-term trials, St. John's wort was significantly more helpful than placebo and comparable to the effects of old- and new-generation antidepressants.

A word of caution: St. John's wort interferes with the metabolism of hundreds of drugs and may reduce the effectiveness of some, such as birth control pills.[13] While these interactions are not a contraindication to using St. John's wort, the risk of drug interactions is significant, and this supplement should be avoided if you are taking immunosuppressants, antiretrovirals, or chemotherapy. Moreover, St. John's wort should not be combined with antidepressant medications, as this combination increases the risk of serotonin syndrome, a potentially life-threatening medical condition which includes elevated blood pressure and body temperature, as well as problems with muscles and a variety of body organs. The bottom line is that given these limitations and the availability of alternative treatments, it appears wise to use St. John's wort as a mono therapy (that is, by itself and *not* in conjunction with other medications) for mild depression. In that situation, a usual starting dose is 200 mg three times daily (using a 0.3 percent hypericin extract), which may be increased up to 1,200 mg a day as needed.

Folate

Folate, a water-soluble B vitamin, enhances the synthesis of neurotransmitters in the brain. You may get folate (dihydrofolate) in your diet from leafy vegetables, legumes, and fruits. Cereals and breads are also commonly fortified with folic acid, the synthetic form of folate.

The body converts folate into methyltetrahydrofolate (L-methylfolate), which is able to cross the blood-brain barrier where it plays a role in synthesizing the neurotransmitters serotonin, norepinephrine, and dopamine. There is a genetic component to the way this substance works in the brain, and if you have specific genetic variants (namely, of the gene encoding for the enzyme methylenetetrahydrofolate reductase, or MTHFR), you may benefit from taking folate supplements. Besides your genetic makeup, there are several other common ways you may develop low levels of folate:

- smoke cigarettes and/or marijuana
- drink significant amounts of alcohol
- take certain medications, including estrogens, anticonvulsants, chemotherapy, metformin, sulfasalazine
- are pregnant or lactating
- have poor nutrition
- are on kidney dialysis
- are anemic
- have a C677T polymorphism of the MTHFR enzyme gene (risk increased in Hispanic and Mediterranean cultures)

Folate deficiency leads to the buildup of homocysteine, a toxic amino-acid metabolite associated with depression severity. Up to one-third of patients with depression have decreased levels of folate. These patients experience more frequent and severe episodes of depression and are significantly less likely to respond to antidepressant medications.[14]

Fortunately, there is a lot of interest and research looking at folate supplementation as a way to improve and accelerate response to treatments for depression. Controlled clinical trials have investigated the safety, tolerability, and efficacy of several forms of folate in patients with depression: folic acid, folinic acid (5,10 methylenetetrahydrofolate, also known as leucovorin), or methyltetrahydrofolate (L-methylfolate, or Deplin). Although more research is needed, these studies generally support using folate supplements as a way to enhance the effectiveness of antidepressants either from the beginning of treatment or augmenting ongoing treatment. Folinic acid and L-methylfolate are available as "medical foods" and thus require a prescription; folic acid is available over the counter. Folinic acid has been used for years as a supplement to chemotherapy; L-methylfolate is a recent preparation.

In terms of safety, there are several concerns.[15] First, folate supplementation may mask the symptoms of anemia and the symptoms of potential vitamin B12 deficiency, thus making you vulnerable to potentially permanent nervous-system damage. Consulting with your health care professional about clinical signs or symptoms of B12 deficiency is wise. Methyltetrahydrofolate may be less likely to mask this deficiency.

Second, concerns have been expressed that folate supplementation may increase risk of cancer. Although recent data questions these concerns, caution is warranted if you have a family history of colorectal cancer.

Third, although there were concerns, folate supplementation does not seem to interfere with zinc homeostasis. Here are the dosages I (Jeff) use as a regular supplement: folic acid, 1 or 2 mg daily; folinic acid, 10 to 15 mg daily; or L-methylfolate, 7.5 mg daily.

SAM-e

SAM-e (S-adenosylmethionine) is a compound formed naturally in the body that, like folate and vitamin B12, is important for the production of the neurotransmitters dopamine, norepinephrine, and serotonin. Depressed patients may have low levels of serum and cerebral spinal fluid SAM-e, and supplementation increases levels of neurotransmitters in the brain. Since the 1970s, SAM-e has been noted to be helpful for the treatment of depression. In trials of clinical depression, the antidepressant effects of SAM-e appear similar to typical antidepressant medications; however, the number and size of trials are too limited to draw firm conclusions.[16] The evidence supporting SAM-e suggests that it's strongest when administered intravenously, although a number of studies also demonstrate its benefit when administered orally at doses of 1,600 mg per day. A 2010 controlled trial showed that SAM-e, in oral doses increased to up to 800 mg twice daily, improved the effectiveness of antidepressant drugs and was well tolerated.[17] Side effects are uncommon, but occasionally nausea, gastrointestinal upset, and anxiety can occur. In patients with bipolar disorder, mania has been reported. Usual doses of oral SAM-e range between 800 and 1,600 mg/day. Here are the main drawbacks of SAM-e:

1. Many manufacturers provide dosages of SAM-e that are only about half the amount used in clinical trials.

2. It is relatively expensive: treatment at therapeutic doses usually costs between $80 and $140 per month.

Magnesium

Magnesium (Mg) is a metal that is abundant in living beings. Magnesium is extensively involved in the regulation of glucose, hormones, calcium, and vitamin D, and literally hundreds of cellular and biochemical reactions.[18]

A variety of common factors may cause your body's magnesium levels to decline. First, the refining of our foods has removed a significant amount of magnesium from what we eat. A recent study found that a low level of dietary magnesium intake was associated with increased symptoms of depression.[19] Furthermore, as we age, magnesium deficiencies become common due to reduced absorption, thinning of bones, and increased urinary losses. These deficits are associated with a wide array of physical disorders, including high blood pressure, strokes, cardiovascular diseases, glucose intolerance, asthma, fatigue, and elevated lipids.[20] A 2012 study found that ongoing use of proton pump inhibitors—medications such as omeprazole (Prilosec), lansoprazole (Prevacid), and esomeprazole (Nexium)—was associated with significantly reduced magnesium levels.[21]

Magnesium plays an important role in a wide array of brain processes, especially those related to stress and immunity. The first use of magnesium to treat depression was described by Dr. P. G. Weston in the *American Journal of Psychiatry* as far back as 1921.[22] Recent reports have described magnesium as a first-line treatment (used alone), an adjunctive treatment (used in combination with antidepressant medicines), and in patients with treatment resistant depression.[23]

There are several ways you can supplement with magnesium: taken by mouth, absorbed into the skin, or injected through the skin or intravenously (IV). The IV form is generally reserved for patients with severe deficiencies or depressions and would not be used in the treatment of almost depression. Taking baths in Epsom salts (which are made from the compound magnesium sulfate) is an inexpensive and easily available way to supplement with magnesium. While the optimal dose is unclear, the aim is usually around 400 mg daily.

The other option is oral supplements. It's important to recognize that the form of magnesium put into many vitamins is magnesium oxide. Unfortunately, this form is not absorbed well by the body and will not be helpful in treating depressive symptoms. It is necessary to use a form of magnesium that will be easily absorbed, such as chloride, malate, citrate, lactate, glycinate, and taurate. We suggest avoiding the glutamate and aspartate forms, as they can be agitating in patients with depression. Likewise, if you have depression, we suggest avoiding foods or drinks containing monosodium glutamate or aspartate. When supplementing with magnesium, be aware that you may experience loose stool or diarrhea. If this happens, stop supplementing for a few days, and then once the problem is resolved, consider restarting at a lower dose.

Acetyl-L-Carnitine

Acetyl-L-carnitine (ALC), derived from the amino acid carnitine, enhances the production of the neurotransmitter acetylcholine (helpful in memory) and helps to regulate energy within cell bodies. In animal models, ALC has been found to enhance neurotransmission of dopamine, gamma-aminobutyric acid (GABA), and serotonin. Preliminary reports show that ALC, in divided doses between 1,000 and 1,500 mg daily, is helpful for dysthymia.[24] Recently, researchers compared ALC to amisulpride, an antidepressant widely used to treat dysthymia in Italy. In this controlled trial of 204 patients, both groups experienced similar reductions in symptoms of dysthymia, but the group receiving the ALC experienced significantly fewer side effects.[25] ALC can also be administered intravenously, a delivery method that may be particularly helpful for alcoholics with liver dysfunction and depression.[26] Although usually well tolerated, nausea, vomiting, or agitation may occur when you take ALC. The bottom line is that in doses of 500 mg twice a day, ALC may be a useful supplement for the treatment of almost depression.

The Role of Light in Almost Depression

Exposure to light is an important regulator of circadian rhythms or biorhythms. Extended periods of reduced exposure to light are associated with depressive symptoms in many people. For example, depression rates are higher in parts of the world that have long periods without sunlight. Considerable evidence indicates that light is an effective therapy for depression. Although it is most well known in the treatment of "winter depression" or seasonal affective disorder (SAD), light therapy is appropriate to use as a primary or supplemental treatment for various forms of depression.[27]

Michael's Story

Michael, age thirty-nine, is a radiologist and married father of three. Since his adolescence, he has suffered through several episodes of mild depressive symptoms, usually beginning some-time in mid to late November. At first, he associated these mild mood fluctuations with going away to school and leaving his family each fall. However, the episodes continued even after Michael finished college and returned to his hometown in Massachusetts to practice at a local hospital. He is worried because, "It's (the depression) coming back." He describes himself as more irritable than usual or than he wants to be. He says, "My sleep is all messed up and I want to sleep a lot, especially after I'm on call." Michael pushes himself to exercise regularly, and he feels more energetic and happier afterward. Nevertheless, he complains, "I really just want to sit on my couch, watch football, eat mint-chocolate-chip ice cream, and brood." Michael has tried several medications, but he tolerates them poorly and so prefers not to take them. His father was a psychologist, and Michael says that he has tried therapy several times over the years. He is looking for an alternative. Michael has a mild variant of seasonal affective disorder. He decided to try light therapy because it has been found to be effective in training circadian rhythms that can be out of balance in people with depression.

. . .

Bright light therapy can be applied through increased exposure to natural light outdoors or through special lamps, visors, or other artificial light sources. The most common type of light therapy (LT) is using a light box, which involves sitting for a certain amount of time each day in front of a panel of therapeutic-strength lights.

The following recommendations about the use of LT are

adapted from doctors at the Center for Environmental Therapeutics, who have been using light therapy for more than twenty-five years.[28]

Before beginning: If you are physically healthy and not taking medications or using supplements, then there is little risk. However, please consider consulting with your health care professional before using LT if you are unsure whether any of the following apply to you:

- Some medications or supplements, such as antipsychotics, psoralen, antiarrhythmics, antimalarials, antirheumatics, porphyrins, and hypericum (St. John's wort), may absorb light and make your skin or eyes photosensitive.

- Some medical conditions may make your retinas more sensitive to LT, including retinal dystrophies, age-related macular degeneration, porphyria, lupus, actinic dermatitis, and solar urticaria.

- Although not fully investigated, there is some concern that because the lenses of older patients may become yellowish, they filter more short-wave blue light than the clear lenses of younger patients, making it difficult for the right light to reach the retina.

Choosing a light box: Please be aware that there are no agencies monitoring or regulating the design or safety of light boxes. We suggest that you carefully research the effectiveness and safety record of several different types. Choose a light box that has been tested in successful peer-reviewed clinical trials or shown by an independent lab to match the qualities of well-tested boxes. You want a box that provides up to 10,000 lux (units of light energy) at a comfortable distance. The lamps should give off soft, broadband white light rather than colored light. Invisible short-wavelength ultraviolet (UV) light energy can damage the skin and eyes (cornea, lens, and retina). Although there are potential theoretical advantages to the blue light spectrum, at this time many experts advise against a blue spectrum light until these claims and the safety of such treatment are fully confirmed. We recommend soft-white fluorescent bulbs over cool-white, daylight, or "full-spectrum" lamps. There are a variety of light boxes available for purchase online at a reasonable price.

Using the light box: LT is a passive experience. The room where you will sit should be lit with "regular" lights. While sitting and facing the light box screen, your eye level should be two-thirds below the top of the screen. Although you do not need to look directly at the light box, LT relies on stimulating the cells on the periphery of your retina, which is most easily accomplished by maintaining a downward gaze (as in reading). The distance from your head to the light box will vary between boxes; however, the prescribed distance should be comfortably maintained. Usual sessions can vary between twenty to thirty minutes using 10,000 lux and sixty minutes using 2,500 lux light.

Michael's Story (continued)

Fortunately, other than his SAD, Michael was healthy. Michael started using a light box for thirty minutes in the morning before work. So he wouldn't be late for work, he made a plan to get up a half hour early. He used that time to read and reply to emails on his computer. Over the course of two weeks, Michael reported feeling better. Michael's wife, Cindy, noticed "a big difference . . . he was energetic and smiling again." Michael continued to use light therapy for five weeks and then had an extra-heavy week at work. He began skipping light box sessions, and two weeks later he wasn't using it at all. Within days of stopping, he noticed his depressive symptoms coming back. He returned to using the box daily, and within three days felt better. Michael continued using the light box daily through the middle of April, when the family took a vacation to Florida. He is now on a schedule of using light therapy from mid-October through mid-April and continues to feel well.

• • •

The information in this chapter is intended to familiarize you with some treatments that *may* benefit you as you address your negative mood symptoms. Before using any of these treatments, please consult with your health care professional to discuss risks, benefits, side effects, titrating schedule, and dosage range.

• • •

In these last two chapters we've highlighted strategies that target almost depression through the biological pathway. The next chapter will help you put it all together and learn some final strategies for improving and brightening your mood.

■ ◆ ■

| 16 |

Stepping into the Light
Increasing Positive Emotion

*In the midst of winter, I finally learned that
there was in me an invincible summer.*
—Albert Camus

We have reviewed many ways to address the difficulties associated with almost depression and reduce its influence in your life. Once you are feeling "normal" again, it is time to go even further—and move from normal to "flourishing." We want you to build a habit of not merely avoiding the negative emotions that come with depression but of experiencing positive emotions in abundance.

Positive emotions bring an array of benefits, enhancing your resilience, improving your mental and emotional health, and increasing creativity and cognitive flexibility. Developing and practicing positive emotions increases the scope of your attention and helps you to respond to difficulties in innovative ways.

Barbara Fredrickson, a psychologist at the University of North Carolina at Chapel Hill, has been instrumental in researching the benefits of positive emotions. Her broaden-and-build theory suggests that positive emotions (such as enjoyment, happiness, joy, and fascination) broaden awareness, increase interest in new things, and increase exploration of your environment. Through this interest and exploration, you gradually build knowledge of new subjects, develop new friendships and social support, and increase physical activity that leads to better health. There is considerable scientific support for this theory.[1]

To benefit from broaden-and-build, it appears necessary to experience positive emotions three times as often as negative ones. Three to one is the "magic ratio" of emotions.

$$\frac{\text{Positive Emotions}}{\text{Negative Emotions}} = \frac{3}{1}$$

That is, you need to spend three times as much time feeling positive compared to feeling negative. How can you do this? Many people mistakenly believe that positive emotions must arise spontaneously to be beneficial. However, the truth is that positive emotions can be intentionally and purposefully generated. Most of the strategies we've discussed in this book increase positive emotions even while reducing symptoms of depression.

Practicing Positive Emotions

There are a number of ways to build and practice positive emotions. Sonja Lyubomirsky, a psychologist at the University of California at Riverside, lists the following ways to practice happiness and positive emotions:[2]

- expressing gratitude
- cultivating optimism*
- nurturing social relationships*
- avoiding social comparisons
- practicing acts of kindness*
- learning to forgive
- savoring life's joys
- setting and working toward goals*
- meditating*
- increasing physical activity*

The methods marked with an asterisk (*) are strategies and skills we have already discussed because of their proven ability to counteract depressive symptoms. However, you will also want to incorporate a couple of these additional strategies into your life as you move from the grays into the brightness of positive well-being.

Gratitude

People who have developed a habit of gratitude are happier, are more energetic, and experience more positive emotions.[3] Here are two exercises in gratitude that have been shown to increase positive emotions and well-being:

1. *Keep a gratitude journal.* Once a week before you go to bed, write down five things you are grateful for that week. (For example, a healthy body, a friendship, a beautiful sunset, or the bird that sings each morning outside your window.) Try to do the gratitude exercise on the same night each week for six weeks. Try not to repeat

the items on your list; come up with new gratitude items each week. You can periodically read over your list to remind yourself of all you have to be grateful for.

2. *Write a gratitude letter.* Write a letter to someone who has helped you or been an inspiration to you but whom you have not actually thanked. You can make the letter as short or as long as you like. While the greatest benefit comes from actually delivering the letter to the object of your gratitude, some studies have shown that you don't actually need to deliver the letter to experience a boost in happiness.[4] If you make a regular practice of writing a letter of gratitude (this can also be in the form of an email or Facebook post), even if you don't always deliver it, you will feel buoyed by positive emotions.

Social Comparisons

Comparing yourself to others can sometimes be beneficial; for example, if you are striving to improve yourself in some way, you can compare your current state to that of someone who models the personal trait or performance level that you strive for. Comparing yourself to someone who is worse off than you (a *downward* comparison) can also make you feel better about yourself when you realize that, compared to the other person, you are relatively well off.[5] However, the bulk of social comparisons are *upward* comparisons, where you compare yourself to someone who has more money, more beauty, a bigger house, a bigger boat, or more success. Upward comparisons can foster envy, jealousy, resentment, and bitterness. Modern culture presents unparalleled opportunities for unfavorable social comparisons; we are steadily bombarded by images of beauty, thinness, superhuman athleticism, and wealth through glossy magazines, the Internet, and round-the-clock television programming. Research has shown that repeated exposure to images of people who are more attractive or more successful than you can damage your self-concept and self-esteem.[6]

Studies show that the number of social comparisons you make is related to both positive and negative emotions. A study conducted by researchers in psychologist Ellen Langer's lab found that men and women between the ages of eighteen and fifty-two who reported making frequent social comparisons experienced more guilt, regret, and blame than those who made less frequent comparisons.[7] Another study conducted at the University of California Riverside found that happy people make fewer social comparisons and pay less attention to such comparisons than people who report being unhappy.[8] There is, then, ample evidence that the less frequently you compare yourself to others, the more positive emotion you are likely to experience—especially if you are basing your self-worth on these comparisons. After all, there will always be someone who is more beautiful, wealthier, or more successful than you are.

There are a number of ways to reduce the frequency of social comparisons.

- *Appreciate what you have.* You can live in one of two spheres: In one sphere, you savor the things that life has provided for you. In the other sphere, you focus on the things you *don't* have that other people may possess, or you focus on the things you don't have that you *used to* have. Sphere 1 is where you will find happiness and positive emotion. Whenever you catch yourself coveting something that you don't have, immediately counter this thought with a statement such as "I appreciate _____ about my life." It is hard to be bitter about what others have when you are appreciating your own personal capital.

- *Distract yourself.* If you find yourself obsessing over how someone else has it better than you or has what you think should have been yours, engage in some activity that will take your mind off those thoughts immediately. Watch a movie, go for a run, get busy with a hobby, or clean the house. The more quickly you can turn to other interests, the less hold the negative comparison will have on you.

- *Set goals.* Rather than ruminating over what someone else has that you don't, take positive steps to obtain what it is that you want. If you are envious of someone else's wealth, make a financial plan and start to implement it. If you are envious of someone else's physique, make a fitness plan for yourself. The principles of problem-focused coping (in which you actively strive to solve a problem in your life) are found in chapter 8. You will be happier if you are working toward a goal than if you are actively resenting others for achieving the same goal. Remember to make your goals attainable so you can experience success and avoid setting yourself up for failure.

Forgiveness

If someone hurts you, either emotionally or physically, your first thought might be to get even. Indeed, retribution and revenge are major themes running throughout human history and are prominent motivating factors in a remarkable number of popular movies and television shows. Fantasies of revenge can be energizing; however, revenge does not lead to positive energy or positive emotions. Modern research shows that holding on to a grudge is truly toxic. Several studies reveal that people who are able to forgive an offense have lower levels of anxiety and higher self-esteem than those who are focused on revenge.[9] Forgiveness does not mean that you excuse someone's behavior or that you deny the hurt. It simply means that you are able to let go of the ill will you hold for that person. Letting go of ill will and resentment is a gift you give yourself, as well as the other person.

One of the best exercises for learning forgiveness and acceptance is the loving-kindness meditation we presented in chapter 11. In this exercise, you meditate on expressing kind and loving thoughts to yourself, which will eventually facilitate self-forgiveness. Over a period of time, you move on to expressing kind and loving thoughts to all people, including those who have hurt you in the past. In neuroimaging studies, the loving-kindness meditation has been shown to activate parts of the brain associated with empathy toward others.[10] And studies of self-reported emotions have associated this meditation with increased positive emotions. In one study conducted by Barbara Frederickson at Chapel Hill, participants who had engaged in the loving-kindness meditation for seven weeks showed significant increases in the positive emotions of amusement, awe, contentment, joy, gratitude, hope, interest, love, and pride compared to the participants in the control group.[11]

You don't need to hurry the process; as you continue to meditate on loving-kindness, you will experience an increase in positive emotions. Eventually, you will likely find that the negativity and anger you feel toward someone who has hurt you have evaporated, replaced by positive emotional energy.

Savoring Moments of Joy

The tendency to experience positive emotions includes two different stages: the ability to *generate* positive emotions and the ability to *maintain* them. Maintenance is important because, like all emotions, positive emotions are relatively short-lived, discrete experiences unless something is done to extend them. The process of "savoring" is one way to maintain positive emotional experience. Savoring involves consciously focusing on and being aware of pleasant moments or experiences. Savoring is associated with high levels of well-being and self-esteem in people of all age groups, from grade school students to the elderly.[12]

Savoring can include reliving memories of happy events, stopping to "smell the roses" as you enjoy the present, or anticipating the future with eagerness and excitement. Here are several exercises based on controlled trials that have been found effective in increasing your ability to savor moments of joy.

- *Relish an ordinary experience.* The act of mindfully participating in everyday experiences renders even the most mundane act pleasurable. A good exercise for mindful enjoyment of the moment is the *mindful eating* meditation described in chapter 10. In this meditation, you fully explore and savor the act of eating a raisin or other simple food. However, this mindful exercise could be applied to any everyday act, including brushing your teeth, taking a shower, or driving to work. The important thing is to pick at least one ordinary act each day and nonjudgmentally give it your whole and undivided attention.

- *Keep a catalog of moments of joy.* The catalog can include written descriptions of joyful moments, as well as photographs, ticket stubs, or other reminders of joyful times. As you live through moments of joy, writing a description of them in your catalog will prolong the joy as well as create a record for future reference. The accumulation of moments of joy also increases gratitude for your life experiences, which further increases positive emotions.

- *Reminisce with family and friends.* Whenever you get together with a person with whom you have shared good times, spend a few minutes reliving the positive experiences. While there are benefits to remembering good times even when you are alone, positive emotions are enhanced when you share the memory with others.[13]

• • •

You are now armed with a tool kit of techniques and learnable skills to assist you as you overcome the symptoms of almost depression. You have additional strategies to help you develop a favorable ratio of positive to negative emotions. If you have implemented some of the skills and strategies from the previous chapters, you are likely already noticing that your depression symptoms are improving. The key is to continue to *practice.* As with all skills and techniques, to be successful the strategies to reduce depressive symptoms need to be practiced as well as learned. If you have put in good effort to practice these techniques and you are still suffering or your symptoms are worsening, please contact a health care professional. There are many treatments available today that go beyond the scope of this book; you do not need to suffer.

We are so happy that you have taken the time to explore with us the many pathways out of almost depression. You will likely find that one of the pathways we have discussed—the behavioral, psychological, social, or biological pathway—works best for you. Perhaps, like Pia (chapter 8), you will find that just reducing your stress load using positive coping strategies is helpful. Perhaps, like Taylor and Betty Ann (chapter 5), you will find that exercise and behavioral activation will give you the lift you need. Like Blake and Loni (chapter 6), you may discover that you need to focus on finding meaning in your work and your activities. Creative activity, as we saw in the cases of Raymond and Sally (chapter 7), may be the antidote that will help you to fight off depression. Like Jason (chapter 9), perhaps you need to reframe a stressful situation as a challenge rather than a threat. Maybe, like Sarah and Mara (chapters 10 and 11), self-acceptance and mindfulness practices will help you find greater well-being. You may find that increasing your social support network and practicing social skills (chapters 12 and 13) will help you, as they did for Inez. Or you may learn that improving your sleep and nutrition is a key for you (chapter 14). Finally, you may find that you need something more, in the form of medication, supplements, or light therapy. These biological aids were very helpful to Kallista and Michael (chapter 15).

Whichever pathway you choose, the strategies in this book will also help you develop resilience against future episodes of almost depression. However, you may refer back to the methods in this book if you ever suspect that your symptoms are returning. You can think of these skills and strategies as a lifelong tool kit for maintaining a healthy emotional life.

Taking action to combat symptoms of almost depression is important not only because it will make you feel better, but also because it will improve your overall physical health and well-being as well as the well-being of those who are closest to you. You don't *have* to be almost depressed. You can take charge of your symptoms and make your way out of the gray shadows and into the full light of good mental health. We wish you a successful journey!

■◆■

appendix A

DSM Disorders on the Depression Continuum

The following are disorders related to depression that appear in the most recent editions of the *Diagnostic and Statistical Manual of Mental Disorders* (*DSM-IV-TR* and *DSM-5*).[1] We are not including the bipolar-spectrum (or manic depression) disorders here, except for the disorder of cyclothymia; if you are almost depressed but also have periods of unusually elevated mood and high self-confidence, there is a possibility that you qualify for this disorder.

Major Depressive Disorder: A history of one or more major depressive episodes. A major depressive episode is a period of more than two weeks of either depressed mood or anhedonia (loss of pleasure) that causes severe distress or inability to function. In addition to this symptom, at least four of the following must also be present: significant weight change (gaining or losing more than 5 percent of body weight without intending to do so), significant changes in sleeping patterns (insomnia or its opposite:

sleeping much more than is usual for the person), psychomotor changes (a noticeable slowing down or speeding up in movements and speech), constant fatigue, feelings of worthlessness or inappropriate guilt, trouble concentrating, and thoughts of death or dying or suicidal thinking.

There are several identified subtypes of major depression. Two of these include *postpartum depression*, in which an episode of depression occurs within four weeks of childbirth, and *seasonal pattern* (often called *seasonal affective disorder*), in which episodes of depression tend to occur at the same time each year and remit as the seasons change. *Bereavement*, or grieving, is also listed under depression in the *DSM-5*. Bereavement is extreme sadness following the death of a loved one. Although criteria for depression may be met during the grieving period, *DSM-5* notes important distinctions. Breavement is recognized as a normal response to loss and is only diagnosed as depression under specific circumstances.

Persistent Depressive Disorder (Dysthymia): A period of depressed mood or anhedonia (loss of pleasure) that is less intense than that experienced in major depression and doesn't include suicidal thinking. However, it lasts much longer—at least two years without remission for longer than a one-month period. It also includes two or more of the following: changes in appetite, changes in sleep patterns, low energy or fatigue, low self-esteem, poor concentration or difficulty making decisions, and feelings of hopelessness.

Depressive Condition Not Elsewhere Classified (CNEC): This diagnosis includes *minor depression*, which is a period of more than two weeks of either depressed mood or anhedonia that causes severe distress or inability to function. It also includes between two and three of the following: significant weight change, significant changes in sleeping patterns, psychomotor changes (a noticeable change in movements and speech), constant fatigue, feelings of worthlessness or inappropriate guilt, trouble concentrating, and suicidal thinking.

Adjustment Disorder with Depressed Mood: Significant distress or inability to function accompanied by depressed mood within three months of experiencing a major life stressor.

Cyclothymia: A period of two years or longer in which the person has recurrent periods of depressive symptoms that cycle with recurrent periods of hypomania. Some features of hypomania include persistent elevated or irritable mood (at least four days at a time), inflated self-esteem, decreased need for sleep, being more talkative than usual, and excessive involvement in pleasurable activities that may have painful consequences (such as shopping sprees, sexual indiscretions, foolish business investments, or reckless speeding). This disorder is classified under Bipolar and Related Disorders in the *DSM-5.*

Depressive Personality Disorder: (This is not currently an official diagnosis but is a condition that was slated for further study in *DSM-IV-TR.*) This is a trait-like pattern of depressive thoughts and behaviors that begins in adolescence and includes five or more of the following: dejected, gloomy, or cheerless mood; low self-esteem; excessive brooding or worry; a blaming or self-critical nature; negative and critical attitude toward others; pessimism; and proneness to feel guilt and remorse.

Premenstrual Dysphoric Disorder: Marked feelings of depression, irritability, anxiety, and/or mood swings that cause significant distress or inability to function and are centered around the week before the onset of menses each month. It also includes some or all of the following: anhedonia, difficulty concentrating, overeating or food cravings, fatigue, changes in sleep patterns, a sense of being overwhelmed or out of control, and physical complaints such as tenderness or joint pain.

The *DSM-5* also includes categories for *substance-induced depressive disorder* and *depressive disorder associated with another medical condition.*

| appendix B |

The Biology of Stress

Stressors are events or situations that are perceived as threatening. They can include emotional, psychological, and infectious threats as well as actual physical threats or challenges. When the brain perceives a potential stressor, a cascade of reactions is initiated in the brain and body. The stress response begins with the release of the brain chemical norepinephrine, which is produced in the brain stem. Norepinephrine (which is also known as *noradrenaline*), in turn, signals two interrelated systems to spring to action. One system, called the sympathomedullary pathway (SAM), activates the sympathetic arm of the autonomic nervous system through the release of the hormone *adrenaline*. Adrenaline causes an increase in heart rate and blood pressure, slows digestion, dilates the pupils, and leads to a surge of energy. (We have all felt that rapid rush of adrenaline when, for instance, someone cuts us off in traffic.) The amount of adrenaline released depends on how threatening you perceive a stressor to be. A stressor that's interpreted as a small challenge may lead to a minimal spike of adrenaline and will be experienced as excitement or mild anxiety; however, a stressor that's interpreted as a dangerous threat will lead to large releases of adrenaline (the knees-knocking kind) and will accompany the emotions of fear and anger. The release of norepinephrine in the brain also has very considerable effects on our thinking processes. A 2011 study in the prestigious journal *Science* confirmed that the release of norepinephrine in the face of stress basically reorders activation in many parts of the brain; it focuses our senses on signs of threat, activates stress-related memories, increases feelings of anxiety or even fear, and disengages our attention from our current tasks.[2] Thus, our innate biology virtually ensures that we can't concentrate on our everyday work or tasks when we're under "too much" stress.

A second response to stress is the activation of a biological system called the HPA axis—HPA stands for hypothalamus-pituitary-adrenal cortex, the three components of the system. Norepinephrine triggers the release of a glucocorticoid hormone (called corticotropin-releasing factor, or CRF) from the hypothalamus in the brain. CRF then stimulates the synthesis of another hormone called adrenocorticotropic hormone (ACTH) in the pituitary gland. ACTH enters the bloodstream and triggers the release of cortisol from the adrenal cortex located on top of the kidneys. Cortisol then circulates in the bloodstream, reducing immune functioning (so that the body can concentrate on the challenge or threat at hand) and mobilizing the conversion of glucose to energy. Eventually, cortisol makes its way back to the brain, where it acts as a negative feedback loop to turn *off* the release of CRF from the hypothalamus, giving the HPA axis a rest and returning the body to its pre-stress state.

The stress system is designed to (1) activate the brain and body to provide extra energy, focus, and strength in the face of threat, and (2) return the body to its normal state (this is the process of *homeostasis*) after a threat has been dealt with. When the system is engaged too often or when it responds without letup to ongoing low-level stressors, cortisol and adrenaline may continue to circulate, and the body doesn't get a chance to return to its baseline state. This increases what is called the "allostatic load" (the physiological consequences to the heart, brain, immune system, and other body tissues that result from a heightened and prolonged stress response) and can lead to both physical illness and a deregulation of brain chemicals associated with depression.[3]

appendix C

Negative Thinking Patterns Associated with Depression

Certain patterns of thinking have been associated with depression. These patterns are called "cognitive distortions"[4] or "cognitive biases." Here are descriptions of some of the most common distortions in thinking that we developed as a handout for use in the military project afterdeployment.org:[5]

- *All-or-nothing thinking (dichotomous thinking):* If you use all-or-nothing thinking when making sense of events, you tend to experience things in black-and-white terms. You may see situations as either entirely "good" or "bad" or view people as either "right" or "wrong" when there's actually a middle ground you aren't considering. You can check to see whether you're using all-or-nothing thinking by putting your thoughts into the "either/or" format. For example, you may decide that a friend is "bad" because he made an insensitive comment about something that is important to you ("*either* Michael supports what I say, *or* he's not someone I can count on").

- *Exaggeration:* Exaggeration is sometimes called "catastrophizing" because when people use this form of thinking, they blow the imagined consequences of an event way out of proportion. They see events and situations as more dire or important than they really are. For example, you might think that getting stuck in traffic is going to completely ruin your day. If you're stuck in this type of thought pattern, you may get accused of "making a mountain out of a molehill." Using words and phrases like "disastrous," "horrible," and "this ruins everything" in your conversation or self-talk may be a sign that you are using exaggeration or catastrophizing.

- *Overgeneralization:* This type of thinking is extremely common. You overgeneralize when you take one isolated experience or piece of information and draw serious, and usually bad, conclusions from your experience. In this way, isolated negative events are viewed as a never-ending pattern of negative events, horror, or defeat. For example, you might interpret a setback in your training as "I am just no good at it and will never get better." Or you might interpret a flat tire as "the car is always falling apart." Using words such as "always" and "never" in your conversation or self-talk are signs that you are overgeneralizing.

- *Mind-reading:* In this type of thinking, you assume you know what another person is thinking (or will think), even though you have no evidence to back up your assumptions. When you're mind-reading, you almost always assume that what someone is thinking about you is negative. For example, if you assume no one wants to hear about what you went through while you were deployed, you are using the negative thinking pattern of mind-reading. Communicating is the only way you will actually find out what anyone else is thinking . . . and it may well be more positive than you assume. Self-talk that includes "she probably thinks . . . " and "he doesn't understand . . ." are signs that you may be using the negative thinking pattern of mind-reading.

- *Minimization:* If you use minimization when making sense of events, you tend to shrink the importance of some events that deserve far more weight than you give them. For example, you may minimize or ignore your successes or personal achievements, or you may skip over your good qualities and only focus on your (or others') weaknesses. You may dwell on the negative events in your life and forget the things that are going well.

- *Emotional reasoning:* If you draw conclusions based on how you feel, you are using emotional reasoning. That is, you interpret your emotions as evidence of some general truth. For example, you may notice that you feel anxious as you are doing some job and infer that there is a definite and true cause for your feelings. You decide that it's dangerous, so you start scanning the environment for threats instead of recognizing that your feelings are a result of how you interpreted your feelings.

notes

Chapter 1: What Is Almost Depression?

1. J. M. Bostwick and V. S. Pankratz, "Affective Disorders and Suicide Risk: A Reexamination," *American Journal of Psychiatry* 157 (2000): 1925–32; Y-W. Chen and S. C. Dilsaver, "Lifetime Rates of Suicide Attempts among Subjects with Bipolar and Unipolar Disorders Relative to Subjects with Other Axis I Disorders," *Biological Psychiatry* 39, no. 10 (1996): 896–99; H. M. Inskip, E. C. Harris, and B. Barraclough, "Lifetime Risk of Suicide for Affective Disorder, Alcoholism and Schizophrenia," *British Journal of Psychiatry* 172 (1998): 35–37.

2. A. J. Rush, M. H. Trivedi, H. M. Ibrahim, T. J. Carmody, B. Arnow, D. N. Klein, J. C. Markowitz, P. T. Ninan, S. Kornstein, R. Manber, M. E. Thase, J. H. Kocsis, M. B. Keller, "The 16-Item Quick Inventory of Depressive Symptomatology (QIDS) Clinician Rating (QIDS-C) and Self-Report (QIDS-SR): A Psychometric Evaluation in Patients with Chronic Major Depression," *Biological Psychiatry* 54 (2003): 573–83.

3. Hippocrates, *Hippocrates, Collected Works I,* part 10, ed. W. H. S. Jones (Cambridge: Harvard University Press, 1868), www.perseus.tufts.edu/hopper/text?doc=Perseus%3Atext%3A1999.01.0251%3Atext%3DAer.%3Asection%3D10. Aristotle, "Problems," in *The Complete Works of Aristotle,* vol. 2, ed. J. Barnes (Princeton, NJ: Princeton University Press, 1984), 1319–1527.

4. American Psychiatric Association, *Diagnostic and Statistical Manual of Mental Disorders,* 5th ed. (Washington, DC: American Psychiatric Association, 2013).

5. Centers for Disease Control and Prevention, "Current Depression among Adults—United States, 2006 and 2008," *Morbidity and Mortality Weekly Report (MMWR)* 59, no. 38 (2010): 1229–35, www.cdc.gov/mmwr/preview/mmwrhtml/mm5938a2.htm?s_cid=mm5938a2_e%0D%0.

6. D. Robert, R. D. Goldney, L. F. Fisher, E. D. Grande, and A. W. Taylor, "Subsyndromal Depression: Prevalence, Use of Health Services and Quality of Life in an Australian Population," *Social Psychiatry and Psychiatric Epidemiology* 39 (2004): 293–98.

7. B. Guan, Y. Deng, P. Cohen, and H. Chen, "Relative Impact of Axis I Mental Disorders on Quality of Life among Adults in the Community," *Journal of Affective Disorders* 131 (2011): 293–98; B. N. Subodh, A. Avasthi, and S. Chakrabarti, "Psychosocial Impact of Dysthymia: A Study among Married Patients," *Journal of Affective Disorders* 109 (2008): 199–204.

Chapter 2: Understanding the Depression Continuum

1. National Institute of Mental Health, *Depression: A Treatable Illness*, NIH Publication No. 03-5299, Washington, DC: NIMH, 2003, www.apps.nimh .nih.gov/health/publications/depression-a-treatable-illness.shtml.

2. R. E. Ingram and D. D. Luxton, "Vulnerability–Stress Models," in *Development of Psychopathology: A Vulnerability–Stress Perspective*, ed. B. L. Hankin and J. R. Zabela (Thousand Oaks, CA: Sage, 2005): 32–46.

3. D. F. Levinson, "Genetics of Major Depression," in *Handbook of Depression*, 2nd ed., ed. I. H. Gotlib and C. L. Hammen (New York: Guilford Press, 2009), 165–86.

4. A. Caspi, K. Sugden, T. E. Moffitt, A. Taylor, I. W. Craig, H. Harrington, J. McClay, J. Mill, J. Martin, A. Braithwaite, and R. Poulton, "Influence of Life Stress on Depression: Moderation by a Polymorphism in the 5HTT Gene," *Science* 301 (2003): 386–89; K. Karg, M. Burmeister, K. Shedden, and S. Sen, "The Serotonin Transporter Promoter Variant (5_HTTLPR), Stress, and Depression Meta-analysis Revisited," *Archives of General Psychiatry* 68 (2011): 444–54.

5. M. E. Thase, "Neurobiological Aspects of Depression," in *Handbook of Depression*, 2nd ed., ed. I. H. Gotlib and C. L. Hammen (New York: Guilford Press, 2009).

6. C. M. Pariante and S. L. Lightman, "The HPA Axis in Major Depression: Classical Theories and New Developments," *Trends in Neuroscience* 39, no. 9 (2009): 464–68.

7. K. J. Miller and S. A. Rogers, *The Estrogen-Depression Connection* (Oakland, CA: New Harbinger Publications, 2007).

8. M. M. Shores, V. M., Moceri, K. L. Sloan, A. J. Matsumoto, and D. R. Kivlahan, "Low testosterone Levels Predict Incident Depressive Illness in

Older Men: Effects of Age and Medical Morbidity," *Journal of Clinical Psychiatry* 66 (2005): 7–14; O. P. Almeida, B. B. Yeap, G. J. Hankey, K. Jamrozik, and L. Flicker, "Low Free Testosterone Concentration as a Potentially Treatable Cause of Depressive Symptoms in Older Men," *Archives of General Psychiatry* 65 (2008): 283–89.

9. R. Davidson, D. Pizzagalli, and J. B. Nitschke, "The Representation and Regulation of Emotion in Depression: Perspectives from Affective Neuroscience," in *Handbook of Depression*, 2nd ed., ed. I. H. Gotlib and C. L. Hammen (New York: Guilford Press, 2009), 218–48; R. Nusslock, A. J. Shackman, E. Harmon-Jones, L. B. Alloy, J. A. Coan, and L. Y. Abramson, "Cognitive Vulnerability and Frontal Brain Asymmetry: Common Predictors of First Prospective Depressive Episode," *Journal of Abnormal Psychology* 120, no. 2 (2011): 497–503.

10. R. J. Gatchel, Y. B. Peng, M. L. Peters, P. N. Fuchs, and D. C. Turk, "The Biopsychosocial Approach to Chronic Pain: Scientific Advances and Future Directions," *Psychological Bulletin* 133, no. 4 (2007): 581–624.

11. A. T. Beck, A. J. Rush, B. F. Shaw, and G. Emery, *Cognitive Therapy of Depression* (New York: Guilford Press, 1979).

12. R. Kotov, W. Gamez, F. Schmidt, and D. Watson, "Linking 'Big' Personality Traits to Anxiety, Depressive, and Substance Use Disorders: A Meta-Analysis," *Psychological Bulletin* 136 (2010): 768–821.

13. N. Schmitz, J. Kugler, and J. Rollnik, "On the Relation between Neuroticism, Self-Esteem, and Depression: Results from The National Comorbidity Survey," *Comprehensive Psychiatry* 44, no. 3 (2003): 169–176.

14. K. S. Kendler, J. W. Kuhn, and C. A. Prescott, "Childhood Sexual Abuse, Stressful Life Events and Risk for Major Depression in Women," *Psychological Medicine* 34 (2004): 1475–82.

15. K. S. Kendler, K. Sheth, C. O. Gardner, and C. A. Prescott, "Childhood Parental Loss and Risk for First-Onset of Major Depression and Alcohol Dependence: The Time-Decay of Risk and Sex Differences," *Psychological Medicine* 32 (2002): 1187–94.

16. W. R. Beardslee, E. M. Versage, and T. R. Galdstone, "Children of Affectively Ill Parents: A Review of the Past 10 Years," *Journal of the American Academy of Child and Adolescent Psychiatry* 37 (1998): 1134–41.

17. S. Galea, J. Ahern, A. Nandi, M. Tracy, J. Beard, and D. Vlahov, "Urban Neighborhood Poverty and the Incidence of Depression in a Population-Based Cohort Study," *Annals of Epidemiology* 17 (2007): 171–79.

Chapter 3: Almost Depression and the Role of Stress

1. H. Eyre and B. T. Baune, "Neuroimmunological Effects of Physical Exercise in Depression," *Brain, Behavior, and Immunity* 26 (2012): 251–66.

2. T. H. Holmes and R. H. Rahe, "The Social Readjustment Rating Scale," *Journal of Psychosomatic Research* 11, no. 2 (1967): 213–18.

3. J. A. Sedgeman, "Health Realization/Innate Health: Can a Quiet Mind and a Positive Feeling State Be Accessible Over the Lifespan without Stress-Relief Techniques?" *Medical Science Monitor* 11, no. 12 (2005): HY47-52.

4. S. S. Wong, "Balanced States of Mind in Psychopathology and Psychological Well-Being," *International Journal of Psychology* 45, no. 4 (2010): 269–77, doi: 10.1080/00207591003683090.

5. R. S. Lazarus and S. Folkman, *Stress, Appraisal and Coping* (New York: Springer, 1984).

6. J. P. Jamieson, M. K. Nock, and W. B. Mendes, "Mind over Matter: Reappraising Arousal Improves Cardiovascular and Cognitive Responses to Stress," *Journal of Experimental Psychology: General* 141, no. 3 (2012): 417–22, doi: 10.1037/a0025719.

7. Ibid.

8. W. B. Mendes, J. Blascovich, S. Hunter, B. Lickel, and J. T. Jost, "Threatened by the Unexpected: Physiological Responses during Social Interactions with Expectancy-Violating Partners," *Journal of Personality and Social Psychology* 92 (2007): 698–716.

9. R. T. Liu and L. B. Alloy, "Stress Generation in Depression: A Systematic Review of the Empirical Literature and Recommendations for Future Study," *Clinical Psychology Review* 30 (2010): 582–93.

10. J. L. Wang and N. Schmitz, "Does Job Strain Interact with Psychosocial Factors outside of the Workplace in Relation to the Risk of Major Depression? The Canadian National Population Health Survey," *Social Psychiatry and Psychiatric Epidemiology* 46, (2011): 577–84, doi: 10.1007/s00127-010-0224-0.

11. Y. K. Goldberg, J. D. Eastwood, J. Laguardia, and J. Danckert, "Boredom: An Emotional Experience Distinct from Apathy, Anhedonia, or Depression," *Journal of Social and Clinical Psychology* 30, no. 6 (2011): 649, doi: 10.1521/jscp.2011.30.6.647.

Chapter 4: Almost Depression . . . or Something Else?

1. J. Jacobsen, G. Maytal, and T. Stern, "Demoralization in Medical Practice," *Primary Care Companion to the Journal of Clinical Psychiatry* 9, no. 2 (2007): 139–43.

2. C. M. Celano, O. Freudenreich, C. Fernandez-Robles, A. Theodore, T. A. Stern, M. A. Caro, and J. C. Huffman, "Depressogenic Effects of Medications: A Review," *Dialogues in Clinical Neuroscience* 13 (2011): 109–25.

3. T. J. Moore, C. D. Furberg, J. Glenmullen, J. T. Maltsberger, and S. Singh, "Suicidal Behavior and Depression in Smoking Cessation Treatments," *PLoS One* 6, no. 11 (2011): e27016.

4. P. A. Frewen, D. J. Dozois, and R. A. Lanius, "Neuroimaging Studies of Psychological Interventions for Mood and Anxiety Disorders: Empirical and Methodological Review," *Clinical Psychology Review* 28, no. 2 (2008): 228–46.

Chapter 5: Enhancing Your Mood through Movement

1. Physical Activity Guidelines Advisory Committee, *Physical Activity Guidelines Advisory Committee Report, 2008* (Washington, DC: U.S. Department of Health and Human Services, 2008).

2. C. A. Elliot, C. Kennedy, G. Morgan, S. K. Anderson, and D. Morris, "Undergraduate Physical Activity and Depressive Symptoms: A National Study," *American Journal of Health Behavior* 36 (2012): 230–41, doi: 10.5993/AJHB.36.2.8.

3. A. H. S. Harris, R. Cronkite, and R. Moos, "Physical Activity, Exercise Coping, and Depression in a 10-Year Cohort Study of Depressed Patients," *Journal of Affective Disorders* 93 (2006): 79–85; J. Mata, C. L. Hogan, J. Joormann, C. E. Waugh, and I. H. Gotlib, "Acute Exercise Attenuates Negative Affect Following Repeated Sad Mood Inductions in Persons Who Have Recovered from Depression," *Journal of Abnormal Psychology*, advance online publication, September 17, 2012, doi: 10.1037/a0029881.

4. M. Babyak, J. A. Blumenthal, S. Herman, P. Khatri, M. Doraiswamy, K. Moore, W. E. Craighead, T. T. Baldewicz, and K. R. Krishnan, "Exercise Treatment for Major Depression: Maintenance of Therapeutic Benefit at 10 Months," *Psychosomatic Medicine* 62 (2000): 633–38 (SMILE Study).

5. G. E. Mead, W. Morley, P. Campbell, C. A. Greig, M. McMurdo, and D. A. Lawlor, "Exercise for Depression," *Cochrane Database of Systematic Reviews*, no. 3 (2009), CD004366, doi: 10.1002/14651858.CD004366.pub4.

6. J. Mota-Pereira, J. Silverio, S. Carvalho, J. C. Ribeiro, D. Fonte, and J. Ramos, "Moderate Exercise Improves Depression Parameters in Treatment-Resistant Patients with Major Depressive Disorder," *Journal of Psychiatric Research* 45 (2011): 1005–11, doi: 10.1016/j.jpsychires.2011.02.005.

7. Eyre and Baune, "Neuroimmunological Effects of Physical Exercise."

8. M. Babyak, J. A. Blumenthal, S. Herman, P. Khatri, M. Doraiswamy, K. Moore, W. E. Craighead, T. T. Baldewicz, and K. R. Krishnan, "Exercise Treatment for Major Depression: Maintenance of Therapeutic Benefit at 10 Months," *Psychosomatic Medicine* 62 (2000): 633–38; H. W. Tsang, E. P. Chan, and W. M. Cheung, "Effects of Mindful and Non-mindful Exercises on People with Depression: A Systematic Review," *British Journal of Clinical Psychology* 47, pt 3 (2008): 303–22, doi: 10.1348/014466508X279260.

9. A. L. Dunn, M. H. Trivedi, J. B. Kampert, C. G. Clark, and H. O. Chambliss, "Exercise Treatment for Depression: Efficacy and Dose Response," *American Journal of Preventative Medicine* 28 (2005): 1–8.

10. G. E. Simon, K. M. Von Korff, K. Saunders, D. L. Miglioretti, P. K. Crane, G. van Belle, and R. C. Kessler, "Association between Obesity and Psychiatric Disorders in the U.S. Adult Population," *Archives of General Psychiatry* 63 (2006): 824–30.

11. S. E. Saarni, S. M. Lehto, J. Hintikka, S. Pirkola, M. A. Heliövaara, J. Lönniqvist, J. Suvisaari, and S. I. Saarni, "Body Composition in Subtypes of Depression—A Population-Based Survey," *Psychological Medicine* 41 (2011): 1113–18, doi: 10.1017/S0033291711000110.

12. J. K. Vallaince, E. A. H. Winkler, P. A. Gardiner, G. N. Healy, B. M. Lynch, and N. Owen, "Associations of Objectively-Assessed Physical Activity and Sedentary Time with Depression: NHANES (2005–2006)," *Preventative Medicine* 53 (2011): 284–88, doi: 10.1016/j.ypmed.2011.07.013.

13. E. K. Nisbet and J. M. Zelenski, "Underestimating Nearby Nature: Affective Forecasting Errors Obscure the Happy Path to Sustainability," *Psychological Science* 22 (2011): 1101–6, doi: 10.1177/0956797611418527.

Chapter 6: Improving Your Mood through Meaning-Based Action

1. D. R. Hopko, J. F. Magidson, and C. W. Lejuez, "Treatment Failure in Behavior Therapy: Focus on Behavioral Activation for Depression," *Journal of Clinical Psychology: In Session* 67 (2011): 1106–16, doi: 10.1002/jclp.20840.

2. S. A. Hadley and A. K. McLeod, "Conditional Goal-Setting, Personal Goals and Hopelessness about the Future," *Cognition and Emotion* 24, no. 7 (2010): 1191–98; N. Bailly, M. Joulain, C. Hervé, and D. Alaphilippe, "Coping with Negative Life Events in Old Age: The Role of Tenacious Goal Pursuit and Flexible Goal Adjustment," *Aging and Mental Health* 16 (2012): 431–37, doi: 10.1080/13607863.2011.630374.

3. C. S. Carver and M. F. Scheier, "Origins and Functions of Positive and Negative Affect: A Control Process Review," *Psychological Review* 97 (1990): 19–35, doi: 10.1037/0033-295X.97.1.19.

4. H. Street, "Exploring Relationships between Goal Setting, Goal Pursuit and Depression: A Review," *Australian Psychologist* 37 (2012): 95–103, doi: 10.1080/00050060210001706736; C. Crane, R. Winder, E. Hargus, M. Amarasinghe, and T. Barnhofer, "Effects of Mindfulness-Based Cognitive Therapy on Specificity of Life Goals," *Cognitive Therapy and Research* 36 (2012): 182–89.

5. P. Muris, H. Schmidt, R. Lambrichs, and C. Meesters, "Protective and Vulnerability Factors of Depression in Normal Adolescents," *Behaviour Research and Therapy* 39 (2001): 555–65.

6. C. Vergara and J. E. Roberts, "Motivation and Goal Orientation in Vulnerability to Depression," *Cognition and Emotion* 25 (2011): 1281–90, doi: 10.1080/02699931.2010.542743.

7. C. Crane, R. Winder, E. Hargus, M. Amarasinghe, and T. Barnhofer, "Effects of Mindfulness-Based Cognitive Therapy on Specificity of Life Goals," *Cognitive Therapy and Research* 36 (2012): 182–89.

Chapter 7: Improving Your Mood through Creative Activity

1. G. Greene, *Ways of Escape* (New York: Simon and Schuster, 1980).

2. B. Newcomb, "The Black Hole of Depression," *Thoughts on Good Therapy* (blog), February 1, 2012, http://brettnewcomb.com/the-black-hole-of-depression.

3. J. Erkkilä, M. Punkanen, J. Fachner, E. Ala-Ruona, I. Pöntiö, M. Tervaniemi, M. Vanhala, and C. Gold, "Individual Music Therapy for Depression: Randomised Controlled Trial," *British Journal of Psychiatry* 199 (2011): 132–39, doi: 10.1192/bjp.bp.110.085431.

4. J. W. Pennebaker, "Writing about Emotional Experiences as a Therapeutic Process," *Psychological Science* 8, no. 3 (1997): 162–66.

5. D. M. Sloan, B. A. Feinstein, and B. P. Marx, "The Durability of Beneficial Health Effects Associated with Expressive Writing," *Anxiety, Stress, & Coping* 22, no. 5 (2009): 509–23, doi: 10.1080/10615800902785608.

6. Adapted from Pennebaker (1997), p.162.

7. C. Grape, M. Sangren, L. O. Hansson, M. Ericson, and T. Theorell, "Does Singing Promote Well-Being?: An Empirical Study of Professional and

Amateur Singers during a Singing Lesson," *Integrative Physiological and Behavioral Science* 38, no. 1 (2003): 65–74.

8. C. Sarao, "The Effects of Singing on Depression," Livestrong.com, October 12, 2010, www.livestrong.com/article/277000-the-effects-of-singing-on-depression.

9. F. Davis, *The History of the Blues* (New York: Hyperion, 1995).

10. T. Mangan, "Pacific Symphony Paints 'Tchaikovsky Portrait' This Week," *Orange County Register*, December 24, 2009, www.ocregister.com/articles/tchaikovsky-225889-symphony-path233tique.html.

Chapter 8: Improving Your Mood by Reducing Stress

1. C. S. Carver, M. E. Scheier, and J. K. Weintraub, "Assessing Coping Strategies: A Theoretically Based Approach," *Journal of Personality and Social Psychology* 56 (1989): 267–83.

2. A. G. Horwitz, R. M. Hill, and C. A. King, "Specific Coping Behaviors in Relation to Adolescent Depression and Suicidal Ideation," *Journal of Adolescence* 34 (2011): 1077–85, doi: 10.1016/j.adolescence.2010.10.004.

3. K. J. Eschleman and N. A. Bowling, "A Meta-Analytic Examination of Hardiness," *International Journal of Stress Management* 17 (2010): 277–307; C. MacCann, A. A. Lipnevich, J. Burrus, and R. D. Roberts, "The Best Years of Our Lives? Coping with Stress Predicts School Grades, Life Satisfaction, and Feelings about High School," *Learning and Individual Differences* 22 (2012): 235–41; S. E. Taylor, "How Psychosocial Resources Enhance Health and Well-Being," in *Applied Positive Psychology: Improving Everyday Life, Health, Schools, Work, and Society*, ed, S. I. Donaldson, M. Csikszentmihalyi, and J. Nakamura (New York: Routledge/Taylor and Francis, 2011), 65–77; G. M. Alarcon, J. B. Lyons, B. R. Schlessman, and A. J. Barelka, "Leadership and Coping among Air Force Officers," *Military Psychology* 24 (2012): 29–47.

4. P. Cuijpers, A. van Straten, G. Andersson, and P. van Oppen, "Psychotherapy for Depression in Adults: A Meta-Analysis of Comparative Outcome Studies," *Journal of Consulting and Clinical Psychology* 76 (2008): 909–22, doi: 10.1037/a0013075; Department of Veterans Affairs, *VA/DoD Clinical Practice Guideline for Management of Major Depressive Disorder* (Washington, DC: Department of Veterans Affairs, 2009).

Chapter 9: Challenging and Reframing Your Depressive Thoughts

1. J. Blascovich and J. Tomaka, "The Biopsychosocial Model of Arousal Regulation," *Advances in Experimental Social Psychology* 28 (1996): 1–51, doi:

10.1016/S0065-2601(08)60235-X; J. P. Jamieson, M. K. Nock, and W. B. Mendes, "Mind over Matter: Reappraising Arousal Improves Cardiovascular and Cognitive Responses to Stress," *Journal of Experimental Psychology: General* 141, no. 3 (2012): 417–22, ePUB Sep 26, 2011, doi: 10.1037/a0025719.

2. A. T. Beck, A. J. Rush, B. F. Shaw, and G. Emery, *Cognitive Therapy of Depression* (New York: Guilford Press, 1987).

3. P. Brickman, D. Coates, and R. Janoff-Bulman, "Lottery Winners and Accident Victims: Is Happiness Relative?" *Journal of Personality and Social Psychology* 35 (1978): 917–27.

4. D. Gilbert, *Stumbling on Happiness* (New York: Knopf, 2006).

5. A. Ellis, "Rational Psychotherapy," *Journal of General Psychology* 59 (1958): 35–49; A. Ellis, *Reason and Emotion in Psychotherapy* (Secaucus, NJ: Citadel, 1962).

6. S. J. Rupke, D. Blecke, and M. Renfroe, "Cogntive Therapy for Depression," *American Family Physician* 73 (2006): 83–86; D. Schuyler, "Short-Term Cognitive Therapy Shows Promise for Dysthymia," *Current Psychiatry* 1 (2002): 43–49.

7. T. E. Joiner, J. M. Cook, M. Hersen, and K. H. Gordon, "Double Depression in Older Adult Psychiatric Outpatients: Hopelessness as a Defining Feature," *Journal of Affective Disorders* 101, no. 1–3 (2007): 235–38.

8. C. Reynaert, P. Janne, A. Bosly, P. Staquet, N. Zdanowiez, M. Vause, B. Chatelain, and D. Lejeune, "From Health Locus of Control to Immune Control: Internal Locus of Control Has a Buffering Effect on Natural Killer Cell Activity Decrease in Major Depression," *Acta Psychiatrica Scandinavica* 92 (1995): 294–300.

9. Charles P. Bosmajian is a psychologist and subject matter expert for the Defense Centers of Excellence for Psychological Health and Traumatic Brain Injury, National Center for Telehealth and Technology.

10. M. E. P. Seligman, *Learned Optimism: How to Change Your Mind and Your Life* (New York: Pocket Books, 1998).

Chapter 10: Improving Your Mood by Applying Mindfulness Strategies

1. J. Kabat-Zinn, *Wherever You Go There You Are* (New York: Hyperion, 1994), 4.

2. M. H. Mason, M. I. Norton, J. D. Van Horn, D. M. Wegner, S. T. Grafton, and C. N. Macrae, "Wandering Minds: The Default Network and Stimulus-Independent Thought," *Science* 315 (2007): 393–95, doi: 10.1126/science

.1131295; M. A. Killingsorth and D. T. Gilbert, "A Wandering Mind Is an Unhappy Mind," *Science* 330 (2010): 932, doi: 10.1126/science.1192439.

3. Z. V. Segal, P. Bieling, T. Young, G. MacQueen, R. Cooke, L. Martin, R. Bloch, and R. D. Levitan, "Antidepressant Monotherapy vs Sequential Pharmacotherapy and Mindfulness-Based Cognitive Therapy, or Placebo, for Relapse Prophylaxis in Recurrent Depression," *Archives of General Psychiatry* 67 (2010): 1256–64, doi: 10.1001/archgenpsychiatry.2010.168.

4. S. W. Lazar, C. Kerr, R. Wasserman, J. R. Gray, D. N. Greve, M. T. Treadway, M. McGarvey, B. T. Quinn, J. A. Dusek, H. Benson, S. L. Rauch, C. I. Moore, and B. Fischl, "Meditation Experience Is Associated with Increased Cortical Thickness," *Neuroreport* 16 (2005): 1893–97; B. K. Hölzel, J. Carmody, M. Vangel, C. Congleton, S. M. Yerramsetti, T. Gard, and S. W. Lazar, "Mindfulness Practice Leads to Increases in Regional Brain Gray Matter Density," *Psychiatry Research* 191 (2011): 36–43, doi: 10.1016/j.pscychresns.2010.08.006; L. A. Kilpatrick, B. Y. Suyenobu, S. R. Smith, J. A. Bueller, T. Goodman, J. D. Creswell, K. Tillisch, E. A. Mayer, and B. D. Naliboff, "Impact of Mindfulness-Based Stress Reduction Training on Intrinsic Brain Connectivity," *NeuroImage* 56 (2011): 290–98, doi: 10.1016/j.neuroimage.2011.02.034; C. E. Kerr, S. R. Jones, Q. Wan, D. L. Pritchett, R. H. Wasserman, A. Wexler, J. J. Villanueva, J. R. Shaw, S. W. Lazar, T. J. Kaptchuk, R. Littenberg, M. S. Hämäläinen, C. I. Moore, "Effects of Mindfulness Meditation Training on Anticipatory Alpha Modulation in Primary Somatosensory Cortex," *Brain Research Bulletin* 85, no. 3–4 (2011): 96–103, doi: 10.1016/j.brainresbull.2011.03.026.

5. J. Kabat-Zinn, *Full Catastrophe Living: Using the Wisdom of Your Body and Mind to Face Stress, Pain and Illness* (New York: Bantam Dell, 1990).

6. J. Joyce, *Dubliners (Modern Library edition)* (New York: Random House, 1993), 130.

7. M. Csikszentmihalyi, *Flow: The Psychology of Optimal Experience* (New York: Harper and Row, 1990), 30.

8. R. Rosen, *The Practice of Pranayama: An In-depth Guide to the Yoga of Breath* (New York: Random House Unabridged Compact Disks, 2010).

9. S. Carson and E. Langer, "Mindful Practice for Clinicians and Patients," in *Handbook of Primary Care Psychology*, ed. L. Haas (London: Oxford, 2004), 173–86.

10. E. J. Langer, *Mindfulness* (Reading, MA: Addison-Wesley, 1989); E. J. Langer, *The Power of Mindful Learning* (Reading, MA: Addison-Wesley, 1997).

11. A. Flodr, S. Carson, and E. J. Langer, "Attitude toward Remission Predicts Health Measures in Breast Cancer Survivors," in preparation for submission.

Chapter 11: Using Mindfulness to Diminish Shame and Foster Self-Acceptance

1. I. E. de Hooge, M. Zeelenberg, and S. M. Breugelmans, "A Functionalist Account of Shame-Induced Behaviour," *Cognition & Emotion* 25, no. 5 (2011): 939–46, doi: 10.1080/02699931.2010.516909.

2. J. P. Tangney, P. E. Wagner, and R. Gramzow, "Proneness to Shame, Proneness to Guilt, and Psychopathology," *Journal of Abnormal Psychology* 101 (1992): 469–78; J. J. Gross and L. F. Barrett, "Emotion Generation and Emotion Regulation: One or Two Depends on Your Point of View," *Emotion Review* 3, no. 1 (2011): 8–16.

3. N. Eisenberg, "Emotion, Regulation, and Moral Development," *Annual Review of Psychology* 51 (2000): 665–97.

4. S. Kim, R. Thibodeau, and R. S. Jorgensen, "Shame, Guilt and Depressive Symptoms: A Meta-Analytic Review," *Psychological Bulletin* 137, no. 1 (2011): 68–96, doi: 10.1037/a0021466.

5. Medline Plus online medical dictionary, www.merriam-webster.com/medlineplus/perfectionism; P. L. Hewitt, G. L. Flett, and E. Ediger, "Perfectionism and Depression: Longitudinal Assessment of a Specific Vulnerability Hypothesis," *Journal of Abnormal Psychology* 105 (1996): 276–80.

6. D. E. Hamachek, "Psychodynamics of Normal and Neurotic Perfectionism," *Psychology* 15 (1978): 27–33; K. G. Rice, J. S. Ashby, and R. Gilman, "Classifying Adolescent Perfectionists," *Psychological Assessment* 23, no. 3 (2011): 563–77, doi: 10.1037/a0022482.

7. P. L. Hewitt, G. L. Flett, E. Ediger, G. R. Norton, and C. A. Flynn, "Perfectionism in Chronic and State Symptoms of Depression," *Canadian Journal of Behavioral Science, Special Issue: Canadian Perspectives on Research in Depression* 30 (1998): 234–42; S. K. Huprich, J. Porcerelli, R. Keaschuk, J. Binienda, and B. Engle, "Depressive Personality Disorder, Dysthymia, and Their Relationship to Perfectionism," *Depression and Anxiety* 25 (2008): 207–17; P. Luyten, S. Kempke, P. Van Wambeke, S. Claes, S. J. Blatt, and B. Van Houdenhove, "Self-Critical Perfectionism, Stress Generation, and Stress Sensitivity in Patients with Chronic Fatigue Syndrome: Relationship with Severity of Depression," *Psychiatry* 74, no. 1 (2011): 21–30, doi: 10.1521/psyc.2011.74.1.21.

8. B. Brown, *Soul without Shame: A Guide to Liberating Yourself from the Judge Within* (Boston: Shambhala Publications, 1998).

9. P. Chödrön, *Start Where You Are: A Guide to Compassionate Living* (Boston: Shambhala, 2004).

10. S. Salzberg, *Lovingkindness: The Revolutionary Art of Happiness* (Boston: Shambhala Publications, 1995).

11. Ibid.

12. P. Gilbert, "Workshop Notes: An Introduction to the Theory and Practice of Compassion Focused Therapy and Compassionate Mind Training for Shame Based Difficulties," on Compassionate Mind Foundation website, accessed July 15, 2012, www.compassionatemind.co.uk.

13. J. Bowlby, *Loss: Sadness and Depression* (vol. 3), London: Hogarth, 1980.

14. C. K. Germer, *The Mindful Path to Self-Compassion: Freeing Yourself from Destructive Thoughts and Emotions* (New York: Guilford Press, 2009); J. Kabat-Zinn, *Wherever You Go, There You Are* (New York: Hyperion, 1994).

15. S. Carson and E. J. Langer, "Mindfulness and Self-Acceptance," *Journal of Rational Emotive Behavioral Therapy* 24, no. 1 (2006): 29–43.

16. Ibid.

17. E. Langer, *On Becoming an Artist: Reinventing Yourself Through Mindful Creativity* (New York: Ballantine Books, 2005).

18. From S. Carson, *Your Creative Brain: Seven Steps to Maximize Imagination, Productivity, and Innovation in Your Life* (San Francisco: Jossey-Bass, 2010), 92–94.

Chapter 12: Increasing Your Social Engagement and Support

1. B. Lakey and A. Cronin, "Low Social Support and Major Depression: Research, Theory, and Methodological Issues," in *Risk Factors for Depression*, ed. K. S. Dobson and D. Dozois (San Diego, CA: Academic Press, 2008) 385–408; M. Barrera, "Distinctions between Social Support Concepts, Measures, and Models," *American Journal of Community Psychology* 14, no. 4 (1986): 413–45; S. E. Taylor, "Social Support: A Review," in *The Handbook of Health Psychology*, ed. M. S. Friedman (New York: Oxford University Press, 2011), 189–214; E. S. Paykel, "Life Events, Social Support and Depression," *Acta Psychiatrica Scandinavica Supplementum* 377 (1994): 50–58.

2. B. N. Uchino, J. T. Cacioppo, and J. K. Kiecolt-Glaser, "The Relationship between Social Support and Physiological Processes: A Review with Emphasis on Underlying Mechanisms and Implications for Health," *Psychological Bulletin* 119 (1996): 488–531; C. Kirschbaum, T. Klauer, S. H. Filipp, and D. H. Hellhammer, "Sex-Specific Effects of Social Support on Cortisol and

Subjective Responses to Acute Psychological Stress," *Psychosomatic Medicine* 57 (1995): 23–31; S. J. Lepore, K. A. Allen, and G. W. Evans, "Social Support Lowers Cardiovascular Reactivity to an Acute Stressor," *Psychosomatic Medicine* 55 (1993): 518–24; A. Steptoe, N. Owen, S. R. Kunz-Ebrecht, and L. Brydon, "Loneliness and Neuroendocrine, Cardiovascular, and Inflammatory Stress Responses in Middle-Aged Men and Women," *Psychoneuroendocrinology* 29 (2004): 593–611; R. M. Sapolsky, *Why Zebras Don't Get Ulcers*, third edition (New York: Henry Holt, 2004).

3. S. Grav, O. Hellzèn, U. Romild, and E. Stordal, "Association between Social Support and Depression in the General Population: The HUNT Study, a Cross-Sectional Survey," *Journal of Clinical Nursing* 21 (2012): 111–20, doi: 10.1111/j.1365-2702.2011.03868.x.

4. K. M. C. Cline, "Psychological Effects of Dog Ownership: Role Strain, Role Enhancement, and Depression," *Journal of Social Psychology* 150, no. 2 (2010): 117–31, doi: 10.1080/00224540903368533.

5. Ibid.

6. R. B. Tower and M. Nokota, "Pet Companionship and Depression: Results from a United States Internet Sample," *Anthrozoos* 19, no. 1 (2006): 50–64.

7. R. D. Putnam, *Bowling Alone: The Collapse and Revival of American Community* (New York: Simon and Schuster, 2000).

8. University of Pennsylvania Collaborative on Community Integration, www.med.upenn.edu/psych/RRTC.html.

Chapter 13: Improving Your Social Skills

1. J. C. Coyne, "Depression and the Response of Others," *Journal of Abnormal Psychology* 85 (1976): 186–93.

2. Reviewed in C. Segrin, "Social Skills Deficits Associated with Depression," *Clinical Psychology Review* 20 (2000): 379–403.

3. C. Segrin, "Social Skills Training," in *General Principles and Empirically Supported Techniques of Cognitive Behavior Therapy*, ed. W. T. O'Donohue and J. Fisher (Hoboken, NJ: John Wiley and Sons, 2009), 600–607.

4. D. Fine, *The Fine Art of Small Talk: How to Start a Conversation, Keep It Going, Build Networking Skills—and Leave a Positive Impression!* (New York: Hyperion, 2005).

5. P. M. Lewinsohn, "A Behavioral Approach to Depression," in *The Psychology of Depression: Contemporary Theory and Research*, ed. R. J. Friedman and M. Katz (Washington, DC: John Wiley and Sons, 1974).

6. A. M. Cusi, G. M. MacQueen, R. M. Spreng, and M. C. McKinnon, "Altered Empathic Responding in Major Depressive Disorder: Relation to Symptom Severity, Illness Burden, and Psychosocial Outcome," *Psychiatric Research* 188 (2011): 231–36, doi: 10.1016/j.psychres.2011.04.013.

7. R. Bolton, *People Skills: How to Assert Yourself, Listen to Others, and Resolve Conflicts* (Englewood Cliffs, NJ: Prentice-Hall, 1979).

Chapter 14: Improving Your Sleep and Diet

1. J. M. Krueger, D. M. Rector, S. Roy, H. P. Van Dongen, G. Belenky, and J. Panksepp, "Sleep as a Fundamental Property of Neuronal Assemblies," *Nature Reviews Neuroscience* 9, no. 12 (2008): 910–19, doi: 10.1038/nrn2521.

2. M. M. Ohayon, "Epidemiology of Insomnia: What We Know and What We Still Need to Learn," *Sleep Medicine Reviews* 6, no. 2 (2002): 97–111.

3. C. Baglionia, G. Battagliese, B. Feigea, K. Spiegelhaldera, C. Nissena, U. Voderholzera, C. Lombardo, and D. Riemann, "Insomnia as a Predictor of Depression: A Meta-analytic Evaluation of Longitudinal Epidemiological Studies," *Journal of Affective Disorders* 135, no. 1–3 (2011): 10–11, doi: 10.1016/j.jad.2011.01.011.

4. C. M. Morin, A. Vallières, B. Guay, H. Ivers, J. Savard, C. Mérette, C. Bastien, and L. Baillargeon, "Cognitive Behavioral Therapy, Singly and Combined with Medication, for Persistent Insomnia: A Randomized Controlled Trial," *Journal of the American Medical Association* 301, no. 19 (2009): 2005–15, doi: 10.1001/jama.2009.682.

5. A. G. Wade, G. Crawford, I. Ford, A. McConnachie, T. Nir, M. Laudon, and N. Zisapel, "Prolonged Release Melatonin in the Treatment of Primary Insomnia: Evaluation of the Age Cut-Off for Short- and Long-Term Response," *Current Medical Research and Opinion* 27, no. 1 (2011): 87–98, doi: 10.1185/03007995.2010.537317.

6. I. B. Hickie and N. L. Rogers, "Novel Melatonin-Based Therapies: Potential Advances in the Treatment of Major Depression," *The Lancet* 378, no. 9791 (2011): 621–31, doi: 10.1016/S0140-6736(11)60095-0.

7. T. N. Akbaraly, E. J. Brunner, J. E. Ferrie, M. G. Marmot, M. Kivimaki, and A. Singh-Manoux, "Dietary Pattern and Depressive Symptoms in Middle Age," *British Journal of Psychiatry* 195 (2009): 408–13, doi: 10.1192/bjp.bp.108.058925; F. N. Jacka, J. A. Pasco, A. Mykletun, L. J. Williams, A. M. Hodge, S. L. O'Reilly, G. C. Nicholson, M. A. Kotowicz, and M. Berk, "Association between Western and Traditional Diets and Depression and Anxiety in Women," *American Journal of Psychiatry* 167 (2010): 305–11,

doi: 10.1176/appi.ajp.2009.09060881; M. F. Kuczmarski, A. Cremer Sees, L. Hotchkiss, N. Cotugna, M. K. Evans, and A. B. Zonderman, "Higher Healthy Eating Index-2005 Scores Associated with Reduced Symptoms of Depression in an Urban Population: Findings from the Healthy Aging in Neighborhoods of Diversity Across the Life Span (HANDLS) Study," *Journal of the American Dietetic Association* 110 (2010): 383–89, doi: 10.1016/j .jada.2009.11.025; A. Nanri, Y. Kimura, Y. Matsushita, M. Ohta, M. Sato, N. Mishima, S. Sasaki, and T. Mizoue, "Dietary Patterns and Depressive Symptoms among Japanese Men and Women," *European Journal of Clinical Nutrition* 64 (2010): 832–39, doi: 10.1038/ejcn.2010.86.

8. A. Sánchez-Villegas, M. Delgado-Rodríguez, A. Alonso, J. Schlatter, F. Lahortiga, L. Serra Majem, and M. A. Martínez-González, "Association of the Mediterranean Dietary Pattern with the Incidence of Depression: The Seguimiento Universidad de Navarra/University of Navarra Follow-Up (SUN) Cohort," *Archives of General Psychiatry* 66 (2009): 1090–98, doi: 10.1001/archgenpsychiatry.2009.129; A. Sánchez-Villegas, E. Toledo, J. de Irala, M. Ruiz-Canela, J. Pla-Vidal, and M. A. Martínez-González, "Fast-Food and Commercial Baked Goods Consumption and the Risk of Depression," *Public Health Nutrition* 15, (2012): 424–32, doi: 10.1017/ S1368980011001856; A. Sánchez-Villegas, L. Verberne, J. De Irala, M. Ruíz-Canela, E. Toledo, L. Serra-Majem, and M. A. Martínez-González, "Dietary Fat Intake and the Risk of Depression: The SUN Project," *PLoS One* 6, no. 1 (2011): e16268, doi: 10.1371/journal.pone.0016268.

9. F. N. Jacka, A. Mykletun, M. Berk, I. Bjelland, and G. S. Tell, "The Association between Habitual Diet Quality and the Common Mental Disorders in Community-Dwelling Adults: The Hordaland Health Study," *Psychosomatic Medicine* 73, no. 6 (2011): 483–90, doi: 10.1097/PSY.0b013e318222831a.

10. M. Lucas, F. Mirzaei, E. J. O'Reilly, A. Pan, W. C. Willett, I. Kawachi, K. Koenen, and A. Ascherio, "Dietary Intake of n-3 and n-6 Fatty Acids and the Risk of Clinical Depression in Women: A 10-yr Prospective Follow-Up Study," *American Journal of Clinical Nutrition* 93 (2011): 1337–43, doi: 10.3945/ ajcn.111.011817; M. E. Sublette, S. Ellis, A. L. Geant, and J. J. Mann, "Meta-analysis of the Effects of Eicosapentaenoic Acid (EPA) in Clinical Trials in Depression," *Journal of Clinical Psychiatry* 72 (2011): 1577–84, doi: 10.4088/ JCP.10m06634; K. M. Appleton, P. J. Rogers, and A. R. Ness, "Updated Systematic Review and Meta-analysis of the Effects of n-3 Long-Chain Poly-unsaturated Fatty Acids on Depressed Mood," *American Journal of Clinical Nutrition* 91, no. 3 (2010): 757–70, doi: 10.3945/ajcn.2009.28313.

11. P. M. Kris-Etherton, W. S. Harris, L. J. Appel, and the AHA Nutrition Committee, "Omega-3 Fatty Acids and Cardiovascular Disease: New Recommendations from the American Heart Association," *Arteriosclerosis, Thrombosis, and Vascular Biology* 23, no. 2 (2003): 151–52.

12. M. Freeman, "Omega-3 Fatty Acids in Major Depressive Disorder," *Journal of Clinical Psychiatry* 70 (suppl 5) (2009): 7–11, doi: 10.4088/JCP.8157su1c.02.

13. M. F. Holick, "Vitamin D Deficiency," *New England Journal of Medicine* 357 (2007): 266–81, doi: 10.1056/NEJMra070553.

14. M. Hoang, L. F. DeFina, B. L. Willis, D. S. Leonard, M. F. Weiner, and E. S. Brown, "Association between Low Serum 25-Hydroxyvitamin D and Depression in a Large Sample of Healthy Adults: The Cooper Center Longitudinal Study," *Mayo Clinic Proceedings* 86, no. 11 (2011): 1050–55, doi: 10.4065/mcp.2011.0208.

15. T. G. Dinan and E. M. M. Quigley, "Probiotics in the Treatment of Depression: Science or Science Fiction?" *Australian and New Zealand Journal of Psychiatry* 45, no. 12 (2011): 1023–25, doi: 10.3109/00048674.2011.613766.

16. W. P. Bowe and A. C. Logan, "Acne Vulgaris, Probiotics and the Gut-Brain-Skin Axis—Back to the Future?" *Gut Pathogens* 3, no. 1 (2011): 1–10, doi: 10.1186/1757-4749-3-1.

17. K. O'Donnell, J. Wardle, C. Dantzer, and A. Steptoe, "Alcohol Consumption and Symptoms of Depression in Young Adults from 20 Countries," *Journal of Studies on Alcohol* 67, no. 6 (2006): 837–40; S. Peele and A. Brodsky, "Exploring the Psychological Benefits Associated with Moderate Alcohol Use: A Necessary Corrective to Assessments of Drinking Outcomes? *Drug and Alcohol Dependence* 60 (2000): 221–47.

18. U.S. Dept of Health and Human Services, U.S. Dept of Agriculture, *Nutrition and Your Health: Dietary Guidelines for Americans*, 5th ed. (Washington, DC: USDA, 2000).

19. M. J. Paschall, B. Freisthler, and R. I. Lipton, "Moderate Alcohol Use and Depression in Young Adults: Findings from a National Longitudinal Study," *American Journal of Public Health* 95, no. 3 (2005): 453–57.

20. M. Lucas, F. Mirzaei, A. Pan, O. I. Okereke, W. C. Willett, E. J. O'Reilly, K. Koenen, and A. Ascherio, "Coffee, Caffeine, and Risk of Depression among Women," *Archives of Internal Medicine* 17 (2011): 1571–78, doi: 10.1001/archinternmed.2011.393.

21. A. Ruusunen, S. M. Lehto, T. Tolmunen, J. Mursul, G. A. Kaplan, and S. Voutilainen, "Coffee, Tea and Caffeine Intake and the Risk of Severe Depression in Middle-Aged Finnish Men: The Kuopio Ischaemic Heart

Disease Risk Factor Study," *Public Health Nutrition* 13, no. 8 (2010): 1215–20, doi: 10.1017/S1368980010000509.

Chapter 15: When You Need More

1. E. Esposito, J. L. Wang, C. E. Adair, J. V. Williams, K. Dobson, D. Schopflocher, C. Mitton, S. Newman, C. Beck, C. Barbui, and S. B. Patten, "Frequency and Adequacy of Depression Treatment in a Canadian Population Sample," *Canadian Journal of Psychiatry* 52, no. 12 (2007): 780–89; K. Demyttenaere, A. Bonnewyn, R. Bruffaerts, G. De Girolamo, I. Gasquet, V. Kovess, J. M. Haro, and J. Alonso, "Clinical Factors Influencing the Prescription of Antidepressants and Benzodiazepines: Results from the European Study of the Epidemiology of Mental Disorders (ESEMeD)," *Journal of Affective Disorders* 110, no. 1–2 (2008): 84–93, doi: 10.1016/j.jad.2008.01.011.

2. C. Barbui, A. Cipriani, V. Patel, J. L. Ayuso-Mateos, and M. van Ommeren, "Efficacy of Antidepressants and Benzodiazepines in Minor Depression: Systematic Review and Meta-analysis," *British Journal of Psychiatry* 198 (2011): 11–16, doi: 10.1192/bjp.bp.109.076448.

3. C. Jay, J. C. Fournier, R. J. DeRubeis, S. D. Hollon, S. Dimidjian, J. D. Amsterdam, R. C. Shelton, and J. Fawcett, "Antidepressant Drug Effects and Depression Severity: A Patient-Level Meta-analysis," *Journal of the American Medical Association* 303, no. 1 (2010): 47–53, doi: 10.1001/jama.2009.1943.

4. Y. Levkovitz, E. Tedeschini, and G. I. Papakostas, "Efficacy of Antidepressants for Dysthymia: A Meta-analysis of Placebo-Controlled Randomized Trials," *Journal of Clinical Psychiatry* 72, no. 4 (2011): 509–14, doi: 10.4088/JCP.09m05949blu.

5. J. A. Stewart, D. A. Deliyannides, D. J. Hellerstein, P. J. McGrath, and J. W. Stewart, "Can People with Nonsevere Major Depression Benefit from Antidepressant Medication?" *Journal of Clinical Psychiatry* 73, no. 4 (2012): 518–25, doi: 10.4088/JCP.10m06760.

6. D. Robert, R. D. Gibbons, K. Hur, C. H. Brown, J. M. Davis, and J. J. Mann, "Benefits from Antidepressants: Synthesis of 6-Week Patient-Level Outcomes from Double-Blind Placebo-Controlled Randomized Trials of Fluoxetine and Venlafaxine," *Archives of General Psychiatry* 69, no. 6 (2012): 572–79, doi: 10.1001/archgenpsychiatry.2011.2044.

7. U.S. Food and Drug Administration. Drugs, accessed July 14, 2012, www.fda.gov/drugs.

8. R. W. Lewis, K. S. Fugl-Meyer, G. Corona, R. D. Hayes, E. O. Laumann, E. D. Moreira Jr., A. H. Rellini, and T. Segraves, "Definitions/Epidemiology/

Risk Factors for Sexual Dysfunction," *Journal of Sexual Medicine* 7 (4 Pt 2) (2010): 1598–1607, doi: 10.1111/j.1743-6109.2010.01778.x.

9. A. Clayon, A. Keller, and E. L. McGarvey, "Burden of Phase-Specific Sexual Dysfunction with SSRIs," *Journal of Affective Disorders* 91 (2006): 27–32.

10. B. C. Shin, M. S. Lee, E. J. Yang, H. S. Lim, and E. Ernst, "Maca (L. Meyenii) for Improving Sexual Function: A Systematic Review," *Complementary and Alternative Medicine* 10, no. 44 (2010), doi: 10.1186/1472-6882-10-44.

11. T. A. Lorenz and C. M. Meston, "Acute Exercise Improves Physical Sexual Arousal in Women Taking Antidepressants," *Annals of Behavioral Medicine* 43, no. 3 (2012): 352–61, doi: 10.1007/s12160-011-9338-1.

12. K. Linde, M. M. Berner, and L. Kriston, "St. John's Wort for Major Depression," *Cochrane Database of Systematic Reviews* no. 4, (2008), CD000448.

13. Y. M. Di, C. G. Li, C. C. Xue, and S. F. Zhou, "Clinical Drugs That Interact with St. John's Wort and Implication in Drug Development," *Current Pharmaceutical Design* 14, no. 17 (2004): 1723–42.

14. M. Fava and D. Mischoulon, "Folate in Depression: Efficacy, Safety, Differences in Formulations, and Clinical Issues," *Journal of Clinical Psychiatry* 70 (suppl 5) (2009): 12–17, doi: 10.4088/JCP.8157su1c.03.

15. N. R. Campbell, "How Safe Are Folic Acid Supplements?" *Archives of Internal Medicine* 156 (1996): 1638–44.

16. G. I. Papakostas, "Evidence for S-Adenosyl-L-Methionine (SAM-e) for the Treatment of Major Depressive Disorder," *Journal of Clinical Psychiatry* 70 (suppl 5) (2009): 18–22, doi: 10.4088/JCP.8157su1c.04.

17. G. I. Papakostas, D. Mischoulon, I. Shyu, J. E. Alpert, and M. Fava, "S-Adenosyl Methionine (SAMe) Augmentation of Serotonin Reuptake Inhibitors for Antidepressant Nonresponders with Major Depressive Disorder: A Double-Blind, Randomized Clinical Trial," *American Journal of Psychiatry* 167 (2010): 942–48.

18. F. Assadi, "Hypomagnesemia: An Evidenced-Based Approach to Clinical Cases," *Iranian Journal of Kidney Diseases* 4, no. 1 (2010): 13–19; B. Szewczyk, E. Poleszak, M. Sowa-Kućma, M. Siwek, D. Dudek, B. Ryszewska-Pokraśniewicz, M. Radziwoń-Zaleska, W. Opoka, J. Czekaj, A. Pilc, and G. Nowak, "Antidepressant Activity of Zinc and Magnesium in View of the Current Hypotheses of Antidepressant Action," *Pharmacological Reports* 60, no. 5 (2008): 588–89.

19. F. N. Jacka, S. Overland, R. Stewart, G. S. Tell, I. Bjelland, and A. Mykletun, "Association between Magnesium Intake and Depression and Anxiety in

Community-Dwelling Adults: The Hordaland Health Study," *Australian and New Zealand Journal of Psychiatry* 43, no.1 (2009): 45–52, doi: 10.1080/00048670802534408.

20. M. Barbagallo, M. Belvedere, and L. J. Dominguez, "Magnesium Homeostasis and Aging," *Magnesium Research* 22, no. 4 (2009): 235–46, doi: 10.1684/mrh.2009.0187.

21. J. T. Gau, Y. X. Yang, R. Chen, and T. C. Kao, "Uses of Proton Pump Inhibitors and Hypomagnesemia," *Pharmacoepidemiology and Drug Safety* 21, no. 5 (2012): 553–59, doi: 10.1002/pds.3224.

22. P. G. Weston, "Magnesium as a Sedative," *American Journal of Psychiatry* 78 (1921): 637–38.

23. G. A. Eby and K. L. Eby, "Magnesium for Treatment-Resistant Depression: A Review and Hypothesis," *Medical Hypotheses* 74 (2010): 649–66, doi: 10.1016/j.mehy.2009.10.051; G. A. Eby and K. L. Eby, "Rapid Recovery from Major Depression Using Magnesium Treatment," *Medical Hypotheses* 67 (2006): 362–70.

24. R. Bella, R. Biondi, R. Fariello, and G. Pennisi, "Effect of Acetyl-L-Carnitine on Geriatric Patients Suffering from Dysthymic Disorders," *International Journal of Clinical Pharmacology Research* 10, no. 6 (1990): 355–60.

25. R. Zanardi and E. Smeraldi, "A Double-Blind, Randomised, Controlled Clinical Trial of Acetyl-L-Carnitine vs. Amisulpride in the Treatment of Dysthymia," *European Neuropsychopharmacology* 16 (2006): 281–87.

26. G. Martinotti, S. Andreoli, D. Reina, M. Di Nicola, I. Ortolani, D. Tedeschi, F. Fanella, G. Pozzi, E. Iannoni, S. D'Iddio, and L. J. Prof, "Acetyl-l-Carnitine in the Treatment of Anhedonia, Melancholic and Negative Symptoms in Alcohol Dependent Subjects," *Progress in Neuro-psychopharmacological and Biological Psychiatry* 35, no. 4 (2011): 953–58, doi: 10.1016/j.pnpbp.2011.01.013.

27. A. Tuunainen, D. F. Kripke, and T. Endo, "Light Therapy for Non-seasonal Depression," *Cochrane Database Systematic Reviews*, no. 2 (2004), CD004050; G. Pail, W. Huf , E. Pjrek, D. Winkler, M. Willeit, N. Praschak-Rieder, and S. Kasper, "Bright-Light Therapy in the Treatment of Mood Disorders," *Neuropsychobiology* 64 (2011): 152–62, doi: 10.1159/000328950. A wonderful and free resource for information on light therapy is the Center for Environmental Therapeutics at www.CET.org.

28. A. Wirz-Justice, F. Benedetti, and M. Terman, *Chronotherapeutics for Affective Disorders: A Clinician's Manual for Light and Wake Therapy* (Basel, Switzerland: S. Karger AG, 2009).

Chapter 16: Stepping into the Light

1. B. L. Fredrickson and M. F. Losada, "Positive Affect and the Complex Dynamics of Human Flourishing," *American Psychologist* 60, no. 7 (2005): 678–86; B. Fredrickson, "What Good Are Positive Emotions?" *Review of General Psychology* 2, no. 3 (1998): 300–19; B. L. Fredrickson, "The Value of Positive Emotions," *American Scientist* 91 (2003): 330–35.

2. S. Lyubomirsky, *The How of Happiness: A Scientific Approach to Getting the Life You Want* (New York: Penguin Press, 2007).

3. R. A. Emmons and M. E. McCullough, "Counting Blessings versus Burdens: An Experimental Investigation of Gratitude and Subjective Well-Being in Daily Life," *Journal of Personality and Social Psychology* 84 (2003): 377–89; A. M. Wood, J. J. Froh, and A. W. A. Geraghty, "Gratitude and Well-Being: A Review and Theoretical Integration," *Clinical Psychology Review* 30 (2010): 890–905, doi: 10.1016/j.cpr.2010.03.005.

4. Lyubomirsky, *The How of Happiness*.

5. T. A. Wills, "Downward Comparison Principles in Social Psychology," *Psychological Bulletin* 90 (1981): 245–71.

6. E. J. Strahan, A. E. Wilson, K. E. Cressman, and V. M. Buote, "Comparing to Perfection: How Cultural Norms for Appearance Affect Social Comparison and Self-Image," *Body Image* 3 (2006): 211–27; S. E. Gutierres, D. T. Kenrick, and J. J. Partch, "Beauty, Dominance, and the Mating Game: Contrast Effects in Self-Assessment Reflect Gender Differences in Mate Selection," *Personality and Social Psychology Bulletin* 25 (1999): 1126–34.

7. J. White, E. Langer, L. Yariv, and J. Welch, "Frequent Social Comparisons and Destructive Emotions and Behaviors: The Dark Side of Social Comparisons," *Journal of Adult Development* 13 (2006): 36–44, doi: 10.1007/s10804-006-9005-0.

8. S. Lyubomirsky and L. Ross, "Hedonic Consequences of Social Comparison: A Contrast of Happy and Unhappy People," *Journal of Personality and Social Psychology* 73 (1997): 1141–57.

9. E. L. Worthington Jr., S. J. Sandage, and J. W. Berry, "Group Interventions to Promote Forgiveness: What Researchers and Clinicians Ought to Know," in *Forgiveness: Theory, Research, and Practice*, ed. M. E. McCullough, K. I. Pargament, and C. T. Thoresen (New York: Guilford, 2000), 228–53; A. H. S. Harris and C. E. Thoresen, "Extending the Influence of Positive Psychology Interventions into Health Care Settings: Lessons from Self-Efficacy and Forgiveness," *Journal of Positive Psychology* 1 (2006): 27–36.

10. A. Lutz, J. Brefczynski-Lewis, T. Johnstone, and R. J. Davidson, "Regulation of the Neural Circuitry of Emotion by Compassion Meditation: Effects of Meditative Expertise," *PLoS One* 3, no. 3 (2008): e1897.

11. B. L. Fredrickson, M. A. Cohn, K. A. Coffey, J. Pek, and S. M. Finkel, "Open Hearts Build Lives: Positive Emotions, Induced through Loving-Kindness Meditation, Build Consequential Personal Resources," *Journal of Personality and Social Psychology* 95, no. 5 (2008): 1045–62, doi: 10.1037/a0013262.

12. F. B. Bryant, "Savoring Beliefs Inventory (SBI): A Scale for Measuring Beliefs about Savouring," *Journal of Mental Health* 12 (2003): 175–96, doi: 10.1080/0963823031000103489; M. M. Tugade and B. L. Frederickson, "Regulation of Positive Emotions: Emotion Regulation Strategies That Promote Resilience," *Journal of Happiness Studies* 8 (2007): 311–33, doi 10.1007/s10902-006-9015-4.

13. M. Pasupathi and L. L. Carstensen, "Age and Emotional Experience during Mutual Reminiscing," *Psychology and Aging* 18 (2003): 430–42.

Appendixes

1. American Psychiatric Association, *Diagnostic and Statistical Manual of Mental Disorders*, 4th ed., text revision (Washington, DC: American Psychiatric Association, 2004); American Psychiatric Association, *Diagnostic and Statistical Manual of Mental Disorders*, 5th ed. (Washington, DC: American Psychiatric Association, 2013).

2. E. J. Hermans, H. J. F. van Marle, L. Ossewaarde, M. J. Henckens, S. Qin, M. T. van Kesteren, V. C. Schoots, H. Cousijn, M. Rijpkema, R. Oostenveld, G. Fernandez, "Stress-Related Noradrenergic Activity Prompts Large-Scale Neural Network Reconfiguration," *Science* 334, no. 6059 (2011): 1151–53, doi: 10.1126/science.1209603.

3. B. S. McEwen, "Allostasis and Allostatic Load: Implications for Neuropsychopharmacology," *Neuropsychopharmacology* 22 (2000): 108–24.

4. D. D. Burns, *The Feeling Good Handbook* (New York: William Morrow and Co., 1989).

5. The website www.afterdeployment.org contains additional information that may be valuable to people who are suffering from almost depression.

about the authors

Jefferson Prince, MD, is an instructor in psychiatry at Harvard Medical School and Massachusetts General Hospital and serves as the director of child psychiatry at MassGeneral for Children at North Shore Medical Center. Dr. Prince earned his medical degree from Emory University School of Medicine and completed his training in psychiatry and child psychiatry at Massachusetts General Hospital and McLean Hospital. Dr. Prince is board certified in general psychiatry and in child and adolescent psychiatry. In addition to his clinical practice and research in traditional hospital settings, Dr. Prince integrates mindfulness practices into his work with children, adolescents, and adults.

Shelley Carson received her doctorate in psychology from Harvard University, where she continues to teach and conduct research in the areas of creativity, psychopathology, and resilience. She has been published widely in both national and international scientific journals, and her work has been featured on the Discovery Channel, CNN, and NPR. She has won multiple teaching awards for her popular course *Creativity: Madmen, Geniuses, and Harvard Students.* Since 2006, she has also served as a senior subject matter expert for the Department of Defense project afterdeployment .org, which provides innovative online mental health assistance to service members returning from Iraq and Afghanistan. Dr. Carson writes the popular *Psychology Today* blog "Life as Art," and is the author of the award-winning book *Your Creative Brain: Seven Steps to Maximize Imagination, Productivity, and Innovation in Your Life*. You can learn more about Dr. Carson and her work on her website: http://ShelleyCarson.com.

■ ◆ ■

Hazelden, a national nonprofit organization founded in 1949, helps people reclaim their lives from the disease of addiction. Built on decades of knowledge and experience, Hazelden offers a comprehensive approach to addiction that addresses the full range of patient, family, and professional needs, including treatment and continuing care for youth and adults, research, higher learning, public education and advocacy, and publishing.

A life of recovery is lived "one day at a time." Hazelden publications, both educational and inspirational, support and strengthen lifelong recovery. In 1954, Hazelden published *Twenty-Four Hours a Day*, the first daily meditation book for recovering alcoholics, and Hazelden continues to publish works to inspire and guide individuals in treatment and recovery, and their loved ones. Professionals who work to prevent and treat addiction also turn to Hazelden for evidence-based curricula, informational materials, and videos for use in schools, treatment programs, and correctional programs.

Through published works, Hazelden extends the reach of hope, encouragement, help, and support to individuals, families, and communities affected by addiction and related issues.

For questions about Hazelden publications,
please call **800-328-9000** or visit us online
at **hazelden.org/bookstore.**

RELATED RESOURCES FROM HAZELDEN PUBLISHING

The *How to Change Your Thinking* Collection
These e-book shorts apply the proven methods of Rational Emotive Behavior Therapy (REBT) to challenge and change the irrational thoughts and beliefs that contribute to the debilitating effects of shame, anger, depression, and anxiety.

How to Change Your Thinking about Depression
A Hazelden Quick Guide
Provides practical strategies from behavioral health experts to change the way we think about and respond to symptoms of depression.
Order No. EB4803

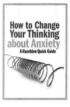

How to Change Your Thinking about Anxiety
A Hazelden Quick Guide
Offers healthy ways to process and change our thoughts, feelings, and behaviors to better deal with anxiety.
Order No. EB4805

Also available:

How to Change Your Thinking about Shame
A Hazelden Quick Guide
Order No. EB4804

How to Change Your Thinking about Anger
A Hazelden Quick Guide
Order No. EB4802

For more information or to order these or other resources
by Hazelden Publishing, call **800-343-4499**
or visit **hazelden.org/bookstore.**

HazeLDen®